INSIDE NGOs

Managing
conflicts between headquarters
and the field offices in non-governmental
organizations

NAOKI SUZUKI

INTERMEDIATE TECHNOLOGY PUBLICATIONS 1998

Published by ITDG Publishing
The Schumacher Centre for Technology and Development
Bourton Hall, Bourton-on-Dunsmore, Rugby, Warwickshire CV23 9QZ, UK
www.itdgpublishing.org.uk

First published in 1998
Print on demand since 2004

ISBN 1 85339 413 0

A catalogue record for this book is available from the British Library

ITDG Publishing is the publishing arm of the Intermediate Technology
Development Group. Our mission is to build the skills and capacity of people in
developing countries through the dissemination of information
in all forms, enabling them to improve the quality of their lives and
that of future generations.

Typeset by Dorwyn Ltd, Rowlands Castle, Hants
Printed in Great Britain by Lightning Source, Milton Keynes

Contents

PART II   DIVERSITY VS. SIMILARITY

List of tables and figure

Preface

THIS BOOK IS the product of many NGO practitioners who care deeply about their daily work in development. To participate in my interview research, they sacrificed valuable time which they would otherwise have directed toward their own goals. In addition, they demonstrated great courage and sincerity during the course of the interviews, sharing their problems, worries, and mistakes more candidly than most people care to do with someone they don't know. Through their willing and honest help with my field research, they gave much and received little in return. I hope that this book can play the role of midwife, returning to them their own voices, to which we can listen together and from which we can learn together to improve our day-to-day practices.

While this book consists of many people's personal accounts, the idea for it originally emerged from my desire to learn from, yet avoid writing about, my own difficult experiences. And yet these experiences both ground this study (and thus provide readers with an understanding of its context) and link me to the practitioners whose stories appear here.

My NGO experience began with a month of predeparture training at the headquarters of an NGO based in Japan. Prior to this job, I had had some volunteer experience in Africa teaching mathematics and physics. But working for an NGO, and particularly as a country director (despite the smallness of the country office), was a whole new experience for me. My training involved assisting a desk officer who supported the field office in Ethiopia in which I would work. Through this training, I learned about the NGO's financial systems, its donor relations, the on-going projects in which I would participate, my colleagues-to-be in the field, and the local situation in which I would live with my wife and our three-month-old son. I also became aware of financial, personnel, and operational issues with which the organization was struggling. Moreover, this training helped me develop relationships with the staff at the organization's headquarters.

The understanding that I gained of the field, and the personal relationships I developed, instilled in me a sense of membership in the organization. This sense, however, did not necessarily relieve my worries about my upcoming work in the field. In contrast to my previous experience as a teacher – work that involved the clearly defined task of teaching students based on assigned textbooks – I could hardly imagine which day-to-day practices might effectively accomplish my project objectives. While a project objective could be as concrete as planting one million trees, for example, I would not actually be planting these trees myself, but rather helping to devise a plan to make it happen.

My training, which enabled me to envision field situations, did not direct me in what (not) to do in the field but, instead, made me realize that I would have substantial autonomy. It was too good for me. Had I known how I wanted to conduct my daily work, I would have been able to enjoy the freedom that such autonomy would entail. But without the ability even to distinguish working effectively from squandering time, I could only hope supportive colleagues would help me out once I went to the field. And yet that prospect only deepened this poor novice's worries: I would have felt much more comfortable if I had had concrete practical suggestions, but I did not want the headquarters to gain control over my work.

The image of field work that I developed during my training remained with me as though it were a picture on a wall. This static picture, no matter how accurate it may have been, did not provide practical guidance to such matters as where to direct my attention, how to make decisions, whom to deal with for which issue, and so forth. But I did have some ideas about what I would be doing daily. I could, at least, assume that my daily work would involve making phone calls, writing letters, visiting project sites, meeting local people, learning a local language, calculating project expenses, preparing project proposals, attending meetings, paying bills, hiring and firing local staff, negotiating with the national government for a project agreement, and so forth.

The problem was that these activities, which would need to be coherently interwoven to be effective, appeared to me as fragmented pieces that offered no clue to their relations or priorities. Envisioning fragmented activities, like pieces of a jigsaw puzzle, was awful. Every jigsaw puzzle comes with a final image that we can refer to when we try to put its pieces together. But in my case, I could only envision the different pieces, with no sense of the final image, and without even a guarantee that they could be assembled into one. I felt I had no way even to discern whether my daily work would be leading the projects in the right or wrong direction. To escape from my growing sense of dread, I subconsciously convinced myself to let my future in the field take care of itself. I decided that only within the context of actual field work could I determine what I should do.

Alas, the field did not offer me practical suggestions either. Once there, I still could not quite tell what I should pay the most attention to, which activities I should prioritize, or how I should organize my daily work.

Thanks to the daily activities that absorbed my mind, energy, and time, my worries disappeared immediately after I assumed the position. At the same time, however, I had to survive every day without any practical guidance, which I had thought I could get in the field. As a novice, I easily became consumed by a daily routine of various small tasks without giving much thought to their meaning. I was lucky that kind and supportive colleagues helped me out whenever I got stuck. But, overall, I was simply responding to, instead of directing, the requirements of my job on a daily basis.

In part, my poor performance had to do with the fact that I could, at least, assuage my discomfort by getting the job done every day, whatever the job was. This superficial satisfaction, embedded as it was in my daily work, discouraged me from making efforts to improve my work beyond what was required to protect myself from feelings of guilt. For example, I could continue to justify my lack of planning in my work as a local way of doing things once I felt (with little careful consideration) that such an approach was common in the local context. Instead of identifying key principles and using them as the basis for organizing my activities, I swiftly learned to excuse and legitimize my haphazard practices.

Just as I lacked co-ordination in my daily activities, I also lacked any motivation to improve my performance of them. Knowing that the government officers could be difficult, I felt that our failure to agree with each other was their problem, not mine. I did not try to develop a strategy to negotiate better with them. I simply presented my proposal, tried to maximize my interests against theirs, and assigned responsibility for dissension to them.

I am not now sure if I improved my performance as I worked. But reflecting seriously on what I experienced in the field has led me to raise practical questions about daily work. In determining the priority of particular activities, for example, surely developing relationships with local staff members was important to working with them effectively. Given that, was it a wise decision to take a day off to attend a funeral ceremony for a relative of the office's gatekeeper with other local staff? What would enable me to make a better judgement and know whether the decision was wise or stupid? Is it an issue of developing better criteria by which I can determine the priority of attending the ceremony in relation to the other things I have to do?

In addition to the priority issue, the quality of each activity can also be questioned. Considering the example of negotiation, again how can I better negotiate with people whose interests differ from mine, instead of blaming their different interests for our dissension? Was an attempt to maximize my own interests a wise negotiating stance? What constitutes high-quality negotiating? What were my resources for the negotiations, and how did I use them? What problems prevented me from identifying and employing those resources? What strategies did I have at hand to address the problems?

At the time, I did not think of these questions. I had a vague sense that completing the immediate tasks before me would eventually accomplish a long-term objective. Again, I felt as if I were attempting to put the pieces of a jigsaw puzzle together without having a clear image of the picture that should ultimately emerge. If I had had practical suggestions to which I could refer in my work, I would have approached situations more attentively, understood them more thoroughly, envisioned a more coherent objective, been more flexible in my perceptions, made more thoughtful decisions, and practised with more confidence, for I would have been better equipped, better informed, less worried, and more honest with myself as well as with others.

Where and how, then, can I acquire practical informative knowledge? I would have felt better equipped if, in addition to the knowledge I gained in the predeparture training, I had had the range of knowledge about development that formal education can offer. This knowledge can greatly help us to conceptualize and understand the messy situations in which we work. However, this knowledge can often be too abstract to apply in practice because it usually tries to explain a variety of situations as economically as possible, at the price of excluding the contextual uniqueness of each situation.

But if the knowledge offered by formal education is not helpful enough, or is easily obtained, can we acquire practical relevant knowledge only through experience and a great deal of trial and error? Can't we acquire it without going through all those miserable experiences? Specifically, can we acquire the knowledge by learning from others' experiences? Are others' experiences too specific and different to apply to our own specific issues at hand?

In working for an NGO, for example, can we acquire knowledge that suggests more than 'participation is important', 'a gap between the rich and the poor is expanding', 'government officers are tough', or 'try to understand local knowledge'? Indeed, the stories of thoughtful NGO colleagues who have experienced and responded to their daily challenges with their own concrete practices are invaluable resources from which we can gain a great deal of practical knowledge.

This book is based on field research that was conducted in the headquarters and four field offices for each of four international NGOs between December 1993 and July 1994. Assuring the confidentiality of the interviews, I took notes and, by agreement with interviewees, tape-recorded 74 out of 76 interviews. Interviewing NGO staff was an amazing learning process for me. I met people who cared about the same things I was struggling with, and I could relate their practices to mine. As I listened to the stories of other practitioners, I felt that I was not totally alone in my daily work. Despite the distinctive contexts in which we live, I believe we can still relate to each other and learn from each other's experiences. While this book introduces specific and concrete problems through voices from the field, it also attempts to identify a sense of commonality among those who care about their daily work in development.

Among the numerous issues associated with the work of NGOs, I have focused particularly on those that emerge from within NGOs themselves. For the purposes of this book, therefore, 'the field' refers not only to project sites but can also refer to headquarters in a US city or a field office in the capital of an African country. This definition of 'the field' might not be attractive to people whose interests lie in community development or people-centred development, because their main concerns involve poor and oppressed people, the unjust societies in which they live, and other matters that emerge in rural areas or big-city slums in the Third World, and which can seem more pressing than issues that emerge within NGOs.

This book is also concerned with poverty, oppression and injustice. But rather than focusing on the form these issues take in the places that usually figure prominently in development literature, this book identifies these issues as they emerge inside NGOs, especially between their head-quarters and field offices. When expatriate staff work with local staff in an NGO, for example, the organization faces the issues of the rich and the poor, a dominating language and a suppressed one, well-served interests and neglected ones, fair employment terms and unfair ones. The headquarters–field office relationship within NGOs embodies and reflects the problems of North–South relations.

Furthermore, these issues that emerge within NGOs can be as problem-atic as the external issues they seek to address, precisely because they make addressing those issues effectively more difficult. First of all, the prime mission of NGOs is to address issues outside NGOs, not inside. Second, NGOs' staff would lose their identities and the rationale for their existence if they themselves were a source of problems. Third, admitting internal problems is not simply tough but, more importantly, threatens NGOs' relationships with their donors, to whom they need to be accountable.

In identifying problems internal to NGOs, however, I do not mean to denigrate the work that they do. The purpose of this book is neither to criticize NGOs for having their own internal problems, nor to argue that all organizations experience internal problems, and that NGOs are hardly unique in this regard. Rather, this book attempts to illustrate the vul-nerability of NGOs when they commit themselves to dealing with their problems. An NGO cannot maintain distance from the poor and the oppressed, or from unjust societies, and exist simply as a means to solve their problems, because it encounters some of these same problems in its internal organization and can effectively address these problems only from within. For example, while NGOs can perform better if expatriates and locals collaborate on equal terms, most of their employment terms establish a vertical distinction, or hierarchy, between the two groups to accommodate different standards of living in the North and the South. Although an NGO without local staff would be ineffective, an NGO in which expatriates and locals form vertically dichotomized groups is also ineffective. The challenge to NGOs is to resist the temptation to ignore these internal issues, and instead to identify them humbly and sincerely, and address them patiently without losing hope, motivation, or concern about those who are suffering.

I hope that this book will benefit those who care about their day-to-day work in NGOs and other organizational contexts. Although it focuses on international NGOs, with a special concentration on the relationships between headquarters and field offices, people in many organizations may find the lessons reflected in these accounts useful for their own daily work. As a 'midwife', the task of this book is to present these accounts as effectively as possible so that we can best learn from them. To enable readers to hear the interviewees' voices clearly, I have tried to use as little jargon and abstract theory as possible in the main text, and to restrict most of my discussion of the literature on development to the Notes. However, I should acknowledge that I was helped significantly by the range of knowledge that literature offers when I examined and clarified the issues that I address here. The development literature helped me to look critically at issues, to develop frameworks through which I could present the accounts more effectively, and to challenge and deepen my initially shallow understanding of the problems I address here. Although I eagerly sought practical knowledge, I was very fortunate to have access to the vast accumulated knowledge the literature represents. It proved to be a very precious resource.

In addition to extending my sincere thanks to the contributors of the personal accounts included in this book, I would like to thank many others as well whose support was vital to my research and writing. In particular, my thanks to my mentor, John Forester, are too deep to express in words. I also received significant support from Merrill Ewert and Porus Olpadwala. I appreciate the invaluable comments on my research ideas that Norman Uphoff and Bob Stern offered. I would also like to thank Milton Esman for his kind help during my revision of the manuscript. I owe much to Stacey Young, who carefully and patiently reviewed and edited this manuscript. My thanks to Dan Kostka for helping with the final edit. The support I received from the Department of City and Regional Planning at Cornell University was essential. I am also grateful to the Foundation for Advanced Studies on International Development (FASID) for granting me a scholarship, which made possible the preparation and research for this book.

My thanks also go to Om and Amrita Gurung, Kosuke Koyama, Peter and Margie Morris, Edwin Oyer, Michael Reynolds, Yoshihiro and Nobuko Saito, Kazuyuki and Megumi Sasaki, Sakae and Mayumi Yamada, and Jaroslav Vanek. I would like to give special thanks to my parents. They have shown me by their excellent example how to deal with life's challenges and have directed me with careful support and patience. Hiroki, Mitsuo and Shinya, through their play, mischief, fights, laughs, smiles, shouts and cries, provided new insights in peculiar ways which people usually do not want to appreciate. Their contribution was unusual yet profound. Finally, thanks to Misako Suzuki, who devoted herself to developing and maintaining an environment in which I could undertake my research and complete this book. None of this would have been possible without her.

CHAPTER 1

NGOs in Tension

We support the field. But we are kind of being part of a funding division, too, and as such, we have to take a lot of cognizance of what the funder wants.

Desk officer

Our priority is to discuss the thing with project managers and field workers, and see how programmes can be improved, while they are interested in satisfying funders.

Field officer

THIS BOOK IS about the practical issues that confront NGO staff and the strategies that those staff use to try to work most effectively. Too often, as we shall see, studies of NGOs treat these complex, far flung organizations from the outside as simple units. In this book we listen closely to the accounts of NGO insiders – in field offices (FOs) and in headquarters (HQ) – to learn about the real world of NGO administration and project implementation.

After setting out the difficulties that NGO staff face in relating FO practice to HQ directives, this chapter then sets out the structure of the book and specifies three major tensions between central management and field implementation. These tensions involve: i) field-oriented versus organization-oriented attitudes, ii) the diversity or similarity of NGO staff, and iii) the flexibility or consistency of their project administration. To provide an overview of these tensions, this chapter finally presents a case study drawn from a couple of personal accounts from the field. This composite case exemplifies the effectiveness of storytelling as a method to address issues within NGOs and sketches structurally-embedded internal tensions that NGO staff face in their day-to-day work.

NGOs in several forms

As used in this book, 'NGOs' refers to non-governmental organizations that attempt to address concerns of the unprivileged and the underserved in the Third World through development activities such as agricultural assistance, primary health care, provision of basic services, and education. Once NGOs multiplied and started to play substantial roles in serving the needs of the Third World, they emerged as a distinctive organizational type and gained attention as a major alternative to

1

government-to-government development. As NGOs established their domain within the development community, a significant gap in knowledge about that domain emerged. The literature on development swiftly shifted a good deal of its focus to NGOs and attempted to understand various aspects of their functioning. This literature focused increasingly on such NGO issues as government relations,[1] donor/public relations,[2] NGO management,[3] institution building,[4] networking,[5] planning and strategies,[6] social change,[7] and NGOs' challenges.[8]

Despite its rapid expansion, the literature on NGOs tends nevertheless to address the concerns of NGO leadership rather than the more immediate interests of the NGO staff who work under them. By contributing more to the knowledge of the leadership than to that of their subordinates, the literature widens, rather than bridges, the gap between NGO leaders and their staff. Serving these staff more directly is work that the literature has yet to explore, much less complete. So far, little of the literature has discussed the internal dynamics of NGOs as organizations:[9] most tends to treat NGOs as single, coherent entities.[10]

In reality, however, an NGO is a complex entity that consists of diverse offices staffed by diverse members who hold diverse values.[11] The

---

[1] See Bebbington and Farrington (1993), Bratton (1989), Clark (1995), Garain (1994), Smith (1990), Steen (1996), Tongsawate and Tips (1988) and Uphoff (1993).

[2] See Dolnick (1987), Fowler (1992b), Lissner (1977), O'Brien (1991), and Suharyanto and Hutabarat (1993).

[3] See Billis (1993), Billis and MacKeith (1992, 1993), Chambers (1985), Esman (1988, 1991), Fowler (1990), Kiggundu (1989), Lovell (1992) and Staudt (1991).

[4] See Bryant and White (1982), Carroll (1992a), Eaton (1972), Hughes (1991), Israel (1987), Postma (1994), Tayko (1988) and Thomas-Slayter (1992).

[5] See Brown (1991a), Fisher (1993) and PACT (1989).

[6] See Brown (1988, 1991b), Edwards and Hulme (1992a, 1992b), Goldsmith (1996), Korten and Klauss (1984), Narkwiboonwong and Tips (1989), Tuckman and Chang (1992) and Uyangoda (1989).

[7] See Fowler (1991, 1993), Magendzo (1990), Ndegwa (1996) and Vansant (1989).

[8] See Drabek (1987), Hodgkinson and Sumariwalla (1992), Korten (1990b), Smillie (1994), Vergara (1994) and Verhagen (1987).

[9] Fowler (1992a) suggests that a serious gap in the understanding of NGO structures and functions exists. Billis and MacKeith (1993) argue that management is a vital missing link in voluntary sector research and is an undervalued element in the overall characterization of the sector (135). However, most literature focuses on the field in the Third World. NGOs usually appear in the literature as agencies to facilitate development processes, but they rarely become the central focus of study. Exceptions include Billis and MacKeith (1992), and DiBella (1992).

[10] For example, De Graaf (1987) uses three criteria regarding NGOs' performance – programme accomplishment, contribution to self-sustaining change outside the NGO, and improvement of performance – to analyse NGO organizations; he does not include NGOs' internal dynamics in the performance components. While Korten (1988) lists a number of principles for an NGO to be effective, he treats NGOs as a unit. As Clegg (1989, 97) says, 'Organizations have typically been regarded as coherent and homogeneous entities.' March and Olsen (1989, 17) argue that 'a claim of coherence is necessary if we wish to treat institutions as decision makers'.

[11] Different interest groups view core organizational issues (i.e. efficiency and effectiveness) significantly differently (Cameron and Whetten, 1983). This research regards an NGO as a complex entity in which agencies, networks, interest groups and so forth are constituted.

complexity of Northern-based international development NGOs (the type of organization to which the term 'NGO' refers throughout the rest of this book) is especially profound due to their globally-dispersed office locations where different socio-economic systems, political structures, and religious and ethnic groups prevail. To the extent that these NGOs work globally, they need to embrace the complexity that these social, political, and ethnic differences involve.

The literature on NGOs operates at three different levels: assessing the NGO sector as a whole, particular kinds of NGOs, or single NGOs taken individually. Analyses that treat NGOs as a sector usually deal with the overall trends within, and the influences upon, the sector. Such literature not only presents aggregated data on NGOs, such as their total number and budget,[12] but also addresses critical issues facing NGOs as a sector. For example, the NGO–government relationship is one major issue that must be addressed not only by each NGO but also by the entire NGO community.[13] Such literature analyses the NGO sector in relation to the larger society in which NGOs operate and suggests roles that the NGO sector can play in society. Because such analyses provide a general understanding of NGOs' status within society, they can be particularly beneficial to the staff of governmental/donor organizations in determining their organizational policies toward NGOs.

Several authors identify key differences that exist among NGOs, and they classify the organizations according to those differences. Such literature questions the term 'NGOs'. The literal meaning of the term 'non-governmental organizations' is so vague and broad that it fails even to distinguish for-profit private firms from non-profit volunteer organizations. Even among non-statutory international development organizations, a huge number of organizations exist and their differences in missions, operations and funding schemes are too substantial to treat them all as the same type of organization.[14] To resolve this confusion, some development scholars have attempted to clarify the term 'NGOs' and to categorize these organizations into small subgroups.[15] These classifications are also helpful to the staff of governmental/donor organizations, because they need to define and categorize NGOs before they formulate their NGO policies.

Still other analyses take individual NGOs as the unit of analysis. This literature attempts to address issues such as accountability and fundraising that matter to NGOs as individual organizations. Such analyses often centre around a particular NGO in its specific context rather than a

---

[12] Clark (1991), Hulme and Edwards (1997), and Smillie (1995) provide well-informed discussions of trends affecting the NGO sector as a whole.

[13] For example, see Uphoff (1996) for the accountability of NGOs as an emerging sectoral issue.

[14] See, for example, Carroll (1992b) and Salamon and Anheier (1996).

[15] For more on their categories, see Appendix A.

group of NGOs with their aggregated or generalized data. Because these case study analyses attempt to address organizational problems in concrete contexts, NGO leaders can fairly easily relate the case to their own organizational experiences and make sense of what the literature discusses in their own contexts. Thus, this literature can benefit NGO leadership when it makes organizational decisions concerning fund-raising policies, the formulation of its development philosophy, and so forth.

These different ways of studying NGOs can clarify differences between the interests of the staff of governmental/donor organizations and those of NGO leadership. While the staff of governmental/donor organizations tend to be interested in the relationships of their organizations with NGOs as a group, NGO leadership tends to be less interested in broader analyses of NGOs. Because NGO leaders are most immediately concerned with their own organizations, they are typically much more interested in the particular issues that they face as individual organizations.

But organizational analyses can still be rather too broad and abstract for NGO staff to make sense of and apply to their actual working situations. For example, a field officer may not easily put the concept of 'institution building' into practice in his or her day-to-day work. The concept is too abstract to put into practice, and the practical constraints that face NGO staff make it difficult for them to act as they wish. Even within an NGO, daily activities and contextual constraints (lack of authority in particular) vary greatly according to staff members' positions. Thus, the knowledge that helps NGO leadership to direct their organizations differs substantially from the knowledge that helps other NGO staff to perform their day-to-day work. While the knowledge that is useful to leadership tends to address issues of an NGO *vis-à-vis* its environments, the knowledge that is useful to staff tends to concern issues internal to NGOs.

The struggle between headquarters and field offices

In an NGO as a complex entity, one prominent area of tension is that between HQ and FOs.[16] The tension that emerges between the two is due mostly to differences in their tasks. This tension is typically observed in international NGOs for two reasons. First, their target groups are entirely different from their funding sources.[17] Second, FOs, which mainly serve

---

[16] Billis and MacKeith (1992) also point out the difficulty of co-ordinating different offices.

[17] Compare NGOs with the government or private firms. In the case of government or private organizations, those that pay money are normally expected to receive some type of direct service. Citizens who pay taxes to the government are supposed to receive some types of social services in return, in theory if not in practice. A client pays a price to a private firm to obtain a commodity or a type of service that the client wants. In both cases, there is an understanding that those who pay are supposed to be the ones who benefit.

4

the target groups, and HQ, which mainly deals with funding, are not only physically distant from each other – they also differ with respect to their cultures, views, interests, concerns, and so forth.

This tension affects HQ and FOs differently. The HQ staff find themselves caught in the tension between funders and FOs. They need to secure funding[18] while simultaneously maintaining accountability to FOs. The FOs' staff, on the other hand, find themselves caught in the tension between HQ and projects. They need to be accountable to the requests of HQ while maintaining the quality of projects in the field.[19]

In addition to the internal tension between HQ and FOs, there are external sources of tension as well. When a donor and an NGO have more or less the same interests, concerns and views regarding projects,

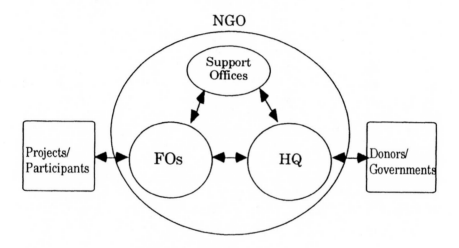

Figure 1. *An NGO and its Environments*[20]

---

[18] The issue of funding is one major concern for NGOs. For discussions of the relationship between the characteristics of donors and amounts raised, see Booth, *et al.* (1989). See, also, Edwards and Hulme (1996) for a discussion of NGOs' accountability to donors. Bowden (1990) discusses NGOs' dishonest practices in securing funds, such as 'double-dipping', i.e. when a project is doubly funded by two donors. Brown and Korten (1989) present guidelines for donors to support voluntary organizations.

[19] For a discussion of external and internal accountability of NGOs, see Kelleher and McLaren (1996, 4–9).

[20] Constituencies of NGOs are not as simple as this figure suggests. Each NGO consists of different kinds of constituencies that would not necessarily fit in this figure. However, because this study particularly focuses on the internal dynamic of an NGO, it intends to show the two main NGO–environments relationships that distinguish headquarters from field offices. As the figure shows, the two relationships are the headquarters–donors/governments relations and the field offices–beneficiaries/participants relations.

the external tension is not serious because no crucial discrepancy exists between them. However, when the donor's own interests differ significantly from the NGO's interests, the differences can become a serious problem in their effects on the NGO.[21] The NGO must either internalize the problem and deal with it between HQ and FOs, or displace the problem to either the donor or the projects. In any case, the tension that the NGO faces is augmented.

Within an NGO, both HQ and FOs may try to release the tension by displacing the problem. For example, HQ may displace the gap in interests on to either donors or FOs, while FOs may displace it on to either HQ or projects. Hence, if HQ wants to be accountable to the donors while FOs want to be accountable to project participants, HQ and FOs must deal with the gap between themselves. Because of internal and external pressures, the HQ–FOs relationships tend to be highly complex and to involve high levels of tension.

However, tensions *per se*, regardless of their levels, are not necessarily negative, so long as they are properly managed to maintain a balance. This study assumes that ways in which an NGO manages internal tensions (mostly between HQ and FOs, but not exclusively so) significantly affect its performance with respect not only to project implementation[22] but also to fund-raising.[23] Beginning from this premise, this study attempts to identify and discuss problems that NGO staff face in their day-to-day work under these tensions,[24] and to identify strategies that they actually use to address those problems. To identify effectively the problems derived from the internal tensions of NGOs, three broadly-defined sets of tensions are described and discussed separately, based on information collected through field research. (See Appendix C for details of this research.)

The structure of this book

Part I focuses on tensions between two opposing pressures: the pressure to be accountable to project activities in the field as the output of the

---

[21] Donor–NGO relations are a major issue that NGOs need to handle carefully. See, for example, Quizon (1989). See James (1989) for the relationship between government funding and accountability of recipient organizations.

[22] Developing organizational capacity is a vital component to improve the quality of community development (Craig, *et al.* 1990).

[23] Fowler (1991) implies the importance of consistency between what an NGO does in the field and what it does to manage itself when he argues that NGOs can become effective agents of democratization if they themselves become more democratic. However, he seems to disregard the internal complexities that make it difficult for NGOs actually to manage themselves as they might intend to. From the donors' point of view, the managerial capacity of NGOs is one of the most important criteria in judging the effectiveness of the organizations (Daniels and Dottridge, 1993).

[24] For discussions of tensions derived from the relationship between an NGO and its environment, see De Graaf (1987).

organization, and the pressure to maintain and develop organizational capacities to ensure quality output over the long term. To identify problems associated with tensions, this Part pays particular attention to NGOs' membership creation because of its vital importance to an NGO's performance in the field as well as in securing funding. When an NGO tries to recruit the staff and train them to allocate the proper people to the proper places in the organization, the NGO needs to consider carefully how that affects donor relations and project implementation.

For example, while donors usually want to make sure that their financial support is properly used in the field and not 'wasted' within the organization, NGOs cannot perform well in the field unless they invest some resources in recruiting and training their staff. Hence, when an NGO attempts to create its membership, it must consider how it can achieve simultaneously two competing objectives: dispensing inputs in order to address immediate needs in the field, and making the investments necessary to develop the staff and the organization. Anticipating the tensions between these two objectives, Part I identifies and discusses strategies for managing the tensions that arise when NGOs recruit and train staff.

The issue in Part II is how an NGO can properly balance – and treat as organizational resources – the two opposing characteristics of their staff: their diversity in having distinctive skills, views, knowledge, backgrounds, and so forth, and their similarity in sharing the same core values and missions. Without a sufficiently diverse staff, an NGO can become homogenized, which restricts its capacity to address disparate, dynamic and unexpected problems. However, without a sufficient degree of similarity, staff members may fail to develop a sense of commonality from which they can co-ordinate tasks and work coherently to achieve their mission goals. Part II identifies and discusses the problems that emerge when the staff attempt to maintain these two characteristics – diversity and similarity – simultaneously;[25] and it presents strategies to address those problems. Although this discussion deals with intraorganizational dynamics, major external factors such as donors/governments and sociopolitical environments can also be taken into account accordingly.[26]

Part III discusses tensions that NGO staff members face when they deal with systems such as rules, regulations and policies, or more broadly when they work with systematic functions such as language, money and

---

[25] 'The ambiguity and multiple cultures views contain a major challenge to the ecological and institutional perspectives, for how can organizations be institutions if they have multiple or ambiguous cultures? If organizations do not cohere as unitary entities, then the "object" or "target" of selection by external forces is no longer clear' (Aldrich, 1992, 25).

[26] When an NGO tries to minimize uncertainty in its relation to environments, the organization is tempted to introduce bureaucracy. Aldrich (1979, 13) argues, 'Bureaucracy tries to eliminate or control all extra-organizational influences on the behavior of its members.'

modus operandi. Systems are important. Without systems, organizations do not function; they suffer from chaos. But blindly following systems can also be destructive. As an organization, an NGO benefits from systems because systems provide standards which form a common ground for staff members and enable them to communicate with each other. However, systems tend by their nature to be rigid and to create problems when situations change rapidly. In an NGO, which must deal with diverse, dynamic local problems, the challenge for the staff is how they can better use systems while maintaining flexibility, adaptability and responsiveness to address diverse, dynamic needs.[27] To address this problem, an NGO should be organized strategically, such that its 'structure should encourage innovation and initiative consistent with the organization's mission under varied and even unanticipated circumstances.'[28] But the staff in HQ and FOs often do not know exactly what and how they practise, under what tensions, to develop this kind of strategic organization. To address this knowledge gap, Part III identifies and discusses the problems that arise when the staff deal with systems, and the strategies that they actually use to tackle those problems.

Part IV first draws lessons learned from the discussions in the preceding Parts[29] and then provides a summary of the study as a conclusion. The discussions in Parts I, II and III are not narrowly framed to focus on the relationship between HQ and FOs because narrow framing may obscure other important issues that are not directly related to the HQ–FOs relationships. However, after discussing the three sets of tensions discussed in the other Parts, Part IV re-introduces the framework of the HQ–FOs relationships and presents the lessons in terms of their applicability to donors and governments, to NGO managers or leadership, and to NGO field staff for their future efforts.

Throughout these Parts, the study continuously focuses on the voices of NGO staff members as the main actors and subjects of this research. To achieve this objective effectively and efficiently, as many stories as possible from the field are presented[30] so that readers are provided not merely with broad conceptualizations of problems and strategies, but also – and more significantly – with contextually rich, vivid and emotional voices as a way of conveying the experiences of the staff.

---

[27] For organizations that face outside complexities and turbulence, a capacity for organizational learning is central to effectiveness (Brown and Covey, 1989). To understand organizational learning, see, for example, Cohen and Sproull (1996).

[28] Korten (1988, 17).

[29] Compare five important organizational factors that contribute to the success of development projects: clarity of project goals, flexibility and responsiveness, autonomy and accountability, learning process approach, and leadership and human resource development (Conyers and Kaul, 1990).

[30] Because many NGO staff members do not speak English as their first language, quotations have been edited for English comprehension without changing their original implications.

Overview of tensions

Before going on to discuss the three kinds of tensions, staff members' problems with them and their strategies for dealing with them, a case from the field may provide an overview of these tensions. This case is taken from interviews with Susan, a desk officer in the HQ of an NGO who works under a department head, and with Beth, who works as a field officer in Ethiopia. They contact each other indirectly via their bosses.

As a desk officer, Susan follows up day-to-day communication with the field office and interacts with donors to secure funding. While her boss is the one who officially takes responsibility for dealing both with donors and the field office, Susan's job is to cover all detailed tasks, such as preparing reports and proposals for donors, monitoring activities in the field, following up questions raised by donors, collecting necessary information for her boss to make wise decisions, etc. Hence, the staff in the field office as well as in donor agencies identify Susan as the contact person in HQ who knows all the details, although their official respondent is her boss. In her position between donors and the field, Susan identifies her roles as follows:

> We support the field. But we are kind of being part of a funding division, too, and as such, we have to take a lot of cognizance of what the funder wants.

Taking her position into account, her response reveals a lot about her relationship with the field:

> We spend quite a lot of time analysing figures, editing reports, so that they can comply with the funders' requirements. We are trying to work out schedules that are largely based on the funders' requirements. We ensure that the field complies with that, and if they don't comply, we would try to find out why. There might be a reason. So we have to really dig hard to find out . . . I was unhappy with a financial report. I was really angry as my first reaction. The second thing would be, 'OK, there are a number of ways of dealing with this.' You either send off a fax immediately, saying, 'I am really, really fed up with this.' That's one option. Now if you go for the first option, what you are going to get at the other end is a person who is sitting 5000 miles away saying, 'There is no way. I'm not going to respond to this. I may have responded if they had asked me politely, but I'm not going to.' So I could have chosen to write a diplomatic letter. In fact, what I did in the end was I decided I would do most of the work here and I'm going to send it back to the field to complete with a letter. What I'm going to do is to write this letter which will say, 'I want you to present your report like this, in the future.'

Susan's letter reaches Beth via her boss. As a field officer, Beth visits project sites, gathers information requested by HQ, and writes reports to HQ. Although all reports are sent to HQ in the name of the country director, the staff in HQ know that Beth deals with report writing. Beth reacts to HQ after the field office presumably received the letter from Susan:

> There was a lot of negative feedback coming from headquarters. 'We feel that reports are not good from the point of view of A, B, C, D, E, F, G.' I think it's also important to have discussions with headquarters on what kind of issues they see that the funder prioritizes. I mean, all the buzzwords are around now, sustainability, community participation, and all those kinds of things. There are issues that headquarters wants very much addressed. Headquarters wants to address them, I think, because their funders are insisting on it. So we have to make that materialize on the ground, which has not brought about much change. They didn't understand our constraints. Their priorities are to have a report or proposal that is very professionally turned out and this is what you are marketing.[31] Our priority is to discuss the thing with project managers and field workers, and see how programmes can be improved, while they are interested in satisfying funders.

Susan's and Beth's comments demonstrate the tensions that arise between HQ and FOs when the organization tries to be accountable both to donors and to projects at the same time. Both Susan and Beth have their own rationales for their assertions. For Susan, the following factors may become the basis for her actions.

First, she feels that whether the organization receives funds or not depends heavily upon her. Although she works under her boss, Susan is the one who actually handles reports from the field and makes sure that reports for donors are of high quality. Consequently, to secure donors' funds, she needs to insist that the field submits high-quality reports that comply with donors' requests.

Second, she does not have enough authority to carry out what she needs to do. She explains her position:

> The only person who really makes phone calls to the field would be the division head. I cannot make a call to the field. I can understand that if everybody is ringing the field over things, things could potentially go crazy. . . . But it can be a bit frustrating when you know you can solve a problem by picking up the phone, or faxing. But I don't feel I should be making decisions for which I'm not getting recognition. I am at development officer level.

As a desk officer, she cannot make a decision to contact donors or the field by herself, although in practice she handles detailed issues from them. Hence, when a donor requests certain information, not only does she not want to question donors – because to do so might leave a negative impression – but she also cannot question the donor because of her limited authority. As a result, her mission becomes one of conveying the donors' request to the field and getting the information from the field.

---

[31] 'Information may be seen by field staff as an activity separate from the "real work" rather than an integral component of effective development activities,' (Edwards, 1994, 120).

Beth has a different view. First, she feels that HQ cares not about what the field does for projects but about what the field staff write. HQ's priority is to serve the donors while the field's priority is to work on projects. What she calls 'buzzwords' make sense for donors but not in the field.

Second, HQ does not understand that the field faces a series of unforeseen circumstances that prevents projects from operating smoothly. Some of these circumstances come about for clear reasons. But when the cumulative result of such small day-to-day events as people not turning up for meetings delays the project as a whole, one cannot explain each small incident to excuse the delay. These non-structural pressures are difficult to convey to people who are not working in the same context. Beth says:

> That type of change needs to be checked with the funders before the change is made. Now, very often you have project managers making decisions on a day-to-day basis which, cumulatively, change the form of the programmes from what the funders or headquarters expect them to be.

While Susan and Beth have their own rationales that fuel the tensions between them, the tensions can be categorized into the three problem areas discussed in the main sections of this book: tensions between the need to maintain the organization and the need to help implement projects in the field; tensions between diversity and similarity among the staff members; and tensions between flexibility and consistency.

Tensions between organizational maintenance and project implementation

Susan experienced the tension between two opposing pressures: one to secure funds by serving donors through submitting high-quality reports and providing necessary information from the field, and one to help the field carry out its projects. While Susan attempted to support the field by providing funds, Beth was not satisfied with Susan's practices and considered Susan a disturbance rather than a help. Funding is important, but supporting the field is also important. How, then, can Susan manage to deal with the two opposing pressures at the same time?

Tensions between diversity and similarity

This second problem area focuses on the similarities and differences among staff members. Susan and Beth exemplify how HQ and FOs staff members view each other differently. Beth feels that HQ works for the sake of donors and not for the field, while Susan tries to support the field by securing funds. Their roles and tasks are different and contradictory in nature. However, they still must share common missions so that they can work together and seek to achieve organizational objectives. They must

11

determine how they can be similar enough to work coherently while at the same time make better use of their distinctive positions, roles, tasks, pressures, values, skills, knowledge, and so forth.

Tensions between flexibility and consistency

This last problem area focuses on the relationship between flexibility in addressing fluid realities and consistency in following structured systems. Looking at the case from this perspective, tensions can be found between rules and regulations imposed by donors and the messy field reality that really does not fit easily into donors' categories. For example, following donors' requests, Susan asks the field to keep HQ informed of decisions that the field makes. However, Beth claims that responding to this systematic request is virtually impossible because, she says, 'project managers are making decisions on a day-to-day basis which cumulatively change the form of programmes.' In the face of fluid realities in the field, systems such as rules and regulations tend to be quite general, yet rigid enough that FOs may often fail to respond to systematic requests from HQ or donors. How can an NGO be flexible enough to address fluid realities while maintaining consistency in treating systems as standards?

The three Parts that follow present an analysis of these problem areas and the strategies NGO staff use to address them.

PART I

Programme-centred vs. Organization-centred Activities

THE RELATIONSHIP BETWEEN an organization's means and ends is a major issue in the study of organizational behaviour.[1] In the case of NGOs, the means and ends may be regarded as organization-centred and programme-centred activities. Organization-centred activities focus on taking care of the organization by acquiring resources, maintaining the staff, and maintaining a safe environment for the organization. These activities are aimed at securing and maintaining the organization itself. Programme-centred activities, on the other hand, focus on accomplishing the organization's goals. Because NGOs cannot ignore either type of activity, they need to maintain a balance between them so that they do not suffer from one of two pathologies: self-destruction or self-perpetuation.

Table 1. Tension in Organizational Activities: Recruitment and Training

Pathology	Area of Tension		Pathology
Self-destruction	Programme-centred	⬅➡ Organization-centred	Self-perpetuation

As Table 1 illustrates, too much emphasis on programme-centred activities at the expense of organization-centred activities can lead the organization to self-destruct. Unless an organization maintains itself, programme activities can destroy the organization, because an organization cannot carry out a project without its own maintenance. On the other hand, too much emphasis on organization-centred activities can lead the organization to act primarily out of an interest in self-perpetuation. In this case, the organization may abandon its primary objectives and seek to maintain itself for its own sake. So, the imbalance of activities can lead to

---

[1] See, for example, Scott (1992).

13

the organizational pathologies of self-destruction and self-perpetuation respectively.

Part I of this book identifies and discusses the problems and strategies of NGO activities in light of the tension between programme-centred and organization-centred activities. This Part pays special attention to the creation and development of NGOs' membership. Although this activity has never drawn much attention from people concerned with development projects,[2] it is crucial in order for the organizations to carry out desirable projects.[3]

The findings of this study focus on two predominant aspects of creating membership – recruitment and staff training – and reveal problems that arise in these areas. Part I examines these two areas of concern in Chapters 2 and 3 respectively.

Chapter 2 identifies and analyses the problems and strategies concerning recruitment. Because this particular research focused only on NGOs that have existed for many years, this chapter's discussion of recruitment applies only to recruiting additional staff members, not to recruiting primary staff to establish a totally new NGO. However, the study is none the less relevant in its discussion of how recruitment influences the organization. The chapter identifies how conventional recruitment practices[4] cause problems related to the tension between programme-centred and organization-centred activities; it then presents alternative recruitment strategies to address these problems.

Chapter 3 identifies and analyses the problems and strategies of creating membership from the point of view of staff training. Staff training is the next step (after recruitment) in ensuring quality membership. The issue of staff training clearly involves a dilemma arising from the tensions between programme-centred and organization-centred activities.

---

[2] Because NGOs have not invested many resources in examining how creating membership influences their activities, recruitment has been treated independently from projects – NGOs' central concerns – as if membership were an external component with little effect on projects. Hence, NGOs do not have their own distinctive theories of creating membership, although their activities have distinctive characteristics compared with other types of organizations. For a discussion of the distinctive features of NGOs, see, for example, Fowler (1991).

[3] Creating membership is the very first step in organizing an NGO and plays a vitally important role in the future of the organization, because NGO staff members are crucial players. The quality of their work affects all activities, including identifying needs in the field, planning development projects, raising funds, writing proposals, making agreements with local governments, carrying out projects, evaluating projects, co-ordinating the organization, and even recruiting new staff members, to name but a few activities.

[4] According to my research, the majority of NGOs have employed conventional approaches that are broadly applied in private sectors to create membership. They recruit and train staff in the same ways that private firms do. However, O'Neill and Young (1988) suggest that training and education for the staff of non-profit organizations (including NGOs) should be distinctive from business and government organizations in terms of the ambiguity of their performance criteria, their legal and financial constraints, their governance structures, and the kinds of personnel they employ.

14

Because NGOs are founded to serve those outside the organizations – as opposed to private firms, which try to maximize their own benefits – NGOs must negotiate these tensions when they train staff. The chapter approaches this problem from several different perspectives and presents strategies for dealing with it.

CHAPTER 2

Recruitment

Human resources are the most difficult, because human beings cannot be programmed to work like computers, giving you specific results. You can provide all the necessary facilities, but the expected outcome is going to be quite different. Some things you cannot foresee . . . so you need a lot of patience and a lot of appreciation.

Local personnel manager

So being willing to be a learner in that situation, for me, is the only way to make any sense.

Senior manager

Introduction

THIS CHAPTER IDENTIFIES and discusses problems that NGO staff members face when they recruit new staff members, and strategies that they use to address these problems. The importance of recruiting staff is not confined to the initial process of forming an organization. Its impact on the future of projects and of the organization as a whole is enormous, because the staff, once recruited, play core roles in planning projects, writing proposals, obtaining funds, negotiating with local governments, implementing projects, and so forth.

Depending upon the intention of recruiters, recruitment can become either a programme-centred or an organization-centred activity. If the staff are more interested in protecting their positions within the organization than in working toward organizational objectives, they tend to use recruitment activities to secure their organizational positions.

In this case, despite the importance of recruitment, NGO staff members are reluctant to question the quality of recruitment because doing so would be tantamount to questioning the quality of recruits, which in turn would imply questions about their own quality, as products of the established recruitment process. Once an NGO recruits a person, that person becomes a member of the organization. Hence, criticizing the recruitment practice implicitly devalues the newly-recruited colleague.

On the other hand, recruitment that over-emphasizes programmes leads NGOs to recruit solely on the basis of programmes' requirements for staff. In this context, recruits may feel unsafe and suffer from fatalism due to their unstable positions, given that the end of the programme means the end of their contracts.

16

Recruitment is a touchy practice, for it can lead to questions about the value of colleagues or even of recruiters themselves. Thus, it can cause many types of problems. For example, an organization may recruit a candidate who is strong in terms of conventional criteria such as expertise, skills and experience, but useless in terms of the organization's actual projects. As a result, the NGO suffers. However, this recruitment is not a simple mistake. This kind of problem occurs for particular reasons, although the reasons are not clarified properly, for clarifying the reasons may result in criticizing the staff themselves. This chapter addresses this knowledge gap by identifying and analysing problems in recruiting and then presenting some alternative recruitment strategies.

Problems: Ambiguity in recruitment

No recruitment process can guarantee that a recruit fits a given position. NGOs employ recruiting criteria, job descriptions, terms of contracts and so forth to regulate the process, to make sure that a suitable person is hired. However, these processes all involve problems that hinder NGOs in recruiting the persons they desire. Moreover, everybody who is involved in recruitment activities has his or her own interests, agendas, pressures, constraints, and limitations that make desirable recruitment (both organization-wise and programme-wise) difficult, if not impossible. Personal accounts from NGO staff members reveal the problems that emerge within the recruitment process.

Inappropriate recruiting criteria
Recruiting based on conventional criteria is not sufficient to recruit suitable persons for the NGO and its projects. Three types of problems derive from recruiting criteria. The first problem is that good CVs do not guarantee desirable persons for the organization. The second problem is that a person with expertise may not fit into the organization due to differences in core values. The third is that the staff may not apply appropriate recruiting criteria to begin with, their own interests taking priority over the interests of the entire organization and its projects. I will address these three problems with examples from personal accounts.

Good CV but undesirable person
A recruitment officer in HQ worries about a gap between what a CV reveals about the person and what the person's actual skills and capabilities are:

> A person might look great on paper, but when I meet him, he might be not a good person, he might have personality conflicts.

17

This officer takes responsibility to recruit expatriates for the field on behalf of country directors because he can communicate with possible candidates more easily than the country directors can. He screens the CVs of applicants and selects several candidates whose CVs appear to fit the request from the field. However, when he meets each of them face-to-face, a person with a better CV may not appear to be a person with a respectable character. He may judge that the person will cause a problem in the field.

People who are experienced or who have professional skills do not necessarily have good characters. They might have strong personal interests that would totally contradict the organization's missions.[1] They may care only about their careers and join the organization merely as a means of career development. They might not care about other staff, and they might try to accomplish their own tasks by exploiting others.

NGOs will often want not to recruit these problematic people regardless of their experience or skills, since they may use their abilities in ways that would only disrupt the organization. However, taking personality into consideration in recruitment criteria is not easy. While we can examine someone's capabilities with little difficulty, we cannot easily know whether the person would use his or her abilities to benefit or exploit the organization. We do not have a clear set of criteria to determine whether 'this person is good for the organization'.

Thus, if the staff care about candidates' personalities, recruiting must rely on a recruiter's subjective judgement, which may be quite different from that of country directors'. But they can identify any discrepancy arising from subjective judgement only when a newly-recruited staff member arrives in the field. By this time it is too late to reconsider the recruitment since the person is already in the field.

Expertise but discrepant values
Another problem is that an NGO has to deal with candidates who have expertise but whose personal values appear to diverge significantly from those of the organization. When an NGO recruits a new staff member it had better look at both professional expertise and personal considerations. NGOs, particularly those based on religion, have their own core values with which all staff are expected to agree. However, these values are not necessarily directly related to their daily activities. For example, making a call to a field office, writing a report for a donor, procuring needed goods, calculating daily expenses, arranging logistics and so on are activities that all NGOs conduct regardless of their core values. Core values do not impinge on day-to-day practical activities, although they

---

[1] Linking personal interests with organizational goals is a classic issue of human services management (Weiner, 1988).

might determine different styles of dealing with activities. Thus, one can conduct daily activities properly without agreeing with the organization's core values.

Ideally, staff should not only have professional skills but should also agree with the core values of the organization. However, the separation of daily tasks from values leads NGOs to use a double standard in recruiting new staff, and thus staff members tend to be divided into two different types. The first type is career-oriented. These members perform their tasks but do not necessarily care about the organization's values. The second type bring with them a strong set of compatible values but insufficient skills to carry out their tasks. For example, a Christian NGO has experienced this difficulty in the field. A local assistant country director says:

> Because a lot of our staff, both local and international, came on due to the fact that they were in the churches, many of these people do not have a professional [background]. Over the years we have tried to develop them but many just can't make it, and this is the major problem. There is a set of people who are very, very powerful, whose Christianity is rather low but who are real professionals. When you are a good Christian, you do not necessarily have the professional skills. Now it is sometimes a tricky issue, having those. We must be able to retrain our people to get them to have both, which is a very difficult job, because we already have a lot of people in-house.

This issue raises different questions at two different stages: the recruiting stage and the training stage. At the recruiting stage, how do NGOs take their two basic needs (i.e. for professional expertise and for shared values) into account? Do they recruit only those who fulfil both needs? How do NGOs look at human potential, which, with appropriate guidance, enables people to grow after they join an organization? If they need to prioritize the two components, how do they do so, and according to what rationale?

At the training stage, two different types of people should be kept in mind. For those who do not have professional backgrounds, training needs can easily be identified. Whether or not the training can achieve the goal is a different question. However, for those with professional expertise but less Christian values, it is unclear how Christian-faith-based NGOs should deal with them. To begin with, whose issue is it anyway? If these staff members can accomplish their tasks, NGOs should not find any problems in their work; personal faith can hardly be regarded as an organizational matter because of its personal and subjective nature. Moreover, judging others' faith is highly dangerous, for nobody can understand another's faith for certain.

On the other hand, can NGOs totally disregard differences in faith simply because staff members work well? This can be a difficult issue

19

from an organizational point of view. An organization needs to have common ground which every staff member can agree with and stand on.[2] Without it, they would lose a sense of membership in the organization. How can an NGO maintain a sense of membership while it does not regulate individuals' faith? In both recruiting and training stages, NGOs face this problem to varying degrees, depending upon their values.

Not for projects but for internal political games

Recruiting for an influential position in an NGO means much to the entire organization, because a person who assumes the position may bring about change in the organization based on his or her intentions. Particularly when different officers in the same organization have different or opposing interests, recruiting a key position is a matter of gaining or losing a colleague with the same interests. If a person who has the same interests as you assumes a key position, your interests gain more power within the organization. But when a person whose interests differ from your own takes the position, your interests are weakened.

For example, recruitment of a country director is not the sole responsibility of the office to which the director is assigned. The recruitment influences other offices as well, including HQ, support offices and even other FOs. If a newly-assigned country director is from HQ, then HQ's influence on the country office may increase. On the other hand, if the position is filled by a person from an office that is not on good terms with HQ, then HQ would expect tougher relationships with the office in the future. Thus, each office tries to get involved in the recruitment process so that their interests can be shared and promoted by other offices.

In the case of a large NGO that has many FOs and many support offices, two major support offices competed for a country director's position. Both of them wanted to have a country director who agreed with their policies, interests, values, culture, etc. Each office struggled to put its own staff up for the position. In the end, one of the two won the competition to have their colleague fill the position. Subsequently, because the position is important to both offices, the new country director has become a focal point of tension between the two offices. He says:

> There is a style of my support office that says, '*No*, this is *our* mission, we do it *our* way.'[3] One of the biggest problems we haven't dealt with is having two headquarters, two heads who have diverging philosophies and priorities. They [the other support office] think that the country director should be a

---

[2] In social change organizations, commitment to values is a key factor in many contexts (Brown and Covey, 1989). Meyer and Zucker (1989, 22–3) argue, '[T]he participation of multiple actors, whose interests sometimes correspond but sometimes conflict, poses significant problems for the ability of owners to impose anything approaching rational utility maximization upon organizations.'

[3] Italics reflect the speaker's emphasis.

person from [their office]. The person should be brought up from there. For me as an outsider – an arrogant outsider – to come in and take a key position is not the way they think it should happen. The other support office [where he is from] doesn't mind that.

When different support offices have different or opposing interests, recruiting to fill a country director's position becomes a battle between these offices to expand their territory.[4] As a result, recruitment takes place without much attention being given to its influence on projects. The opinions of local staff, the situations in the field and the types of projects operating in the country do not become major considerations in recruiting the country director. The recruiting serves the support offices instead of the field.

Discrepant employment terms

Most NGOs have applied different terms of employment for expatriate and local staff. The difference clearly divides an NGO in two. It embodies the South–North relationship within an NGO. It also intensifies the employee–employer relationship between the two. As a result, field staff members suffer while expatriates enjoy secure job contracts.

The difference also exists among expatriates. Paid and unpaid expatriates face different employment conditions. Although they sign their contracts with an understanding of the differences, that does not guarantee that those differences will not create any tensions. In real working situations, the differences between paid and unpaid staff can harm the relationships between the two.

Expatriate vs. local staff

Expatriate and local staff usually have different terms of contract. The salary scales for expatriates are better than those for locals. But the differences extend beyond salary scales. The two groups are likely to experience an employer–employee relationship. To list but a few of the imbalances that typically operate: expatriates usually employ and fire locals but not vice versa; expatriates have authority to make decisions, and only when they delegate that authority to the local staff can the locals make decisions; and expatriates can leave a country in case of emergency, but locals typically cannot. These features characterize the dichotomized organization based on the employer–employee relationship. This relationship contrasts starkly with the values that NGOs generally espouse, such as a grassroots-oriented approach, decentralization, serving the poor, and situating core NGO experiences in the field.

---

[4] Mintz and Schwartz (1981) suggest that interlocking staff at higher levels of organizations significantly influence the formation of interest groups among the organizations. In Japan, a serious political game takes place when former government officials obtain executive posts in private firms or quasi-governmental organizations. Each ministry struggles and competes with the others to fill the posts with their own ex-staff members to expand or maintain their territory.

An expatriate country director observes the local staff's frustration:

> They know the organization very, very well. But there is a glass ceiling and they are never going to move beyond a certain level within the organization. You have expatriates moving in constantly to manage the whole organization. This creates a tremendous amount of frustration, a tremendous amount of potential bitterness that they are never able to make that jump to senior management positions in the country office.

In Third World countries where job opportunities are scarce, the term of a contract is of major interest to local employees.[5] For them, it is a matter of their own survival. They need to keep the job as long as possible because they do not know when they can get another. While this is the story of local employees, on the employer side, expatriates view the contracts of local staff differently. They relate local staff members' contracts to funds and projects, but not to locals' survival. Recruiting and extending local staff has to come with secured funding. If they have funding for two years, the contracts would be for two years, and if the funding continues for five years, then the contracts may also be for five years. Their primary concern is not the local staff members' lives but the financial balance sheet.

Local employees find themselves in a weak and vulnerable position. They must follow whatever is decided at their manager's level in conjunction with the availability of funds. If the organization receives enough funds to continue projects, managers may extend their contracts. But once the funds stop, the organization has to make a tough decision to dismiss staff members. Usually local staff members who are involved in projects are the first to be fired, followed by local project managers. Expatriate staff do not usually become targets of dismissal until most of the local staff are dismissed. Even in NGOs, the weak are the first to be affected by negative circumstances within the organization.

> It was really hilarious when our budget was chopped. There was one chop that was about 60 per cent right off. It meant dismissing staff. It meant getting rid of several projects. So the local staff was very upset, very angry. There was a lot of yelling, shouting, things like that. And there was a sense of fatalism about their work.[6]

When the field office experienced a sudden huge budget cut it had a significant negative impact on the local staff and projects, but not so

---

[5] Handy (1988) suggests that an ideal working situation in a voluntary organization is a co-operative one, in which people come to work because they agree with the missions of the organization and because they are neither made to do so nor paid to do so. However, people in countries where jobs are scarce tend work for NGOs for their own survival.

[6] Fox (1974) argues that trust and distrust in the attitudes of subordinates strongly affect their performance and co-operation. This specific budget cut, however, ended up bringing about a change for the better in the organization. See 'Using tensions', in Chapter 7.

much on expatriates. NGOs' terms of contracts almost always favour expatriates over local staff. Local staff and projects remain insecure despite the fact that a senior manager regards the field as 'the core place of experience in terms of who we [the NGOs] are and how we define ourselves.'[7]

Paid vs. unpaid expatriate staff

Paid and unpaid expatriates work in most NGOs and the difference sometimes causes problems. The difference is fair in one sense but not fair in another. It sometimes causes unnecessary tensions between the two. Paid staff are supported financially by the organization and usually play the core roles within the organization. Unpaid expatriates are usually volunteers in the USA.[8] They work in either the field, support offices or HQ without any financial support from the organization. Those unpaid staff who work in HQ or in support offices normally have their own jobs by which they support themselves, and can therefore contribute part of their time to the organization without receiving any remuneration.

Unpaid expatriates in the field are different. Because they do not usually earn money in the field, they have to rely on outside financial sources. In the case of the USA, the typical method involves getting support from one's friends, church and family while one is in the field. Hence, although these expatriates are unpaid from the organizational point of view, they have financial support from other sources.

If staff members have understood this difference and have still agreed to their terms of contracts, the difference should not be unfair. They have chosen their unpaid or paid positions themselves. NGOs neither hide the difference nor impose the contract. In reality, however, even if they have understood the terms and still signed the contract – and thus made a fair contract with the organization – tensions may still arise between staff members based on differences in their financial status.

In practice, if two people work as colleagues together on the same project, and one is paid while the other is unpaid, the situation is likely to create tensions between them, particularly if the unpaid person performs better than the paid one. Moreover, if the unpaid staff member does not get enough support from outside the organization, tensions can be magnified. A country director observes the double standard:

> It is not inconsistent in the sense that there have always been unpaid staff. So when someone chooses to do that they understand that up front. That's what

---

[7] Brown (1988, 22) argues, 'The core is at the periphery.'

[8] The status of 'volunteer' varies by country. In Britain, for example, volunteers usually receive only allowances from the organization. The situation in Japan is similar. In the USA, in contrast, volunteers usually do not receive any payment from the organization. They are expected to raise their own support in order to work for the organization.

they are doing. It is not a secret. If you choose to do it, you choose to do it. So that way it is not inconsistent. But the reality in the field is that it actually depends on whether their support is consistent or not. If they are short of support, then it becomes awkward for me.

The issue is not whether they agree about the differences but whether they are supported properly or not. This implies a different level of responsibility that NGOs should assume in addition to following the terms of contracts. Even after they agree with their own terms of contract, NGOs cannot ignore an unbalanced situation where one staff member is paid properly while another suffers from lack of financial support. A staff member's 'unpaid' status does not mean that the organization does not care for the person.

Problems in matching a person to a position

Filling a position is not simply a mechanical process of identifying a person who has expertise to execute a position's required tasks. Rather, it involves a number of components that influence a recruited person, the organization as a whole, the recruiter and other staff. Interviewees identified several important issues to consider. These relate to the effectiveness of a recruited person; recruiting methods; the nature of the position; and the continuity and change of the position.

Scarcity of effective local staff

Finding an effective local staff member is much more difficult than most NGO staff realize. NGOs employ two main strategies to fill a position: recruiting from outside the organization, and transferring from within the organization. Usually, an NGO looks within the organization for a suitable person for a post before it starts searching outside. It is both cost-effective and safe when an organization already has contact with the person and understands his or her skills and characteristics. Only when there seems to be no suitable person in-house do NGOs consider recruiting a person from outside.[9]

In local contexts, however, going outside to look for an effective person is usually a fruitless endeavour. Several country directors express frustration in finding an effective local candidate; this country director provides a clue to why finding an effective local recruit is difficult:

> What I have found is that what looks on paper like adequate education is not proving to be so in reality, so I can assume almost nothing about their educational background. The reality is that you can't find people who are already effective in this kind of work. Because this kind of work is not a matter of, 'I'm an accountant, I just do it.' You can't get training for this kind of work in

---

[9] For a discussion of tensions between developing staff and recruiting skilled people, see Handy (1993, 236).

school very much. You learn by experience. You can get some training, but usually it only makes sense after you have some initial experience. Then you go back and build on it. Because you have to have a mental framework to understand. So I usually don't find people who can already do the job – we don't have many.

An effective person is not necessarily a person who has some kind of specialized expertise, for the work that NGOs do is broad and cannot clearly be framed in terms of narrow specialties, except in the case of such jobs as accounting. Thus, as the director suggests, if 'learning by experience' is required for staff to be effective, NGOs have two alternatives. One is to look inside the organization. The other is to recruit a person without having high expectations, and to then develop the person's effectiveness by letting the person 'learn by experience' in the organization. In any case, if these are the only available strategies for securing effective staff, they will work only where longer-term contracts are concerned. Thus, NGOs that employ local staff on short-term contracts to complete a specific job will never have effective staff, apart from luring effective ones from other NGOs.

Playing with chessmen
An NGO often reshuffles personnel to fulfil its needs without considering staff members' personal interests. Reshuffling is attractive because it does not require additional recruitment from outside. From an organizational point of view, this strategy has several advantages, as the preceding discussion indicates. However, a field officer takes a different view:

> There is no one who can work in this position, so my boss just transferred me here. I said, 'May I be in the field and work with people? That's what I love.' But this director really transfers staff without asking whether you would like it or not. This is not good. There are some staff members who are transferred to other positions against their will. That really troubles us, discourages us. I cried when I was transferred to this position. Every night, crying and crying. 'What's wrong?' I really loved what I did. I did my best and everyone said that I was really good at the position.

Her current position is higher within the organizational structure than her previous one was. But she cares more about her job at a project site than about her status in the organization. Thus, transferring her from her niche to a new position disturbs her significantly, even though it is a promotion. In NGOs, where many people join in order to have work that embodies their values, what matters most may not be promotion but having a job that they care about (although they do not view promotion *per se* negatively).

In this officer's particular case, she is discouraged not only because she was transferred but also because of the way in which the director made her transfer. She felt that the director cared only for the organization and did not regard her as a person who has her own preferences. Through such positioning of staff members, the authoritarian relationship between bosses and subordinates is reinforced. Bosses' accountability to the entire organization tends to result in shuffling their subordinates like chess pieces on a board in the name of promotion.

Responsibility without authority
When a position does not carry enough authority for the person who holds it to do their job responsibly and effectively, the person who takes the position faces a problem. The person may receive unwarranted blame for not accomplishing a task that requires more authority. Those who work in the lower positions within an organization often face this gap between what they are responsible for and what they have the authority to do.

For example, these people cannot themselves contact donors, governments or FOs to conduct the NGO's business. Yet, in a practical sense, they are the ones to deal with detailed matters between the parties. They are the ones to write proposals and reports, plan budgets, follow up on projects and so on, although their bosses sign these reports and proposals and represent the organization. Thus, once a problem is found in a report, for example, it can be attributed to them despite their lack of authority to contact the field, and despite the fact that their bosses officially take the responsibility *vis-à-vis* outside parties.

A desk officer at HQ describes the dilemma in which she finds herself. That she does not have authority to make an overseas call negatively influences her performance of her job:

> The only person who really makes phone calls to the field would be the division head. I cannot make a call to the field. I can understand that if everybody is ringing the field over things, things could potentially go crazy. It's important to have a structure, and that's quite justifiable. But it can be a bit frustrating when you know you can solve a problem by picking up the phone, or faxing. But I don't feel I should be making decisions for which I'm not getting recognition. I am at development officer level. That's partly why I can accept that I don't make phone calls. But there are times with funders and the field when it would be easier to make a phone call rather than waiting for somebody to be here. You could just pick up phone and say, 'What do you mean in your report when you say, blah, blah, blah.'

Her colleagues explain that many staff members have a lot of ability and a lot of experience in the field. But once they come back to HQ, they are posted at a lower level on the organizational ladder where the limited authority they are given hinders them in using their abilities properly. Yet, they are still expected to perform well without sufficient authority. As a

26

result, the discrepancy between authority and responsibility[10] discourages them from working effectively. As this officer's case illustrates, the gap can lead workers to lose their motivation to solve a problem, even if they know how to solve it. They tend to be contented with day-to-day mechanical work.[11]

Change and continuity

Recruiting for a replacement for an important position, such as country director, provides a good opportunity to change organizational dynamics. At the same time, it can be an unwelcome challenge if the organization seeks only to maintain the *status quo*. In fact, in any organization, while some aspects need to be changed, other aspects should be kept the way they are. So the issue actually is not whether or not a replacement should make a change in the organization, but how this replacement can better change aspects that need to be changed, and maintain other aspects unchanged. This proposition, however, is much more difficult to put into practice than it appears to be, due to the nature of NGOs.

If an NGO were coherent enough to be able to identify its positive and negative points without any internal conflicts, it could at least plan, if not execute easily, to change the negative aspects while leaving the positive aspects unchanged. However, in practice, different offices in an NGO have discrepant views, ideas and interests that make the use of a replacement as a source of a planned change very difficult.[12] Consequently, the change and continuity derived from replacing the person in a key position become products of chance.

Although an organization has broad missions with which all the staff members should agree, each member not only has different ways of interpreting missions but also has different ways of executing them. On the one hand, the differences should be appreciated as productive of diversity. They provide alternative approaches, broaden the perspectives of the staff members, and provide staff with the opportunity to interact with each other when they would not ordinarily do so. On the other hand, the differences are not merely differences between individuals; nor are they always appreciated in real organizational contexts. When particular ways of interpreting missions and particular ways of engaging in development are valued by the leadership of an organization, staff under the leadership try to shape their behaviour to fit those interpretations and practices.

---

[10] Baum's (1987) clarification about ambiguous authority and responsibility in the bureaucratic structure provides valuable insights into the discrepancy between authority and responsibility.
[11] Cf. Chamberlain and Kuhn's (1965, 435) 'conjunctive bargaining': 'it provides no incentive to the parties to do more than carry out the minimum terms of the agreement which has temporarily resolved their divergent interests.' Quoted from Fox (1974, 29).
[12] See March and Olsen (1989, 57–8).

I'm the third country director in five years here. Every country director has a different philosophy of management, of work, and of development. So my field co-ordinator said, 'How much longer will you be here? Because you've asked us to do things in very different ways, which is OK, but if the next guy comes, will he allow us [to do it this way]?'

Apparently, his staff are confused by the change in leadership. They have principles that are loosely defined, but their methodologies are all different. The previous country director focused more on concrete projects while the new director encourages the staff to play facilitating rather than managerial roles to get the job done. Even within the same organization, inconsistency in the different directors' approaches diminishes staff members' motivation to adapt to changing strategies, for they feel that what they do may be disregarded after another new country director arrives in the near future.

Can these kinds of policy differences experienced by the staff be regarded as a matter of diversity? If not, how can staff, including leadership, co-ordinate activities to secure continuity in key operations while not compromising productive diversity? Do staff members or the country director identify what needs to be changed and what needs to remain constant when a new country director assumes the position? Is there any mechanism by which an organization can maintain its continuity regardless of a change in leadership? Many important questions emerge and remain unanswered. No clear processes can address these practical issues. Diversity is important, continuity is important, and change is important when necessary. How, then, do the staff manage the paradox? In the strategy section in the second half of this chapter, I discuss how NGO staff attempt to respond to these challenges. First, however, I address one more recruitment problem.

Ambiguous recruiting processes

In most NGOs, country directors take full responsibility for recruiting both expatriate and local staff in their assigned countries. However, because the information available in the field is often incomplete, country directors normally have to delegate to HQs the task of selecting candidates when they hire an expatriate staff member for the field. Thus, the director has little influence beyond approving or disapproving of choices already made elsewhere. This recruiting process sometimes causes problems.

If a country director had sufficient information to select appropriate candidates and make a final selection of the best person among them there would be no organizational problem, with the possible exception of his or her bad judgement resulting in a poor choice. However, in practice, because country directors are in the field where they do not have much access to information on prospective expatriate candidates, their ability to handle recruitment effectively is limited.

As a result, they have to depend on HQ to look for candidates. The delegation of this task to HQ renders recruitment an organizational issue. The task requires interaction between HQ and the country director and thus makes the process more complex than if it were done solely by the country director. An assistant country director describes the tensions that the recruiting process entails:

> We needed an agronomist. We would say, 'Yes,' or 'No,' or whatever. Headquarters would come back and say, 'We were having people such and such and we made a decision at the end.' But it was difficult because they had all the interaction with the persons and information. But they did not have current information or the job description. There was a communication breakdown. The person came with his own expectations, which might differ from the situation in the field. That was always a big problem. We could not hire directly. We had to go through the headquarters. So from time to time they went into that problem. It is not easy to say, 'Yes' or, 'No.' For example, one person was an engineer. He was about 65 years old and his wife was about 70. And we gave the recommendation that it was not a good idea [to hire him]. But he came anyway. Because unless you say absolutely, 'No, we won't stand for this . . .' And if you say, 'No,' too many times, you cannot say, 'No,' again. They may be unclear about us: 'Who are these people?' You know?

Delegation of the recruiting process to HQ makes the process more complex and difficult than it would otherwise be. First, a gap between reality and available information always exists on both sides. HQ may lack the updated country information necessary to communicate with candidates properly. It must rely on job descriptions sent from the field. On the other hand, the field also does not have much information concerning candidates except their profiles, which cover technical aspects only. HQ cannot foresee how the candidates fit into the actual field context.

Second, a gap between what the field expects of a recruit and what the person's capabilities actually are tends to remain unclear until the person arrives in the field. By the time staff realize that the gap between expectations and reality is too much to tolerate, it is too late to reconsider the decision, for the person is already in the field.

Third, although country directors officially have a final say in hiring a person, they cannot easily reject a candidate that HQ has chosen. They need to take into account the effort expended by HQ to select the candidate. They are obliged to accept the selected candidate as positively as possible, for they delegated to HQ responsibility for looking for candidates on their behalf. They are implicitly expected to appreciate the HQ's selection by approving the candidate.

Fourth, unless the field staff come to a strong and clear consensus against a candidate – which is very unlikely, due to the insufficient information available to them to judge in advance – they will not be able to reject the candidate. If they do not do so, HQ assumes that they accept the candidate and sends the person to the field.

These four situations explain how an undesirable person can be sent to the field when the field delegates the candidate selection process to HQ. The field does not have other, better alternatives.

In the first half of this chapter, I have identified problems that NGO staff face when they recruit additional staff. Inappropriate recruiting criteria, discrepant employment terms, problems in matching a person to a position, and an ambiguous recruiting process have been discussed and illustrated with personal accounts. I now turn to the strategies that NGO staff employ to address these problems.

Strategies: Alternative recruitment

To tackle recruitment problems, several recruitment strategies can be used. Introducing alternative criteria, recruiting based on trust, and dealing with organizational consistency and change are among the strategies that NGO staff practise. The three types of strategies are all independent and can be applied simultaneously. However, because these strategies are applied in specific contexts, their relevance varies according to the situation. They might even cause a problem in some situations. Thus, contextualizing these strategies within specific situations is left to the person who wants to apply them. Nevertheless, that does not devalue the strategies.

Introducing alternative criteria
To supplement conventional criteria, I suggest several alternative criteria as ways to look at applicants from different perspectives. These include sensitivity, the ability to listen and learn, active patience, and honesty – criteria that can be used as strategic tools to improve the quality of recruitment. NGO staff identify these factors as important attributes to improve the quality of work in NGOs. Although they do not suggest these recruiting criteria, they are worth considering.

Sensitivity
Sensitivity can be a crucial alternative criterion when recruiting staff. Sensitivity, according to *Webster's Third New International Dictionary*, 'is the capacity of a person to respond emotionally to changes in his interpersonal or social relationships.' According to this definition, noticing a change is an initial step; subsequent response should emerge from one's feelings about the change. I will assess how sensitivity is important in NGOs in two phases: notification and response.

The initial step of recognizing change merits special attention in the case of NGOs. Their working environments, both physical and social, are dynamic. For example, they might face severe drought that would force them to shift their activities from development to relief. There might be a political turnover that would void their project agreement with a local government. Moreover, an NGO's internal complexity makes the organization itself dynamic. For example, internal interactions between HQ and an FO involve different cultures and socio-political environments. Furthermore, the two offices may have different or even opposing interests.

When an NGO itself is changing, how can the staff better deal with their daily work in order to recognize changes? A field administrator says:

> I don't look at people as a subject. In treating individuals as persons knowing that they have feelings just like you, you affect them to a great extent. Sometimes you do things which affect people beyond themselves. So, in dealing with people, you are dealing with more than persons. Somebody might be in a financial problem, and their children are out of school. So when you are dealing with such a situation, you also have to know how the problem affects them, how it would affect their work, how would you help. Sometimes you find you cannot help in an official capacity; then I go out of my way and deal with the person . . . not as an official, but as myself.

Sensitivity to change in others would mean that one is able to put oneself in another's position and view things from their perspective. This process in fact leads to the second part of sensitivity: response based on feelings. By mentally putting oneself in another's position, one is more likely to be involved in and moved by the other person's concerns. As this administrator explains, it is important to try to understand issues behind the scenes, more so than if one is concerned only about problems and not the persons experiencing them.

The two phases of sensitivity together involve the ability to be human-oriented rather than task-oriented. With sensitivity, people can better understand another person's circumstances, position, feelings, interests, problems, and so forth. However, this does not mean ignoring tasks, rules and regulations in organizations. As a strategy, the administrator explains the art of finding a balance between what he calls the people's world and organization's world:

> I find myself trying to balance between people's worlds and the organization's policies and needs. It's the kind of balance that can't always be done. When there is a conflict between the two interests, the interests of the organization have to be taken care of first. But when the interests of the organization are not adversely affected, then something good is being done for the staff member in every way, not just personnel-wise, but in every way that it matters. Sometimes, it could even be a telephone call. The policy may be that no personal calls should be made. But somebody makes one personal call home or to somebody he or she wants. So you have to figure out what difference it makes to the person or to the organization. You may find that, by making that

31

call, she will feel comfortable the rest of the afternoon and work properly. If you stick to the policy, she would not work properly because you've denied that call, and you find now you are affecting the organization. So it's a tricky situation.

One noteworthy point is that taking care of people's interests before the organization's interests is not necessarily costly to the organization. Rather, it may sometimes have a positive impact on the organization. Sensitivity can facilitate good working relationships among the staff, and this, in turn, can informally but significantly contribute to the performance of the organization as a whole.

So, how can NGOs find or train sensitive people? A senior manager reluctantly characterizes sensitivity as 'good heart', which cannot easily, if at all, be instilled through official training. In this sense, 'good heart' should be distinguished from technical skills that can be obtained by training.

On the other hand, to say that 'good heart' can never be learned is also not true. In responding to the question of how to develop sensitivity, a local manager told this story:

> I was told about a girl. Everyone thought that she was terrible. But this couple said, 'She is a nice little girl. She left her country to come to work for this family overseas.' The girl said, 'Who said that? Nobody ever thinks that I'm good.' One day the couple said, 'Dear, would you like to come to our house for dinner?' She came and she felt that she was loved. Now she is very well and supports many people. She changed completely. People may not appear to be good, but don't think that they are bad all the time. [We need to have] a new way of looking, love and understanding. Because of love, we try to understand why they do such things. And if I try to do my best and people misunderstand or react to me badly, which I get very often, I thank God, for these things keep me humble.

The strategy of this couple was not to blame the girl but to emphasize her positive aspects and show their love by having informal, friendly interactions with her. While this seems to be a powerful story, the narrator does not ignore the possibility of misunderstanding and failure that may result from such an attempt. However, she internalizes it strategically as a positive side effect by regarding the possible unpleasant results as a lesson to keep one humble. This strategy is not only a powerful tool to develop a person's sensitivity; it also takes care of risks on the side of the practitioner.

Ability to listen and learn
Another alternative criterion is the ability to listen and learn. As with sensitivity, this criterion also characterizes the attitude of the prospective staff member to explore something beyond the static knowledge,

expertise, skills, and experiences that conventional criteria emphasize. However, the ability to listen and learn should not necessarily over-shadow knowledge, expertise, skills and experiences. They are different, but not opposites.

Skill-oriented recruiting criteria assume that an NGO has a set of clearly defined, framed and specialized tasks for newcomers. For ex-ample, accounting and auto mechanics are tasks that require spe-cialized skills. However, jobs with NGOs do not always entail clear-cut tasks. Specialized skills do not contribute much to administrators, be-cause administrative jobs require a variety of different tasks. Moreover, administrators never know what issues they may have to deal with in the future. For example, emergency situations may suddenly arise, bud-get cuts may unexpectedly hit the organization, or local governments may strictly regulate the organization, to name but a few possible cases. Hence, jobs with NGOs are full of irregularity and uncertainty. And this is the reason to emphasize listening and learning abilities as important recruiting criteria. Stipulating these abilities as important criteria implies that the staff do not know what is crucial to understand. A senior man-ager explains:

> When I was working in education evaluation, there were a lot of standards and a lot of theories, a lot of stuff that people generally agreed with, and so you could answer those questions, not easily but more or less straightfor-wardly . . . But when you go into a rural village in Africa and say, 'What does quality of life mean here?', what is meant to improve quality is not so obvious. So being willing to be a learner in that situation, for me, is the only way to make any sense.

He clarifies the relationship between *what* to do and *how* to do it. De-pending upon what you want to do, you have different ways of achieving it effectively. Thus, if you have a clear task in your mind, then you may easily identify which skills and experiences are required for accomplish-ing the task. However, as the manager indicates, if what you want to do is not clear at the beginning, you need the ability to explore and identify an initial issue. Therefore, the ability to listen and learn, in fact, does not conflict with specialized skills that staff members already have.

The danger may be that in acquiring specialized skills, one could lose the ability to examine the relevance of those skills to the issue at hand. Once acquired, a skill tends to become the primary technique for tackling any and all issues, regardless of their nature. One might fail to examine a better combination of what to do and how to do it. In the face of this tendency, the ability to listen and learn contributes invaluably to self-criticism. Particularly in the field of development, this ability is crucial, for we do not know in advance whether or not the skills people bring with them are relevant. Only through a co-operative learning process may the staff and the local beneficiaries explore possible combinations of what to do and how to do it.

Active patience
Patience can be another valuable alternative criterion. Several staff members, both local and expatriate, cite patience as a crucial criterion for those who are involved in development projects because the projects are long term and often face unexpected diversions. Implicit in this concept of patience is a kind of bearing. This, however, is not the only meaning of the term.

While patience can be defined as 'the bearing of provocation, annoyance, misfortune, or pain without complaint, loss of temper, or anger',[13] many NGO staff members use the term differently. Many attribute 'patience' to an active and persistent involvement with an issue without giving up easily. This important involvement based on patience characterizes ways in which they deal with issues.

In an NGO, staff members whose values, cultures, interests and agendas differ from those of the organization almost always create problems no matter how strong the organizational culture is. The staff members' interactions may frequently be unpredictable and upsetting to them.

However, a local senior manager claims, 'NGO staff should not stop dealing with issues but [should] keep on interacting . . . despite the differences.' Patience, in this sense, is interpreted as an open mind – open to criticism and misunderstanding. This would also suggest that patience is a kind of tolerance of being opposed by others.

The above analyses indicate that patience may include active and persistent involvement, on the one hand, and openness to criticism and misunderstanding, on the other. Therefore, patience takes work, not just waiting. It helps the staff undertake both action and reflection processes simultaneously. It helps the staff complete the circle of the action-reflection learning processes[14] in the midst of problems.

Honesty
Honesty is another criterion that a recruiter should take into account. If a staff member describes only the positive aspects of a project and does not discuss its negative side, they cannot be trusted. However, discussing the negative aspects of a project is difficult; as one staff member says, 'you can only admit your mistake if you feel you wouldn't be penalized.' Even under this pressure, honest persons try to tell the entire story of the project rather than trying to please the boss by describing only its positive aspects. Persons who can honestly tell the whole story can earn trust from

---

[13] *Webster's Third New International Dictionary* (1981).
[14] See Schön (1982), Schön and Rein (1994).

their bosses, although they need to take a risk to reveal the project's negative aspects. A country director explains how an honest person can gain trust while a person who presents only positive aspects loses trust:

> If I go into a programme, and somebody is continually pointing out to me only good and successful points, and I don't hear any of the negative aspects, then I have a problem with this. Then I would begin to ask questions, and if the story that keeps on coming back is a very, very positive one, then I will begin to mistrust the person, because I think they are not telling the full story. But if they can tell me good things and bad things and explain to me why we should continue, then I have much more trust in that person because I feel they have been open.

If NGOs want to recruit people who are trustworthy, they have to recruit honest people who can tell the entire story even if doing so conflicts with their own interests.

Recruiting based on trust

This strategy assumes that job descriptions and required expertise explain too little to judge a person's suitability, and suggests that the recruiter intentionally and actively use his or her personal judgement based on basic information such as job description, CVs, and the situation in the field. This strategy does not consider job descriptions and CVs as the core judgement resources. The resources can only help the recruiter judge suitable persons. The recruiter makes a final decision based on his or her personal interactions with candidates. Therefore, to take this recruiting strategy, the field needs to trust the recruiter and delegate full authority and responsibility to the recruiter.

What kind of people should be responsible for recruitment, then? The recruiter should not be a person who only follows the established set of criteria. The person should be trustworthy in the sense of caring about people in the field and thinking carefully about how a recruited person fits into the field context.

The three passages that follow represent the different views of a recruiter, a recruit and a country director respectively. They help to clarify what needs to be addressed when the recruiter at HQ recruits staff for the field. The recruiter says:

> I can give you a person who I am confident with in terms of their character and ability to learn, and I'm sure their general parameters and skills may not be exactly what you are looking for. But I think that they will be a better person [for the job].

The recruit says:

> I was a volunteer here many years ago. So with a number of people I had a relationship already. Ben was my boss and Tom was my peer. So initially they

were very helpful in saying nice things about me because of my past performance. If Ben says, 'He is a good man,' he is a good man. If Tom says, 'We should hire him,' we should hire him.

The country director says:

I've worked with Lisa in the field. So I know her well and respect her judgement. She knows my programmes here and she knows me and she knows the staff here, and if she meets somebody and tells me that this person is good, then I will take her word for it.

Overall, these voices suggest that trust between a recruiter in HQ and the field staff who delegate the recruitment task to HQ is a determining factor in the success of the recruitment. Trust can alter relations remarkably. Individuals will – to the extent to which they trust others with whom they have contact – like what the others like.[15]

First, the recruiter selects a person about whom she or he feels confident instead of others who have better qualifications on paper. Without trust, one cannot dare to take this action. Introducing a criterion like 'feeling confident' is totally subjective; therefore, the recruiter cannot defend and justify him- or herself if the field is not satisfied with the selected recruit.

Second, establishing a trustworthy relationship between the HQ staff and the recruit is a clear plus for the recruit when she or he goes to work in the field. The field staff welcome the recruit without much doubt if they hear good things about the recruit from HQ. Especially when a person whom the field staff can trust admires the recruit, the field can easily take their word, such as, 'If Ben says he is a good man, he is a good man'. With trust, they can go beyond narrowly defined criteria and look at a candidate as a whole person.

Third, with trust, the field can accept a recruit selected by HQ without doubts. When a country director says, 'if she meets somebody and tells me that this person is good, then I will take her word for it,' the director welcomes the person based on the trust between the director and the recruiter. Trust, however, is not mere faith in another. As the country director indicates, trust more likely develops when the staff understand not only each other's personality but also each other's working situations.

Dealing with consistency and changes

In-house recruiting
Another recruiting strategy is in-house recruiting that consistently maintains the organizational intention. This differs from maintaining the *status quo*. Instead of being simply conservative, the strategy emphasizes consistent changes to meet organizational missions, regardless of staff turnover.

---

[15] See March and Olsen (1989, 44).

Maintaining consistency in an NGO does not conflict with making a change in the organization to increase effectiveness. On the contrary, to make changes effectively an organization must maintain consistent objectives. Consistency should be clearly distinguished from conservatism, or maintaining the *status quo*. If important positions in the organization are filled by people with different stances or opposing ideas concerning organizational change, the inconsistency could become a major obstacle to change.

In view of the importance of consistency, one may conclude that recruiting staff from within the organization for key positions is a wise way to maintain consistency and organizational culture, and to ease the transition from predecessor to successor.

> Most of the country directors in the organization have had at least 15 years of experience with the organization. I think that sense of commitment[16] to the organization is very important when it comes to people who fulfil the roles of country directors because we are not like cookie-cutters, we are not exactly the same. But there is something of our corporate culture which has influenced us, and that means although some of us have very different skills and abilities and approaches, there is a consistency, a great consistency in the organization.

This director is from a large NGO, where in-house recruitment would be valued more than in smaller organizations. For larger organizations, staff who share objectives and understand particular ways to put objectives into practice are more difficult to come by than in smaller organizations, in which the staff can understand each other more easily. For the sake of maintaining organizational consistency and culture, in-house recruiting may be an important strategy for larger NGOs.

A likely challenge for those NGOs, then, would be how practically to distinguish consistency from the *status quo*. While they strive to maintain consistency, they need to avoid being trapped within the *status quo*. They maintain a challenging spirit, and continually work to make the organization better and more effective. Bearing this in mind is very important because in-house recruiting does not require intensive interactions outside the organization and this narrowed focus can often make the organization more conservative.

Balancing consistency and change in transition
The last recruiting strategy argues that the types of transition from a predecessor to a successor affect the characteristics of recruitment. For example, a long transition period may be an effective strategy to ensure organizational consistency while a short one may be relevant if the

---

[16] Drucker (1990) lists opportunities, competence and commitment as the three 'musts' of a successful mission of non-profit organizations.

organization seeks to make significant changes.[17] The strategy assumes that an appropriate transition should not only seek organizational consistency but should also, if necessary, motivate organizational changes. The strategy suggests that, in addition to a recruit's selection, a proper transition process be selected and applied to ensure successful recruitment. Three transition types can be identified, based on the length of the transition period. Because different lengths of transition affect the organization in different ways, each strategy has both advantages and disadvantages.

Starting from scratch. The first transition type involves no hand-over from a predecessor to his or her successor to teach the tasks that the position entails. This transition requires the successor to start from scratch. Although no hand-over is usually considered unfortunate and is not usually applied strategically, this transition would probably result in introducing virtually new styles of work to the position by unlinking the predecessor and successor. A field administration manager describes her experience:

> [It was like] I was thrown into the sea to swim or sink. I didn't meet my predecessor. There was nobody. There was just a clerical person trying to handle issues. So I had a big backlog of things. I wasn't given any orientation. There was no booklet to tell me about what projects get what annually. You come and you don't know what you are coming for. I just found my way from someone. I just survived.

As nobody told this manager what to do when she assumed the position, she had to struggle to survive. She had to ask everybody for everything for the first three months to deal with her daily work. In her case, however, as she learned what she was expected to do, she established her own management style and became satisfied with working in her own style.

Many staff members who experienced no hand-over describe their difficult and arduous time as novices without any guidance. Most of them do not recommend no hand-over. Although they can learn the job from other staff and can go through the files to study the history of the job, a huge cache of valuable experiences can never be retrieved.

However, as this case illustrates, despite their reluctance to accept no hand-over, officers who assume their positions in this way are more likely to put their own ideas, *modus operandi* and values into practice than if they had been influenced by their predecessors. In fact, people in leadership positions do not need to care much about hand-over to the degree that they consider their tasks as embodying their visions in practice rather than simply following whatever they are told to do.

---

[17] Staudt (1991) purports that a key component to enhance the transformation of organizational culture is staff replacement and renewal.

Therefore, the tough transition at the beginning that comes from being 'thrown into the sea to swim or sink' will reward the staff members as they begin to create their own styles of work. However, the lack of opportunities to learn from their predecessors the organization's unwritten history – such as mistakes that were made in the past, interpersonal conflicts within the office, the organization's relationship with external constituents, and so on – may be a great loss.

Emphasizing consistency. In contrast to the scenario of no hand-over, the majority of NGO staff members support a moderate period of hand-over. Unlike leadership, for those who work as specialists, such as accountants, procurement officers and logistics officers, no hand-over is disastrous. Because their job requires them to follow clearly-established procedures, learning the procedures from their predecessors is far more important than developing their own methods. They cannot apply any brilliant ideas of their own without understanding how the established procedures function.

Yet, predecessors emphasize the benefit of long hand-over more than successors do. Many predecessors feel that they do not want to see their successors having trouble due to the lack of hand-over. This good intention, however, seems not to take into account the will of their successors. That is, the stance almost implies that successors need to be taught, for they do not know the job. This intention, as opposed to their expectation, may result in devaluing other resources that the successor has access to, and discouraging alternative ways of doing the job that would better fit the successor's desires and capabilities.

The hand-over transfers a predecessor's experience to a successor as a part of corporate memory. Inheriting past experiences is a precious tool to avoid what a staff member calls 'corporate amnesia'. The hand-over, however, is not only an occasion for transferring experiences. It also shapes the successor's behaviours so that she or he will follow certain ways of doing things and thereby reproduce both positive and negative aspects of behaviour patterns in the organization and its culture. Thus, a moderate-length hand-over is an effective tool to ensure organizational consistency; at the same time, however, it is an obstacle to change.

Balancing changes and consistency. No hand-over tends to encourage change but discourage consistency. A long hand-over tends to encourage consistency but discourage change. The third transition type takes a path between these two, in an effort to retain the positive aspects of each. It simultaneously tries to convey accumulated corporate memory and also opportunities to make changes. A country director suggested short hand-over with a remarkable insight. Although my research interviews show that short hand-over is not popular among the staff, the director's account offers a valuable insight into the dynamics of the interpersonal relationships between a predecessor and a successor:

> I think a long handover can be very destructive, like for six weeks or longer. It makes it very difficult for the person taking over as well as for the person who is leaving because the person coming in is coming in with a lot of new ideas, and fresh thoughts, and fresh ways of looking at things, the person who is handing over has been here for a number of years, has attained the level that he or she wants. And some person coming in with new ideas can be a little bit disturbing. You are not taking over an empty voyage, you are taking over with a lot of people around and lot of support, and lot of staff and lot of documentation. And you can learn as you go along.

While most staff members worry about losing consistency, the director worries about losing a chance to bring in new views. The director claims that a short hand-over is better than a long hand-over or no hand-over. It can maintain organizational consistency and bring in new ideas at the same time. Consistency can be maintained without depending upon the predecessor too much when a variety of resources are available to support the successor. As a result, a short hand-over is used only for learning about important issues and relevant experiences from the predecessor briefly, not in detail.

The fresh ideas of the successor can be protected when the predecessor refrains from explaining everything in excessive detail to the successor, with the goal of making the latter a copy of the former. While a longer hand-over tends not only to provide a rich corporate memory but also to shape the behaviour of the successor, a shorter one would provide more opportunities for the successor to bring his or her own experiences, values, cultures, interests, knowledge and so forth to the organization.

This strategy is designed to retain the benefits of both long hand-over and no hand-over. But what if the strategy ends up retaining the negative aspects of both? If the successor does not have enough resources to maintain corporate memory, or if the successor does not have enough opportunities to make a change due to some type of strict constraint, a short hand-over may be disastrous, with neither new views nor corporate memories.

All three types of hand-over have both positive and negative aspects. We cannot say one type is better than another without taking into account the context in which each is used. A good hand-over retains valuable information, experiences and ideas, but it also provides enough room for successors to attempt to improve practices in their own ways. The challenge for predecessors is to be able to transfer their valuable experiences and knowledge without imposing their style and behaviour. The challenge for successors is to determine how they can better balance hand-over from predecessors and the valuable originality that they bring with them.

Conclusion

This chapter has discussed problems that NGO staff face when they deal with recruitment and strategies that they employ to tackle problems, according to their personal accounts. Problems of inappropriate recruiting criteria, discrepant employment terms, mismatching people to positions, and ambiguous recruiting processes have been identified and analysed. The second half of the chapter has presented strategies involving the alternative criteria of recruiting based on trust, and dealing with consistency and change.

When NGOs want to succeed in recruiting, they should understand expected problems and be ready to apply a suitable alternative recruiting strategy that fits a given situation. Although no strategy is a panacea, and a strategy's relevance depends upon the context in which it is employed, several general guidelines can be identified.

First, NGOs need to consider broader recruiting criteria that include personal aspects in addition to conventional ones, rather than solely applying the conventional criteria. These criteria include: sensitivity and understanding others from their perspective; ability to listen and learn from others regardless of one's knowledge, experiences, and organizational position; active patience and persistent involvement with issues; and honesty in telling the entire story even if that goes against one's own interests.

Second, to take into account personal aspects as major criteria, staff members should develop trust in each other so that they can delegate recruiting tasks to other staff members with confidence. Without developing trust between the field staff and the recruiters at HQ, NGOs cannot successfully apply these recruiting criteria because evaluation based on the criteria depends heavily on the judgement of recruiters.

Third, NGOs should employ the staff in such a way that the staff do not suffer from problems that arise from the employment terms. This issue is not whether the distinction between paid and unpaid staff members is reasonable or not, but how each staff member's needs are met.

Fourth, when an NGO rotates its staff members between HQ and the field, the organization should carefully arrange HQ's positions so that skills, knowledge and experiences that the staff bring back from field can be effectively and efficiently used as resources. In particular, the balance between authority and responsibility should be carefully taken into account.

Fifth and finally, NGOs should use recruiting opportunities strategically to maintain organizational consistency and make necessary changes. To manage the consistency and changes, transitions from predecessors to successors should be carefully planned. The more a predecessor and a successor share time together, the more likely it is that consistency will be maintained, and the less likely it is that changes will be brought about.

41

These problems and challenges are specific to each context and cannot easily be applied to other situations. However, when the staff are equipped with knowledge regarding expected problems and possible strategies, they are more likely to handle recruitment better.

CHAPTER 3

Staff Training

The project is surrounded by so much uncertainty, and the staff, therefore, feel that 'I'm only in the organization for a short time.' That is the feeling that I would like to remove in the training.

Local personnel manager

A development organization has to focus on developing its own people, or it cuts its own throat.

Country director

Introduction

TRAINING STAFF INVOLVES a paradox. Unlike training beneficiaries in the field, training the staff is designed to develop people within the organization. Thus, from the point of view of the organization, training can be an organization-centred activity insofar as it serves to develop staff for the organization's purposes. However, at the same time, training can be regarded as a programme-centred activity and as an organization's provision of services to new recruits insofar as the organization does not expect staff to perform well in the field without it.

This chapter examines problems that derive from staff training and presents strategies that staff employ to respond to these problems. Based on personal accounts from NGO staff, these problems fall into three categories: short-range return vs. long-range return; locals vs. expatriates; and direction vs. manipulation. Although these categories illustrate different aspects of the problems, they all refer to the same problems. As the core cause of the problems, they refer to the tensions between serving programmes and serving the organization.

Four strategies for responding to these problems are presented here. These strategies are also taken from accounts by people in the field; they demonstrate the possibility of going beyond the problems by employing training that serves broader interests.

Problems: Serving programmes vs. serving the NGO[1]

Ideally, NGOs do not serve themselves or donors. They are founded to promote the development of the Third World in one way or another.

---

[1] See Billis (1993) for a discussion of organizational tensions between self-serving and service providing.

Although the kinds of development they promote vary from distributing needed goods to helping local people support themselves, all NGOs are targeted to serve people outside the organization, not inside. In light of this basic principle, staff training is paradoxical, for it can be regarded as serving the NGO, although NGOs train the staff in the hope that they will better execute their missions.[2] The first half of this chapter examines the problems derived from the tension between serving programmes and serving the organization from three different perspectives: the timing of expected benefits; types of training needs; and types of influences on the staff.

Hard to expect long-range returns

The first problem is that NGOs cannot expect long-range returns from staff training because of the high turnover among staff members, uncertainty about the relevance of the training in rapidly changing contexts, and cost-effectiveness of training the staff versus recruiting skilled workers. In a circumstance in which donors strictly monitor the effectiveness and efficiency with which NGOs spend their funds, investing funds in their own staff members is a risky practice for NGOs, due to unpromising long-range returns. When NGOs cannot expect long-range returns, they are induced to modify the training they provide to target short-range returns even if they do not give up the training. A local staff member describes the training:

> Our training is less person-oriented; it's task-oriented. Our sense of satisfaction is when we accomplish our tasks even if other persons get slighted. But this doesn't last; relationships last.[3]

If his opinion, 'It [seeking immediate gain] doesn't last; relationships last,' is not unrealistic, training for immediate gain hardly makes sense. This type of training offers few lasting benefits and comes at the expense of valuable relationships among the staff that, according to him, last longer. However, understanding this trade-off *per se* may still not be sufficient to motivate NGOs to redirect their training to long-range goals, given the unpromising returns associated with doing so. Only if NGOs can reasonably expect that today's training will produce a significant return in the long run will they bring a long-range perspective to their training.[4] Yet

---

[2] In the study of organizational behaviour, this issue – means and ends of an organization – has been a central theme. For example, Levy (1982, 53) describes this type of tension as the tension between organizational maintenance and organizational effectiveness; he underscores their tricky relationship when he quotes (Gouldner, 1963, 162): 'one of the groups which the welfare agencies help, and for whom they provide basic gratification, are the social workers themselves.'

[3] Handy (1990, 145) suggests that 'short-term profit at the expense of quality will lead to short-term lives.'

[4] Drucker (1990) argues that we identify what to do today based on feedback from the long range.

44

NGOs can easily be discouraged from investing in their own staff for the future.

Training under conditions of high turnover

The high turnover of local staff, which is mainly attributable to NGOs' unstable working situations, discourages organizations from investing in staff training.[5] For example, at a time of emergency in the field, many donors are interested in donating funds to NGOs. To meet donors' requests and the field's needs, NGOs hire new staff members and expand projects. But as the emergency develops into a chronic, long-term situation, donors lose interest and withdraw funding or start to look for another emergency case. The result is that NGOs are forced to close projects and fire the extra staff. High turnover is caused mostly by fluctuations in external resource flows and is unfortunately a common phenomenon in unstable NGO contexts.

In the high-turnover situation, staff training is not expected to contribute to an NGO's projects because the trained staff may leave at any time. In this situation, training is designed to achieve a different goal. One local personnel officer fights staff members' short-term fatalism through training. His contextually rich and vivid account is worth quoting at length:

> I know what the staff members think. They are here only for a short time. We have a very high turnover, and basically this has nothing to do with firing staff indiscriminately or things like that. We do have projects that are funded only for a limited time. The refugee project, for example, is something that is surrounded by so much uncertainty and the staff, therefore, feel that 'I'm only in the organization for a short time.' That is the feeling that I would like to remove in the training. You would like to give staff the feeling that they belong and they can grow within the organization. That feeling is not there right now. The number of staff over the last two years has grown 100 per cent, from about 250 to about 570 currently. Staff members do not know what the organization is doing about getting other projects, because this one is about to wind up or this one is about to move to another phase. [They are asking,] 'Can I be absorbed into some other area of operations?' We have had lots of staff coming in and going out. There is a feeling of a lot of job insecurity. You cannot really think of yourself as part of an organization. There is no guarantee. Judging from my experience, the possibility is not always there.

Because staff members stay in the organization for only a short time before they leave, the organization cannot count staff members' skills, expertise and experiences among the organization's assets. For example, staff who are hired in a relief situation and trained to meet related needs usually have to leave the organization after the relief operation is

---

[5] See Baker (1989) for an example of the contradictions between pressures regarding financial security and the long-term considerations of project objectives.

terminated because funding ends with the end of the operation. As a result, if another relief situation arises in the future, the organization must repeat the same process of recruiting staff and providing them with relief-oriented training.

Moreover, changing needs in the field make it difficult for NGOs to carry out long-term training. Especially in a relief situation, where needs in the field change daily, timing becomes an important factor in order for training to be relevant. Skills required at the outset might not be important after a month in such a dynamic situation. Consequently, NGOs are not willing to invest time and resources in staff training that might simply be wasted.

Discrepancies exist between training requirements and organizational requirements. Training normally requires the staff to stay with the organization for the long term while the organization's changing situation requires flexibility in hiring and firing. In most cases, including the scenario described above, organizational requirements for meeting needs in the field and *vis-à-vis* donors are prioritized over training requirements.

Often, meeting organizational requirements does not result in contributing to the organizations or their projects. When NGOs try to respond to changing needs in the field and the changing interests of donors by hiring and firing staff each time, the result is a high turnover rate among staff, which in turn instils fatalism in staff members. This fatalism can disrupt projects.

In the face of staff members' fatalism, training can be introduced to tackle its negative influences. When the officer says that staff members are 'surrounded by so much uncertainty and . . . therefore, feel that "I'm only in the organization for a short time." That is the feeling that I would like to remove in the training,' staff training loses its initial objective to serve projects and becomes merely a tool to counter fatalism.

In a high-turnover situation, NGOs cannot focus training on improving staff members' abilities. Instead, the organizations try to combat fatalism through training. As a result, the staff members, through the training they receive, are encouraged to be content with an insecure work environment.

Training for one's own career development
Another factor that makes NGOs hesitant to invest in staff training is that the staff members are strongly tempted to use the training they receive as a tool to get a better job in another organization. A senior manager who has served with an NGO for more than 15 years reflects on the personnel issue of the organization:

[Our organization] has consciously gone that way to both attract quality people and keep them. In the field, we pay just about the highest salaries and benefits of any of the organizations and, as a result, we end up many times stealing staff from other organizations because we have better security, a higher salary scale.

This account suggests that quality staff can be hired with an appropriate salary scale. Or taking the salary as the subject, the salary level may determine the quality of staff that an NGO can hire. If this relationship is typically observed in most NGOs, training staff does not make sense, because the salary, not training, determines the quality of staff.

In fact, interactions between the staff members and the NGO leadership establish the direct relationship between salary and staff quality. From staff members' point of view, they never feel secure in their positions, for the organization can hire a better quality person with an appropriate salary and fire them anytime. The staff members feel that the organization does not care about them apart from assessing them based on the salary–staff quality relationship. This feeling can motivate them to look for better job opportunities even though they are still employed. As a result, they become career-oriented. Training then can easily become an instrumental tool to develop their careers through seeking a better position in a different organization. Their commitment[6] to the organization can hardly be developed through the training.

On the other hand, once the organization's leadership comes to understand that staff members always look for better job opportunities, the leadership cannot expect the staff to remain in the organization even if the organization trains them. On the contrary, the leadership would think that training may even provide a good chance for the staff to look for better job opportunities in other organizations. The leadership, therefore, is discouraged from training the staff. Instead, with reasonable salary scales, they would hire quality staff who do not need training. Organizations begin hiring and firing staff solely according to their ability at the time.

These two perceptions contrast the career orientation of the staff and the job orientation of the leadership. These meet only in terms of selling and buying the abilities of the staff and an important concept of training – growing together with the organization – is lost.

In addition, difficult living circumstances in the Third World contribute to the divergence of interests between NGO leadership and staff. For those who struggle for daily survival at a subsistence level, striving for a better job is not a luxury but a matter of necessity. Unless the organization secures their livelihoods, staff members have to put their needs before those of the organization. In fact, one major motivation of the local staff to

---

[6] 'Commitment to values is a key factor in high-performing organizations in many contexts.' (Brown and Covey, 1989, 36).

work for an NGO is salaries. Without enough income for daily survival, they would not be able to attend to the organization's missions. If NGOs fail to offer reasonable benefits and job security, and fail to show commitment to those staff who are struggling for their own survival, NGOs cannot expect the trained staff to stay with the organization.[7]

Locals vs. expatriates

Local staff training may cause internal problems between locals and expatriates. The training clarifies the boundary between the two and distinguishes them in terms of skills, language and perspectives. These areas of difference all show, from different viewpoints, how locals and expatriates interact with each other in the context of the tension between serving the organization and serving programmes.

Local skills vs. imported skills[8]

Training that brings skills into the field from outside results in undesirable influences in the field. Significant portions of staff training are aimed at developing local staff members' administrative abilities, such as computer skills, accounting, secretarial work, English writing, and so on. These skills, which are beneficial for international NGOs, however, are not necessarily important qualities for the staff of local NGOs. The discrepancy exists between international NGOs and local NGOs with respect to required skills.

International NGOs should ask themselves how their FOs should deal with local skills and skills from outside. Should the FOs import skills from HQ, for example, to establish and maintain the same administrative capacity as that of HQ? Or should they rely on local skills to maintain coherence in local contexts? Depending upon the answers to these questions, NGOs should train the local staff either to acquire skills from outside or to manage their jobs with the skills available in the local context. Choosing between the different types of training – acquiring new skills and learning to manage with the skills the staff already possess – is vitally important because its impact on the organization is profound. Each of these choices implies a distinct type of training, each of which in turn influences the quality of the staff as well as the nature of the relationship between HQ and FOs.[9] A regional officer observes how a sophisticated

---

[7] The tension between staff capacity and career development is one of the major issues that Billis and MacKeith (1992) have identified.

[8] See Berman (1980), Weiler (1991), and Ward (1989) for the critique of imported skills and knowledge. 'Real development can only begin from where you are, from your own culture; it has to come from within, it cannot be imposed, bought, or borrowed from outside.' (Ward, 1989).

[9] Fowler (1992b) argues that gaps in knowledge and skills create persistent tension between the field and headquarters.

accounting system worked to centralize power and reinforce the top-down structure of the organization:[10]

> The organization introduced high-tech software for accounting. And then we have introduced computers to the rural area. They didn't dream about this sophistication. But what we were increasingly seeing was a hindrance. What happened was that a group of people were sent around to all these high-tech systems and began to exert influence, saying, 'If this system is to be successful, you guys have to follow the line.' It created a lot of internal controversies. So what eventually happened was that [these people] began to take over and control at every level possible. And then unconsciously [they] got a lot of power, because knowledge is powerful. [They] know this system, [they] know the implications of this system. That unconsciously built a lot of centralized control. So eventually local people became a victim of that, and what's happening is delays because it's centralized, it becomes bureaucratic, because most power centres around the head office. So local staff lost their innovativeness because [they think,] 'Why should I take pains with this compulsive bureaucratic system to get something done? So let me remain and just do whatever is given to me.' So it's beginning to kill the initiative of these grassroots-level people.

The local staff training often reinforces an old development assumption among both local and expatriate staff members that expatriates should bring skills from outside to train locals. While NGOs usually agree to encouraging bottom-up development in the field, in which the organization plays a facilitating role, in practice they often do not mind applying a top-down model to local staff training. As a result, in the name of staff training, the top-down relationship between HQ and the FOs may be amplified.[11]

Local language vs. working language
Language training is a major training subject in NGOs but causes another problem between the field and HQ. Because NGOs work in various countries where different languages are spoken, they prefer to establish a common language for efficient communication. Most NGOs[12] encourage their staff to use English due to its international coverage.[13] However, although it may make communication within an NGO more efficient, it will also impose the culture of English at the expense of the local cultures

---

[10] See Barley (1986, 1990) for discussions of the impact of technology on the organization.
[11] 'We produced results that were not only unhelpful, but actually exacerbated the very conditions we were trying to work against . . .' (Ellsworth, 1989, 298).
[12] Exceptions include Japanese and French NGOs, for example, which typically use Japanese and French as their respective working languages.
[13] See Laponce (1987) for a discussion of how English language influences the world. See Khleif and Durham (1993) for an analysis of marginalized languages in the context of the trends of global homogenization as multinational co-operation and modern communications technology make peoples more alike.

that local languages convey.[14] Moreover, it may enhance the top-down structure between HQ and the field.

However, despite these negative aspects of English use and training, staff members are unable to communicate with each other without a common language. Consequently, this country director has made a commitment to invest in language training:

A big problem we face, or probably any international organization faces, is that English is our official language. But in many of our countries in operation, many of our staff do not speak English. So, I have renewed my commitment and taken steps to get my staff English training. But that has to be understood very carefully. We are, for instance, not trying to get Thai people to speak English because we think English is better than Thai. But we want to help them and enhance their English skills. They work for an international organization whose medium is English. My staff are at an unfair disadvantage in participating in the marketplace of ideas if they can't express their particular ideas. If everything is top-down, no problem. But if you want people to interact and participate, there has to be dialogue, back and forth many times. In two languages, it's very difficult. [There are] many logistical problems. So, I think the best solution is to equip my Thai staff with English skills.

He commits to investing in the training with the honest intention of supporting the staff. Through language training, he intends to encourage dialogue between locals and expatriates, encourage locals' participation in organizational matters, and establish a partner relationship between locals and expatriates rather than a top-down one. The issue is not that NGO leaders are cruel and benefit unjustifiably from the training. The issue, rather, is that negative side effects are ingrained in the language training regardless of leaders' intentions.

One considerable side effect is that language training indirectly introduces a scale for measuring the quality of staff. Staff members with advanced English skills are preferred over those who lack such skills. Once this scale is established, NGOs start to apply it to recruitment, selecting people who already possess English language skills. Consequently, these skills become one significant condition for employment by the organization. Although this resolves the language problem, the scale systematically excludes non-English speakers regardless of their experiences, skills, personality, and so forth.[15]

The other side effect is that the language training is likely to reinforce the top-down relationship between expatriate staff and local staff. In addition to their structured advantage as suppliers of funds, expatriates gain another advantage over locals in terms of their ability

---

14 See Mazrui (1975).
15 Non-English speakers would be regarded as illiterates. See Carr (1990).

to communicate in their own language. Language training is a double-edged sword: it provides locals with access to outside information,[16] but it also justifies expatriates in using English and requiring the local staff to use it.

Local staff members are at a disadvantage when they are required to express themselves in a foreign language. A Thai staff member, who works to co-ordinate projects and communicate with the HQ, expresses her frustration at administrative burdens imposed by the use of English as the *lingua franca* of the organization:

> We receive funds from other countries. The only way to make them know the results of the programmes is if we do the reporting. The reporting from the projects is in the Thai language. And then we have all the donors from foreign countries. We have to do all the translation. We have more than 20 projects and all the projects have to be translated. And one report is quite thick.

HQs have a legitimate rationale for requiring the field to translate reports. Once they invest in the language training of the local staff, they expect a return on that investment from the field. The locals must demonstrate their accountability by taking care of all additional, arduous, language-related tasks. This worker seems to feel that she serves donors and HQ rather than beneficiaries. In the name of language training, what gets reinforced is the top-down structure, as opposed to the partnership, participation and dialogue between HQ and FOs.

Language training causes frustration on the part of field staff in two ways. First, it officially devalues their own cultures; and second, it treats an unfair communication mode as a fair one. The frustration of local staff who suffer from this disadvantage is paramount. However, if they want to indicate their frustration to HQ, they still have to express it in English. In English words, a local staff member expresses his frustration which would have been expressed better in his own tongue:

> Sometimes it's very frustrating; you want to express your feelings but you don't know the words. For the technical language, we can communicate, but for expressing feelings, it's very frustrating.

Bottom-up vs. top-down

Many NGO staff members would agree that processes are just as important as results in development projects.[17] NGO staff, especially those who consider development as learning processes, would like to see proper processes being followed in project implementation. Because they care

---

[16] Equal access to language is a critical component of democracy. See Barber's (1984, 178–98) nine functions of strong democratic talk.

[17] For discussions of the learning process approach in NGO contexts, see, for example, Korten (1980), and Edwards (1994).

about that, they mind about not only what project they implement but also how they implement it.[18]

However, when different offices in an NGO have different approaches to the same project, problems emerge. For example, a typical one is observed between bottom-up processes and top-down processes. A Thai field staff member states:

> Westerners [pointing to headquarters] expect us not only to implement but also to do it in a theoretical way. If we are Thai, we are doing like Thai do. But they expect us to do it in a theoretical way to be up to their standards. If we don't do it one, two, three, four, five, six, like this, they expect that it is not the standard they want. But we sometimes have to do step one, step four, step two, step three, something like that. Different ways. But Westerners say, 'You must do like this, this, this, this, this.' If not, they don't accept us as standard.

The account does not clarify whether the Thai methods of working in this case are authoritative or participatory. But even if they are authoritative, the intervention by HQ in the field in the name of training is problematic. When people at HQ have a strong preference for the bottom-up approach, they would like to see this type of process in the field. However, the field does not necessarily take that approach. Different FOs have different cultures, and one may find that the top-down approach is the dominant approach in field contexts.

Suggesting a bottom-up approach to those who practise the top-down approach creates conflict arising from discrepancies between the two approaches. This conflict is problematic in another important sense: imposing the bottom-up approach contradicts the very spirit of the democratic process embodied in the bottom-up approach. To avoid this contradiction, the bottom-up approach should never be imposed from the top. The second half of this chapter attempts to address this issue.

Direction vs. manipulation

Training provides staff members not only with technical skills, but also with a sense of commonality among the membership in the organization which leads them to comply with the organization's missions. However, there is a danger that, in the name of training, the staff can be manipulated, indoctrinated or even brainwashed.[19] This possibility illustrates the problem derived from the subtle but important difference between direction and manipulation.[20]

---

18 'We might observe that life is not only, or primarily, choice but also interpretation. Outcomes can be less significant – both behaviourally and ethically – than process. The process gives meaning to life, and meaning is a major part of life.' (March and Olsen, 1989, 51)
19 Franks (1989) suggests that the political environment of an NGO should be a major consideration in designing training.
20 Jurmo (1985, 14) cites Freire's distinction between manipulation and directives, and suggests the necessity of directives in education.

Some types of training attempt to bring individuals into the membership of organizations. Through this instruction, NGOs try to train workers both formally and informally to understand what behaviour is appropriate within the organization, and what its group norms and values are, and then induce them to behave as expected without close supervision. While this training brings individuals into the membership of the organization, it can also subtly require staff members to give up some of their personal values and characteristics to submerge themselves within the organization.

Can NGOs train their staff members to reflect the direction of the organization without requiring them to sacrifice their own values and characteristics? The following two accounts look at the issue from different angles, one from the organization's point of view, and the other from the staff members' point of view.

A senior manager emphasizes the importance of inheriting organizational ways of thinking:

> As we expand, we are getting less of those people [who have been with the organization for a long time], and we haven't trained to socialize people from outside. One of our challenges is how to get these [new] people to think like this. Some of the ideas we have are to do it through informal training, indoctrination. We are actually talking about bringing people, basing them here, and moving them quite frequently between fields, three months in Somalia, three months in Angola, three months in Bangladesh. Loans are given for sending them off to universities to do Master's degrees, but I'm against that. I'd rather they do that Master's later. Let's do the indoctrination and socialization process first.

While this view implies that instilling a sense of membership in the organization is the major reason for the training, or 'indoctrination', another perspective places the staff at the centre. A desk officer in HQ says:

> . . . depends on the predeparture thing. Obviously they [trainees] want to feel that they can do the job. But there has to be an atmosphere of 'It's all right to admit that things are going wrong.' That atmosphere, we try to create through the predeparture training.

Instead of telling the trainees what they are expected to do in the field, he tries to instil the sense that HQ cares about the field staff. This would develop a favourable disposition among the trainees toward HQ and induce them to work voluntarily to support HQ. Although this officer does not indoctrinate the staff, interviews with other staff in the same organization indicate that he seems to have succeeded in sharing with the staff what the organization expects them to do in the field without actually telling it to them. His direction is achieved by establishing a secure environment in which the staff can act without worrying much about their mistakes.

In most NGOs' working contexts, however, the organizations employ some type of regulation to assure that the quality of performance remains at an acceptable level. Because they face pressures and constraints from various sources, such as donors, local governments, beneficiaries and so forth, they cannot easily rely on staff members' voluntary performance in practice. Easier ways to guarantee their performance involve regulating it, instead of expecting their voluntary actions to comply with organizational expectations.

For example, most NGOs, in theory if not in practice, value a participatory management style over an authoritative one. They value the process-oriented approach rather than the blue-print approach.[21] Therefore they expect their staff to comply with these norms, values and roles, which are not necessarily the same as the individuals' own. Thus, the objective of training is not merely to familiarize the staff with the organization, but rather, subtly or explicitly, to induce the staff to adopt the organization's values and goals. Is it manipulation, direction, or a combination of both? Do staff members have to give up or change some of their values to serve the organizations? If so, isn't that authoritative as opposed to participatory?

A cross-cultural relationship between HQ and FOs offers an ideal example to illustrate this problem because their differences are significantly broad and deep. A country director vividly expresses the challenge he faces to find common ground without requiring staff to give up their values and without being authoritative:

When I come to Asia, in Thai culture, some of the things that I would conceive of as servant leadership as an American confused the local staff, because that's not the way leaders are supposed to act. In American culture, a servant leader is someone who is willing to do anything that you ask other people to do. So if I ask people, 'Please move those boxes,' I do it with them, and they say, 'Oh, he is not looking down, we have an equal relationship.' I try to demonstrate that 'I value you as equal.' For instance, when we had field meetings up country, we all sleep on the floor. So when I sleep on the floor with others, to me that's what I should do to demonstrate servant leadership. The Thai staff say, 'He is not very much of a leader. He doesn't even know he is supposed to hold himself in higher esteem than he holds us.' So the intention is interpreted almost as a sign of weakness as a leader as opposed to a sign of a good leader. [It's a] tricky part of the challenge, I don't want to water down my values just because this is the way Thai things are. At the same time, I have to remember that that's my interpretation of what the Bible says. It's not what the Bible says. It's my interpretation. So I have to figure out, in the Thai context, what would servant leadership look like? And that's the challenge for me. So if I want to be a servant, I do it in a way that is understood by Thai. If I act as a servant in ways Americans understand, it either doesn't have any meaning to Thai or it actually has the opposite meaning. There is a cultural model of leadership, which is different from what the Biblical model is. But again, that's a simplistic

---

[21] See Korten (1980).

way of looking at it. So what we have to find out is what is the Thai Christian interpretation of Biblical leadership. I'm not sure if that has been well defined or articulated even among Thai Christians. Because what Thai Christians have tended to do is one of two things: follow the Thai cultural model, which seems to have something that would appear to be not Biblical, or just buy the Western model of leadership and follow that.

His challenge is that he has to take both cultural diversity and Christian values into account. He does not want to disregard cultural differences, but at the same time he does not want to dilute Christian values.[22] Looking at it from another angle, he is seeking a third alternative that is neither non-Biblical nor simply Western. To understand the issue clearly, it is relevant to examine the characteristics of core values, the Biblical value of servant leadership in this case.

Does this leader's interpretation and enactment of servant leadership imply a challenge to his staff members' core values? In particular, is he manipulating non-Christian staff by imposing on them the Christian value of servant leadership? Is he manipulating Thai staff by imposing on them a Western vision of servant leadership?

People who support a dynamic concept of core values may argue that he is not necessarily manipulative. He tries to communicate his values to field staff as an initial step in dynamic interactions in the hope of developing new insight into the issue for both sides. Thus the issue becomes whether we can tell which aspects of Christian values can be changed and which cannot in the face of cultural diversity.

This example involving Christian values illustrates the more general tension between organizational values and individual differences. When an NGO conducts staff training, the characteristics of trainer–trainee interactions are the key to avoid indoctrination. Trainers, despite their position as trainers, should be attuned to the individual differences among the trainees and be ready to adapt their own stances to find common ground that does not sacrifice the essence of the core values of either the trainers or the trainees. But how is this possible in practice?

The first half of this chapter has addressed problems that NGO staff face when they carry out staff training, analysing those problems broadly in three different aspects: uncertain returns on training; different training interests between locals and expatriates; and the danger of manipulation in the name of the training. The analyses have explored the causes of problems and examined their characteristics. The problems are broadly considered to involve serving the organization and serving programmes, raising the question of whose interests are served through the staff

---

[22] See Ingram and King (1995) for a case of conflict that the mission statement of a church-supported college creates.

training. The second half of the chapter responds to the problems by presenting strategies that the NGO staff employ.

Strategies: For broader (not narrower) interests

Formal training that is targeted to achieve clear objectives is focused and thus serves relatively narrow interests. Training to improve certain areas of expertise, language skills, managerial skills and so forth is not itself a problem. But because these types of training embody clear, focused objectives and are tailored to the particular needs of particular people, the staff participating in the training are tempted to ignore those parts of the training that require them to shift their focus away from their immediate task areas. Consequently, the staff under training tend to ignore either the maintenance of the organization or their missions due to the narrowness of the training.

Alternative training strategies can broaden narrowly-focused training. Broadening views, drawing on latent abilities, training in projects, and predeparture training are four alternative strategies. Compared with clearly-targeted training, these training strategies can serve the broader interests of the entire organization rather than just one part of the organization. They serve all those who are involved in projects, regardless of their positions in the organization, rather than serving selected staff. And they serve development in general rather than particular, narrower interests. Details of the four strategies are illustrated with personal accounts from the field.

Broadening views to identify the right questions
Training to identify key questions is more important than training to elicit a particular response to a given question without examining its value. If teaching how to fish is better than giving fish, as it is often said, a question like 'Which fish is it better to give?' is not a relevant question. Rather, a better question can be posed in terms of the quality of teaching, not types of fish. In the same way, an NGO newsletter editor has discovered the importance of being able to find the information one needs, rather than possessing the information itself:

> I would teach local staff that much more important than actual information is knowing where to look for it and how to ask for it. People are always calling me for information, and it's not that I know so much, but I know where to find it and how to ask.

How, then, can one be trained in the ability to look for information rather than being taught the information itself, in this case? Or more generally, how can one be trained to know the right questions to ask and answer? A country director suggests:

[I]f you know how programmes are supposed to run, if you have worked in some types of programmes before, you will also be very aware of what can go wrong. So experience will help you to ask the right questions. And then depending on the answers, that would lead on to more questions, I think, both to question people and then to go on to see it yourself. That would be my strategy. If I told you, 'We are running credit programmes all over the country,' and if you had no idea what a credit programme was and I gave you a brief description of what it was, you might think it's wonderful. But then if you had experienced this before, you might start asking questions like, 'How the groups are formed? Who pays? How is the interest level set? Who maintains it? Where is the money stored?' A whole stream of questions will follow. But if you weren't familiar with it, then you wouldn't really know what questions to ask, and it's only through asking questions and really sort of digging into things that you find the positive and negative.

Valuable questions can expose sensitive areas of programmes where things can easily go wrong, and then clarify their positive and negative aspects. Thus, according to this country director, understanding where the sensitive areas are is crucial for posing the right questions. To do this, familiarizing oneself with the programme is an important initial step.

In NGO contexts, where a project consists of a variety of components, staff are specialized in their assigned areas and hence find it difficult to understand the entire project as a whole. Because of the lack of broader perspective, staff members can easily miss other important areas that need to be taken care of.

A typical gap can be found between programme and finance. Staff members in each area often fail to identify issues that are important to the other, although their mutual understanding is a vital condition for quality projects. To bridge the gap, NGOs strategically broaden their views from both ends. A regional financial manager approaches programme managers to broaden their views:

When I first got here, accounting was on one side, the programme was on the other side. They never combined. Programme people worked on programmes, finance [people] worked on finance. But that's not a good way to run a programme. Accounting doesn't know what's going on out in the field. The programme managers didn't monitor the budgets. So now, slowly but surely, we are training the programme managers to think about their finances to know that they are the ones who are in charge of the budget.

On the other hand, a field officer suggests that finance people should go to project sites to broaden their views:

Finance people don't get out to see what field conditions are like. So they don't really know what it's like out in these remote places. And the other thing is that finance people think like finance people, whether it's people in headquarters, or whether it's people in a country office, or even someone in a project site. They look at figures more than looking at people and that's where the real problem is. For them, at the end, everything has to balance, but in some of these conditions, things just don't. I think it would be good for them generally to come and visit in the field even if they are not doing any work, it's good for them just to see, 'Oh, you mean this. This is what we've been doing.' Or when they are just looking at numbers, they can now see faces, people. They can see a water system in place, they can see a beautiful farm where people have food now. So I think that would help them in their perspective, too.

Although the financial manager and the field officer each suggest ways to minimize the gap in perspective from the other's point of view and not from their own, both understand equally well that the gap is a serious problem, and both propose solutions based on their experience and not on their own specialization. This ability to identify key issues is crucial. No matter how competent someone is in their own field of specialization, they cannot develop their ability to identify key issues without familiarity with the entire situation.

Familiarizing themselves with the overall situation helps these people transform the types of questions they ask. They step back from issues directly related to their areas of expertise and identify concerns in their relationships to the entire organization. Although training to familiarize staff members with the organization as a whole is so general that it appears to be irrelevant to resolving particular issues, it can instil the valuable practice of asking fundamental questions about the organization's projects.[23] Because all issues are not equally crucial to the organization or its projects, focusing a good deal of effort on a particular issue without critically evaluating its importance to the organization as a whole does not make sense. This practice wastes time and energy on an unimportant problem while an urgent and important issue may be left untouched. Taking this risk into account, the training strategy is designed not to resolve an already-identified issue, but rather to examine critically and identify the key issues in which staff members' and the organization's limited resources should be invested.

What kind of practical changes can be brought about by this training strategy? The above example of programme and finance reflects one change this strategy can make: programme people may become more careful in spending money when they take financial concerns into account as they implement a project. Financial people, by the same token, may be able to take into account the difficulties that the financial preparation entails in the field. This training strategy alters the broad organizational framework and enhances inter-departmental relationships.

---

[23] To enhance organizational effectiveness, training for value and attitude change is at least as important as skill and knowledge transmission (Blunt, 1990).

Drawing on latent abilities

The object of training is not only to impart skills, knowledge, techniques and so forth to the staff. It also draws on staff members' latent abilities and helps them appreciate those abilities. This strategy tries to make better use of human capacities.[24] In the following passages, two types of strategies are addressed by NGO staff.

'Don't ask me but do it'

A director of operations describes a unique and powerful strategy for drawing on the latent abilities of the staff:

> I'm trying to create an environment where they don't ask me. If they feel that they need to go to the office, they should go to the office. If you feel that you need it, I trust you. Maybe somebody is flying abroad. It's expensive. But I would be saying, 'OK. Don't ask me permission for that, you know it, do it.' That's where trust begins. Otherwise, say, 'OK, I value you that you are not going to waste money or whatever on an air flight, just go and have a break.' . . . people [are] not impotent like oxen. I'm going into this person's territory saying, 'We know what's there. But do it. And if there are problems, I live with problems. If it creates problems, then I deal with problems, but I'm not going to stop the process.' I think these are the kinds of informal ways that we can develop concepts of what we are. They must be part of decision making. Otherwise, it's not a decision. It's something handed down.

This is not the usual type of training. The director trains his staff by deliberately not giving them directions. In a sense, he trains the staff by 'not training'. He provocatively challenges his staff to determine their own work plans by themselves. He gives them the authority to plan, to decide, and to practise as they see fit. The training component comes in the form of responsibility after they are given full authority. When staff members have authority, they have to be responsible for plans, decisions and practices. As a result, they need to be more conscious in their daily work than if they had asked for his directives.

His training strategy is targeted at inculcating in staff members the ability to use authority responsibly. To do this, the director initiates the training by offering authority. He then hopes that responsibility will follow – 'people are not oxen'. This strategy is based on the trust relationship, not calculation. Allowing the staff to make decisions without consulting him may be risky and may appear irrational. However, he argues that this very risk taking is the major reason that the organization has been successful:

---

[24] See Fox (1974) to understand how what he calls the 'low-discretion syndrome', which is generated by a mutually reinforcing circle between close supervision and bureaucratic rules, discourages the staff's incentive to do more than what is minimally required.

This organization has been successful, because people have been taking risks. Because people have not done the normal things. People say, 'You can't do that.' I say, 'Why not?' We've done unpopular things very often. The organization has been driven by that kind of, we would say, guts freedom. It's from the heart, it's not from head.

That he openly advocates this view produces and reproduces the notion within the organization that conventional responses to an issue are not always right. This critical view legitimizes a variety of unpopular efforts by the staff. The trust that 'people are not impotent like oxen' works in a novel way to change the staff. The director's training strategy is to take a risk to bet on human capacity, and the very action of betting would touch and change the staff.

Modelling exemplary life

Training is not effective if a trainer does not practise what he or she suggests.[25] The gap between what trainers preach and what they practise instils in trainees negative feelings toward the trainer and discourages them from listening to what the trainer says. A desk officer believes that 'one should never expect someone to do a job if one hasn't done it oneself'. For example, a senior manager of an NGO reflects on the organization's earlier history when people from HQ routinely expected to stay at the best hotel in town. However, this attitude, he said, caused enormous resentment because there was a gap between their behaviour and their words. Preaching a beautiful theory does not have value as far as the staff are concerned unless those preaching it demonstrate its value by practising it. A country director neatly articulates this point and proposes an alternative training strategy:

How can we ask our staff to be involved in promoting development with beneficiaries if we are not doing it with them? We have to model the way we want them to interact with people in the community. If we are hiring them and just saying, 'Do it,' and not enhancing their lives, nor stimulating them, promoting critical reflection, and asking them to think, then what can they do? They can do the same thing we do now. They are not going to ask people to think, they are just going to say, 'Here is the money.' And there is just a project. So we have to model what we want to see.

This training strategy aims at inducing the staff to carry out development projects in the same manner in which the leadership interacts with the staff. Because the quality of the staff's work in the field is a reflection of

[25] Brinkerhoff (1979, 7) says, '. . . if there is a low level of participation on the part of bureaucrats/managers within their own organization, then the level of involvement of clients/ target groups in development programs administered by those bureaucrats is also likely to be low.' Fowler (1993, 336) claims, '[The] challenge to NGOs, both African and international, is to include the dimension of citizenship into their development efforts, particularly in approaches to people's participation. Such a move is necessary because this political factor is commonly missing in their development thinking and strategies.'

the leadership, the leaders cannot simply criticize the staff without critically examining their own practices.

A case from the field illustrates the impact on the staff of the leadership's practices. When a country director made a decision to withdraw from a project area, this project was favoured by a support office. The country director narrates:

> That decision was a political decision. The word got to the board level that 'You are drawing out of the place? That's where our big projects are that we would like to take all our funders [to see].'[26] And the president went to the vice president and said, 'What are we doing?' And the vice president said, 'When we hired him, we told him to go and do what he thinks is best. And he thinks this is what's best. So we will stand by him.' The president said, 'You are right.' He went back to the board and gave this message. Well, that is why I have enjoyed working in this organization so far.

The relationship between the leadership and the staff is a model of the relationship between the staff and local beneficiaries. Thus, when an NGO wants the staff to carry out development work in the field, the leadership has to develop the staff in the same way as the staff implements the projects. Although training the staff can appear to be serving the NGO, this modelling strategy implies that NGOs must be actively involved in developing their staff if they want to make sure that the staff implement projects as expected. The same country director explicates his position:

> A development organization has to focus on developing its own people, or cuts its own throat. Because you have to model what you are telling people to do. If they are getting one message from their own experience within the organization, it's going to be very hard for them to do the opposite with the beneficiaries. So I think it's both/and. And I can't be either/or. People say, 'Oh, well, you are focusing too much on your staff.' If I don't focus on my staff, they can never do a good job with the beneficiaries. Now, I think there is a time when you do more or less. There's an art in finding the balance.

This modelling strategy emphasizes the necessity of staff training. For the staff to be able to model, their training is essential prior to going to the field. The modelling strategy counteracts the notion of training as just serving the organization because it is essential to the staff's ability to carry out development projects in an appropriate manner.[27]

---

[26] 'Programme changes can be motivated by considerations other than, or in addition to, financial viability, but they almost always have financial effects. Many of the programme events, especially new programme developments, were undertaken explicitly on the basis of their financial implications.' (Herman, and Heimovics, 1989, 129)

[27] Kabeer (1991, 194) argues for the importance of beginning from people's own established ways of being: 'Empowering women must therefore begin with the individual consciousness and with the imaginative construction of alternative ways of being, living, and relating.' De Senillosa (1992) argues that, to be effective, non-governmental development organizations (NGDOs) should also challenge inequality in their own societies at the same time that they work in other countries.

Training in projects

Training in projects is an efficient strategy when NGOs have to be careful about the way they spend their funds. NGOs do not need to worry about funds for this type of training. Moreover, the strategy is effective because the training takes place within the real working context. Two types of training in projects are examined here.

On-the-job training

On-the-job training is a popular training strategy. In a well-systematized organization, training is included in project plans.

> Most of our projects, once they are at the designing stage, they have training components. You find many projects training officers to train the staff, give the staff skills they need for the extension work.

For NGOs, this strategy has several advantages. One is that they do not need to allocate separate and independent resources (time, money and staff) for training. Because they are mostly funded based on project proposals, they may not use the funds for different (training) purposes. Second, the relevance of the training can easily be examined through daily jobs. In other words, conceptually valuable but practically irrelevant training can easily be discredited in a real job situation. While this approach involves inserting a training component into projects, a more direct way to merge training and projects is implemented by some NGOs as a form of project evaluation.[28] An evaluation director of an NGO contends that the evaluation can succeed not only in improving projects but also in developing the staff:

> The more the project staff are involved in the entire evaluation process, the more the evaluation events influence what happens in the projects. [It's] not necessarily the written reports. [It's] the experience of having thought through, 'What are we really trying to accomplish with this project, what would be good evidence for that, what kind of evidence do we have, what is the meaning of that evidence?' And it has to do with the experience of that two weeks or three weeks or eight days or whatever it is. It's that experience that influences what they do after the event is over, it's not so much the written reports. Evidence I have comes from folks who were on the evaluation team that I see a year later and they say, 'Because of what we did in that evaluation, this is what I'm now doing differently', or, 'This is what the community decided to do after that evaluation.'

In this evaluation, the project and training are so integrated that it is difficult to draw a line between the staff, who are usually the initial organizers, and the participants, who are supposed to be the target group

---

[28] See Howes (1992) for trends and key issues in the evaluation of NGO projects.

of the projects.[29] Who gets trained, then? All those who participated in the evaluation.[30] In this particular evaluation event, project staff, representatives from the fundraising offices, representatives from the local field office, folks from other experiment programmes, and representatives from the head office participated and learned. In this evaluation, everybody becomes a learner, regardless of their status. Therefore, this type of training can effectively diminish the top-down gaps that exist between HQ and FOs, between donors and the NGO, or between the NGO and its beneficiaries.[31] Having the same experience and process together for the same objective would develop a sense of commonality and reduce the top-down gap among the participants.

As the director says, meta-evaluation, the evaluation of evaluation processes, would not be presented as a written form, because evaluation reports mostly cover the results of evaluation and rarely describe its process. However, the process of the evaluation would be the key to understanding how participants get training. The same director continues:

> Probably the most significant outcome of that process doesn't show up in the evaluation report. I have had a development worker come to me and say, 'You know, I was ready to quit and I was really scared by this evaluation. But gee, after we've gone through the evaluation, I decided not to quit.' I would not put that in the evaluation report. That's a personal kind of communication.

The evaluation played a training role, changing the person through the evaluation process. This change in the staff is as significant an objective as the initial objective of evaluation – to get feedback on projects. Evaluation is not an attempt to discover objectively something out in the field. It is a learning process for the staff themselves. They are trained as they carry out the evaluation.

Regarding staff training as a project
So far, staff training has been treated as an organizational issue. The question that this chapter has addressed is whether the training is serving only the organization, is designed to maintain the organization, or contributes to serving programmes based on the organization's missions. In either case, the issue has been examined in its relationship to organizations.

The last novel training strategy separates the training from organizational issues and directly links it with development. Here, development is not undertaken in the narrow sense of supporting people in need but is

---

[29] In the social learning tradition, Friedmann (1987, 185) says, 'actor and learner are assumed to be one and the same.'
[30] Cf. participatory action research. For example, see Collion and Kissi (1993).
[31] See Béjar and Oakley (1996), and Fowler (1996, 176–82).

used as a means of building people's capacity in the hope that they can better serve development objectives and support needy people in one way or another. The strategy goes beyond the issue of serving the organization and serving programmes to address a fundamental question: 'How can staff training contribute to development?' This reframing offers new insight into the way NGOs should treat staff training. It breaks through the tensions between serving the organization and serving programmes. It encourages the staff to treat the training itself as development, not as a tool of organizations to carry out better projects. A country director offers this insight into the way the alternative strategy influences the organization and the staff:

> Everyone profits. But if we have trained people who leave, I do not have a problem with that because our goal is to promote development. Our goal is not to grow the organization. So I said this to a staff member who has worked for us for seven years now. He comes to me saying, 'You know, another organization has a position that I applied for.' A part of me would be disappointed but the other part would say, 'I would not consider this a loss because he is still contributing to the development and needs of the country.' If I am only training him for the organization, I think that is short-sighted. But he knows I am training him whether he stays in the organization or not. That does something for him, too. He realizes that he as a person is important. Again, that is another thing that we are trying to set up.

This radical training strategy goes beyond the issue of serving the organization vs. serving programmes, and aims at NGOs' fundamental goals. Because NGOs are set up to achieve their mission objectives, the bottom line is that the training must contribute to those objectives. Thus, so long as training aims at the objectives, it should be regarded as valuable, whether it seeks to achieve the objectives indirectly via NGOs or directly without them.

The country director shows that he prioritizes the contribution of this individual to development more than his own ability to retain staff in his organization. This very act of taking a risk and respecting the staff as persons who dedicate themselves to development has a novel impact. It does not necessarily result in losing staff. The director continues:

> It [the commitment of the organization to invest in the staff] makes people want to work and is sure to attract better people. So you know, it's like a parable of the guy with talents.[32] Those who used it got more, those who didn't lost it all. And I think growing an organization is like that. Once you begin to keep good people, then you attract more good people.

He suggests that this paradoxical organizational dynamic, 'those who used it got more', be strategically applied for the staff training to develop

---

[32] He refers to the parable of the talents in Matthew 25:14–30 or Luke 19:11–27.

both the staff and the organization simultaneously. This strategy assumes that while instrumentally investing in organizational development would ironically not lead to organizational development, investing instead purely for development may attract quality people and lead indirectly to organizational development.

Taking risks in training staff members is a genuine way for NGO leaders to demonstrate the extent to which they are faithful to their missions and care about the staff as opposed to being interested in using the staff instrumentally. The staff members would be willing to serve the organizations because the organizations care about them. This strategy is long-term, risk-taking and mission-centred. This strategy can induce both an NGO and its staff members to retreat from short-sighted, narrow perspectives based on financial investment and opt instead for the social stance (caring about persons and missions even at their own expense). Expenses that are incurred for the development of people are well spent, whether the people are staff members or project participants. Any individual can be the means and ends of development.

Predeparture training

Predeparture training for those new recruits who start to work in the field plays an important role in establishing relationships between the field and HQ. Through the training, the recruits get overviews of the organization. Before the new recruits go into the field, desk officers in HQ introduce themselves to the recruits and attempt to construct relationships with them. Because new recruits do not face any field issues yet, they can discuss the issues objectively without feeling any pressure. The new recruits may listen carefully to and understand the desk officers. A desk officer uses this opportunity strategically to orientate the recruits:

> You are going out to work on the project, and we have a funding contract with a funder, so we must implement that project. But if you feel that the project is not going in the right direction, or it needs to be redirected, there is a procedure. Because we are involved in a contract with funding agencies, we have to do that. But you can certainly approach us to say, 'We are doing A, B, C, we should be doing X, Y, Z.' Then, we approach the funders and suggest that it should be redirected this way. In that situation, I don't know any case where funders say, 'No, you can't do it.' Funders are reasonable, they accept that working in difficult, pressured situations – some of the most difficult working environments in the world – they realize things could go wrong, and things don't happen for various reasons, and things do happen in a very unanticipated way. So the project has to change. We go back to the field and say, 'Yes, you can do it.' All projects are dynamic. If it is necessary to change, we need to change.

65

Set the first impression.[33] Predeparture training is an excellent opportunity for desk officers to convey their vision to each of the staff. The training may be the only opportunity for new recruits to listen carefully to the desk officers, since they will be constrained by a variety of issues once they go into the field.

Share issues of funders as common issues. The desk officer tries to share constraints that the HQ faces *vis-à-vis* funders and to construct them as a common issue for the entire organization. Having a common issue helps the staff develop common ground on which they stand together.

Put the field first. The officer prioritizes what the field thinks about the direction of projects. The officer demonstrates that he or she is ready to back up the field staff if they need some changes to be made. The officer's expression of this support helps those who go into the field to co-operate with the officer's requests.

Tell the field that donors are reasonable. The desk officer describes donors as an important advisory source and as participants rather than as constraints. This explanation gives the trainees an image of a co-operative relationship between the NGO and donors. The officer impresses upon the trainees that answering questions from donors is reasonable and even beneficial for the trainees themselves.

Inquire in a constructive manner. Asking a staff member to write a report to donors is usually regarded as something extra that people do not want to do if they are not asked. Instead of saying 'reporting is your obligation,' the desk officer explains it in a constructive way:

> The report is the core part of your work, it's not something that you do on a Saturday night, before you go for a few beers. You do the report on Monday, Tuesday, Wednesday. It's not only so that we can prove it to funders, it's so that the project staff can see you are right. This project is actually making progress toward the object, rather than not really knowing whether it's having benefits or not.

The desk officer encourages the staff to look at reporting as a good management tool instead of something extra required from outside.

Tell staff members not to worry about mistakes beforehand. In writing reports, the staff usually do not want to write things that affect them negatively. They tend to write reports only about successful work and

---

[33] On the importance of the first impression, see Brown (1965), for example.

neglect things that are not going well or that have failed. In the predeparture training, before the staff members face failures, mistakes and problems, he attempts to remove the staff members' fears about revealing negative information:

> There has to be an atmosphere of, 'It's all right to admit that things are going wrong.' We are sort of saying, 'Well, look, we are reasonable people. If they fail, that didn't happen without reasons. They have reasons, so tell us what the reasons are.' We would say that to the funders, and the funders usually accept our reasons.

Conclusion

The first part of this chapter analyses the problems that arise from staff training. Although three different aspects are categorized to characterize the problems differently, they originate from the same root: the tensions between serving the organization and serving programmes. The tensions are the underlying causes of these problems that the staff face when they carry out staff training.

The second part of the chapter discusses alternative strategies for tackling the problems. Personal accounts from NGO staff members have presented four different training strategies: broadening views, drawing on latent abilities, training in projects, and predeparture training. Although the staff members who execute the strategies do not necessarily face the same problems as above, the strategies indicate alternative training that would more likely avoid the problems. All four training strategies are designed to break a barrier that exists between serving the organization and serving programmes, although they employ different approaches and specifically tackle different aspects of the barrier.

PART II

Diversity vs. Similarity

ONCE AN NGO creates its membership, its next step is to co-ordinate staff members so that they can better serve the organization's objectives. Although the literature on NGO project management often treats the NGO as the unit of analysis, NGOs are complex and diverse organizations. An NGO usually consists of headquarters, support offices, field offices and project sites.[1] Moreover, the staff members have different positions, roles and tasks within the organization. Thus, because of its complex organizational features, an NGO cannot always function as the development literature prescribes. How can we tackle the discrepancies between the ideal promoted in the literature and the actual behaviour of the organization?

Through Chapters 4 and 5, Part II attempts to address these discrepancies by examining the dynamics among the staff members within an organization. The dynamics of staff interactions are characterized by the tension between diversity and similarity. An NGO simultaneously tries to maintain both diversity and similarity. Diversity of staff members is vital to remaining flexible, adaptable and responsive to diverse local problems. Sufficient similarity is a necessary precondition for the staff members from a variety of backgrounds, interests and values to work together effectively. The staff should be similar in sharing the identity and objectives of their organizations to work coherently as the members of the same organization. However, satisfying these two characteristics at the same time is a challenging task.

When NGO staff members emphasize diversity more than similarity, they tend to value differences more than shared senses, with fragmented performance being the likely result (see Table 2). In this case, the

---

[1] Support offices are usually located in industrialized countries; their function is to provide financial support to projects. Headquarters support the field in various ways such as recruiting, raising funds, representing the organization to donors and governments, providing technical support, advocating with the public, connecting the field with other related constituencies, and so forth. Field offices are usually situated in the major city of each field country; their function is to support project sites by providing a variety of resources, planning projects, writing proposals, mediating between the project sites and headquarters, contacting local governments, and so forth. Project sites are the places where actual development projects are carried out.

Table 2. Tension among the Staff

Pathology	Area of Tension			Pathology
Fragmented performance	Diversity	◄─────►	Similarity	Restricted performance

organization loses its coherence as a unit. Instead of working toward commonly shared objectives, fragmented staff may seek to achieve different, even opposing, objectives. But when staff members' primary concern is fragmentation, they may then emphasize the importance of similarity to the exclusion of valuing differences, and they may consequently introduce some kind of control mechanism, seeking to achieve similarity by homogenizing the organization. In this case, restricted performance is likely to be the result. In the name of similarity, the organization excludes various precious resources that are provided in the form of diversity.[2] Consequently, the organization loses its capacity to address diverse, dynamic and unpredictable problems in the field.

The theme of this part of the book is how to maintain both diversity and similarity at the same time.[3] Although they are not necessarily mutually exclusive,[4] maintaining them both requires a subtle balance. A slight shift in emphasis on either of the two characteristics can easily disrupt any equilibrium between them and result in organizational pathology: fragmented performance or restricted performance.

Chapter 4 identifies and discusses how fragmentation takes place when an NGO attempts to maintain and develop its diversity. The first half of the chapter describes how well-intentioned practices to promote diversity can ultimately subvert similarity in sharing common senses and result in fragmentation. As strategies to address this problem, several methods of establishing a sense of shared purpose are introduced and discussed.

Chapter 5 identifies and discusses how restriction results when an NGO attempts to retain and develop similarity among the staff members. The chapter first discusses how an emphasis on similarity devalues organizational diversity and brings about homogeneity, exclusion, and restricted performance. The rest of the chapter presents strategies to avoid restricted performance without sacrificing the staff's diversity.

---

[2] Korten (1995, 268) discusses the values of differentiation and diversity based on Toynbee's argument (1947). According to Toynbee, civilizations in decline are characterized by a 'tendency toward standardization and uniformity,' (555) while civilizations in the growth stage are characterized by 'the tendency toward differentiation and diversity' (555).

[3] See Mizrahi and Rosenthal (1993) for a similar example of tensions between unity and diversity in the case of coalition-building.

[4] The staff members can remain distinctive while they are similar in sharing the same missions or core values as the members of the same organization.

CHAPTER 4

Managing Diversity

Many of the things that I have done are North American . . . My actions do not result in the outcome that I desire. It does not occur to them because they are viewing leadership from a different mindset . . . My exercise of leadership has created confusion for them and ultimately that undermines my authority and my ability.

Country director

I was warned by a guy, 'Max, going into the office is very difficult . . . People have mixed cultural backgrounds. Your assumptions about what's important can be all mixed up. So I would encourage you to be open and patient. Re-examine your own values, and listen to people, and plan on being frustrated by that. That's gonna slow you down.' But it's OK.

Associate director in headquarters

Introduction

FRAGMENTATION OF THE organization appears to be the main problem NGO staff face when they deal with diversity. When the organization is fragmented, it is unable to carry out coherent, co-operative endeavours. Staff members tend to act based on their own interests and goals, even at the risk of obstructing organizational goals. Fragmented performance is far less effective and efficient than coherent performance. Developing a sense of commonality is a potentially effective strategy to address this problem.

Diversity is significant for NGOs for several reasons. First, NGOs' working environments are highly diverse. An NGO usually conducts projects in many countries, each with its own natural and social setting. Thus, when each field office adjusts itself to each field context, the NGO becomes a group of offices that differ from each other in many important respects.

Second, NGOs' target groups are diverse. In fact, one major mission for NGOs is to ensure sustainable social and economic development by bridging gaps between diverse constituencies.[1] This goal inevitably leads them to encounter diverse external constituencies as their target groups.[2]

---

[1] See Brown (1991a).
[2] See Brown (1988), Fowler (1991), and Scott (1992).

Third, NGO staffs are multinational and hence diverse, with members from a variety of countries each bringing their own background and expectations to the organization.[3] An NGO needs to address these differences among staff in order to function smoothly as a single entity.

Diversity in environment, in target groups, and in staff poses a challenge to NGOs. A senior manager of an NGO characterizes diversity as something fragile yet valuable:

> I do not think you can have diversity unless you have unity. Because if all you have is diversity, we can spread apart. We are going to have 20 different organizations.

When he referred to unity, he meant 'a whole totality as combining all its parts into one' among several meanings.[4] He identified one of the challenges that NGOs face as the task of maintaining diversity and totality, or unity, at the same time. Because diversity differs from fragmentation, this suggestion makes sense, conceptually at least. In practice, however, their subtle differences and tricky characteristics make it easy to mix them up. The first half of this chapter identifies fragmenting forces and discusses how they can become a destructive force in an organization in the name of diversity; it then introduces possible strategies to address fragmentation without damaging diversity.

Problems: Fragmented performance in the name of diversity

When an NGO values diversity and tries to embody its character in the organization, it creates a culture that values differences more than similarities. However, differences are more fragile and difficult to maintain than are similarities.[5] Consequently, the organization suffers from fragmentation in the name of diversity. For example, when an NGO supports the autonomy of FOs to be able to address different needs in different contexts, those offices may lose a sense of sharing the mission of the organization as a whole and seek to address only locally identified issues, even if working on those issues does not make sense from the point of view of the entire organization. Based on the findings of this research, this part of the book examines decentralization, cultural

---

[3] Diversity is a valuable resource which can help the NGO to address a wide range of problems. Compared with homogeneous NGOs, those with diverse resources are more likely to be able to explore new views, insights and perspectives rather than relying on established assumptions (Davis, 1971), and to develop appropriate solutions to a variety of unexpected problems.

[4] *Webster's College Dictionary* (1991).

[5] This can be compared with North–South NGO partnerships. Postma (1994) addresses several specific problems with respect to the partnerships. The problems include uneven North–South expectations and demands, information dependency, distrust, resource imbalances, the lack of understanding of local context, and Northern manipulation of Southern NGOs.

differences, and differences in scope, respectively, as causes of organizational fragmentation.

Decentralization and loss of order

Decentralization[6] is a major way to expand the organization's diversity, an expansion from which NGOs benefit in several ways. First, decentralization relieves HQ of heavy administrative burdens; second, the field can make quick decisions; and third, communication demands between HQ and FOs are reduced. However, decentralization can also contribute to disorder in the organization. When an NGO decentralizes, it not only increases its diversity but also typically undermines co-ordination[7] between offices, fragmenting the NGO into multiple small organizations. Two underlying forces account for disorganization.

First, extremists can demand that organizational hierarchies be abandoned entirely. A manager who deals with organizational systems worries about extreme decentralization:

> I agree that pushing the decision closer to where the actions are is more effective. I don't have any trouble with that. But you still need centralized standards,[8] and policies, and priorities, as far as goals go. Where are we going to put our resources, where are we focusing? But there are some people who think we need to do that in the extreme, and throw away any international co-ordination, or any international hierarchy. It wouldn't surprise me that that happens. But it's, damn, I think it's a mistake. And I'd think that, in another five years, that went back again. We need a certain amount of hierarchy to make wise decisions. If we are completely decentralized, we will begin to fragment in terms of our objectives.

This analysis implicitly raises the issue of how to balance decentralization and hierarchy in order to maintain the organization's ability to co-ordinate. Unfortunately, there are no simple answers.[9]

Second, NGOs lack the co-ordination capacity required to deal with the decentralization issue as an event that involves the entire

---

[6] For a discussion of the general concept of organizational decentralization, see, for example, Mintzberg (1979) or Rondinelli (1989). Nadler and Tushman (1988, 110) argue that 'the fundamental question in decentralization and centralization is where decisions are made in the organization'. For discussions of NGOs' decentralization, see Asian NGO Coalition for Agrarian Reform and Rural Development (1987), Edwards (1994), Fowler (1992a) and Tongsawate and Tips (1988).

[7] Weiss (1988) explains that co-ordination is difficult to implement in any organization because an organization tends to resist change and to maximize autonomy.

[8] In the case of development NGOs, standards cannot easily be introduced because, as a desk officer puts it, 'about how to work with other institutions, how to be extremely cost-effective, how to be extremely efficient, no one has a standard.' But this does not mean that there is no order. For influences that drive national voluntary organizations to standardize and centralize themselves, see Young (1989).

[9] See DiBella (1992).

organization. Although HQ, FOs and support offices belong to the same single organization, their interests in decentralization vary greatly.[10]

Generally, FOs are ready to be actively involved in the issue because they benefit most. HQ would agree, even if not willingly, to work on decentralization if it were strongly induced to do so by the field. Support offices, however, may not show any interest in the issue for two reasons. First, they do not have much interest in spending time on decentralization because they have their own agendas that occupy their time. Second, they do not feel obliged to work co-operatively with FOs, for they depend on neither HQ nor FOs, at least financially.

Therefore, from the beginning, even before attempting to deal with the issue, the organization would already be fragmented. Ironically, the degree of fragmentation is already so high that the NGO's members may be unable to co-operate to resolve the fragmentation issue. Simply speaking, fragmentation can make their discussions about fragmentation virtually impossible. A staff member at HQ expresses his frustration with the situation:

> We have no power over the fund-raising offices, we have some power with the field, and that dichotomy or imbalance creates havoc in the system of organization. Support offices come to a meeting once a year, and we talk about the systems. In between times, we have a phone conference every two months. It's not enough, because in between those annual meetings, we kind of all lose our enthusiasm and go our own ways. The individual offices tend to do their own things and worry about their own agenda, and they lose track of the whole partnership.

When an NGO faces fragmentation, its leadership tends strongly to seek organizational order and standards to maintain organizational integration. The objective of maintaining integration tempts HQ to reinstate a hierarchical order, with HQ at the top to regulate the organization. But this temptation can easily lead to another pitfall: the negation of diversity. The difference between fragmentation and diversity is subtle but vital.[11] While fragmentation implies disorganization, diversity does not. Rather, the latter emphasizes the capacity to have different parts that can still be integrated.

Distinguishing these two dimensions – the degree of disorganization or organization, and the degree of fragmentation – is essential to judging the characteristics of an NGO. NGOs do not seek to be disorganized. In fact,

[10] Policy designing has a double meaning: one is to keep in mind the interests of others, and the other, which is not so obvious but is nevertheless significant, is to create and maintain a level of mutuality that may sustain co-operative enquiry (Schön and Rein, 1994, 170).

[11] Fragmentation is the act or process of breaking into disorganized pieces, while diversity is the condition of having differences, yet not necessarily being disorganized (*Webster's Third New International Dictionary*, 1981).

decentralization does not necessarily entail disorganization, but is rather an alternative form of organization.

On the other hand, an NGO wants to keep 'having various pieces' in the organization: although this is one aspect of fragmentation, it is also an important characteristic of diversity. Having various different pieces does not necessarily lead directly to disorganization. It is in the interests of NGOs to have different pieces within the organization, but in an organized way. The problem is that although NGOs want to retain both the characteristics, many discover the hard way that the more different pieces exist in an organization, the more disorganized it is likely to become.

Cultural[12] differences

Cultural differences are another major set of forces that can fragment an organization.[13] Cultural differences contribute to fragmentation in several respects.

Promoting distrust

Cultural differences can easily lead staff members to distrust each other's abilities.[14] The process may start with a minor misinterpretation of a single piece of a person's behaviour and develop into a set of misinterpretations that form a more general misunderstanding of the person's overall behaviour. The misunderstood meaning does not remain a mere difference, but rather results in assigning negative values to the person as well as to their behaviour, with consequent distrust of the person's abilities. The following account from a country director exemplifies how cultural differences lead to distrust of people's abilities:

> Many of the things that I have done are North American. I have done things based on what I think would generate trust. For instance, in an American context, if a leader does the dirty work with his subordinates, everybody is kind of impressed with that. People feel, 'Hey, he is one of us.' So for instance, I do not stay at a hotel – I sleep on the floor. What's been interesting is [the reaction]: 'What's he doing? He is not a leader.' When they ask me a question, I say, 'I am not sure, what do you think?' And they say, 'He is a leader, he is supposed to know the answer.' So this idea has been invalid. The intention is interpreted almost as a sign of weakness as a leader as opposed to a sign of a good leader.[15] My actions do not result in the outcome that I desire. It does not occur to them because they are viewing leadership from a different

---

[12] Culture is often defined as something that is shared by, and unique to, a given organization or group. For example, see Schein (1985).

[13] Meyerson and Martin (1987) view cultures from three different angles: integration, differentiation and ambiguity. The more a culture is internally integrated, the more it differs from other cultures.

[14] Miller (1991) analyses how religious uniformity minimizes flexibility and undermines interpersonal co-operation.

[15] See DiBella (1993).

mindset. Some of my staff who have been around American people there understand it, but they still do not think that's the way. My exercise of leadership has created confusion for them and ultimately that undermines my authority and my ability.

Several factors contribute to situations in which cultural differences lead to value differences.[16] First, it matters whether there are opportunities for further clarification after the original misinterpretation or misunderstanding. Whether lack of clarification is due to a lack of interest or a simple lack of opportunity is not clear. In any event, cultural differences can quickly go beyond mere differences to depreciate different values in the absence of efforts or opportunities to clarify the situation.

Second, one cannot easily foresee which mindset or framework informs the behaviour of a person from a cultural background that differs from one's own. Despite this inability, people tend quickly to assign meanings to other people's behaviour based on their own mindsets.

Third, the inflexibility of people's mindsets prevents them from attempting to view things differently. The perspective illustrated in the above account – 'they understand it but they still do not think that's the way' – demonstrates that changing one's view is much more difficult than understanding it. Changing a historically developed mindset may be impossible; and even if such change is possible, it requires a long time.

Fourth and finally, mindsets are not only inflexible but also value-laden. People are not free from values. While they have their own value scales, they tend to put their own mindsets at the top of the scale. Thus, different mindsets are vertically distinguished and devalued. The above quote – 'he is supposed to know the answer' – indicates that the person apparently does not have any doubt about his definition of a leader. A concept like 'a leader as a facilitator' neither makes sense nor has value.

Cultural differences are not only an attribute of organizational diversity. Unless staff members are ready to wrestle with different ways of thinking and are ready to challenge their own assumptions, cultural differences may operate simply to fragment the organization; their benefits may be lost.

Serving to dichotomize
Due to their complexity and multi-dimensionality, cultural differences may also dichotomize an organization. A conceptual framework that can shed light on a certain culture might be irrelevant to understanding another one. Moreover, not only do cultures differ from each other; their stances toward other cultures also differ. A typical case involves general differences between Western cultures and Asian cultures. An Asian staff member who works with Western colleagues asserts these differences:

---

[16] Urban (1993) argues that when distinct cultures interact, the relationship that develops between them tends to be hierarchical rather than equal.

Usually, Western people speak very directly, and [make their points] very strongly. Like when they see problems, they always say, 'OK, fix it now.' That's typical, whereas Asians have more patience if there is a problem. Then they tend to look at the causes, and discuss them informally, so it's very, very different. They bring it to the formal level just for finalization. So it's a different way of doing things.

This particular case suggests that cultural differences are derived not only from the cultures' own attributes, such as languages, religions, societies, ethnicity and so on, but also and more importantly from different ways of dealing with pressing issues. Members of these different cultures have different styles of interacting. They do not take the same approach to understanding each other. Therefore, each tries to understand the interaction style of the other from within their own style. Consequently, their cultural differences can be reinforced through the very practice of attempting to understand each other.

In this particular example, Westerners, according to the Asian staff member, tend to approach target groups proactively in the hope of gaining some clue to understanding them. Asians,[17] on the other hand, tend to observe carefully what other people do. So the relationship is not a two-way interaction, but more like an actor-audience relationship, where one acts while the other observes. Through their own modes of interacting, people in intercultural relationships adopt different roles: Westerners as actors and Asians as audiences. The roles are not just arbitrarily assigned. Depending upon types of cultural differences, interactions will form one-way, actor–audience relationships, as the account explains.

Therefore, the problem is that the very acts of trying to understand each other do not always facilitate mutual understanding. On the contrary, they may end up augmenting cultural gaps. In many cases, well-intentioned attempts to communicate may ironically result in dichotomizing the organization. This contradictory relationship raises a critical question about each group's mode of communication *vis-à-vis* that of others. How can staff members possibly change their interaction styles so that they find common ground without dichotomizing the organization? The strategy section of this chapter addresses this question.

Differences in scope
People's perspectives are significantly influenced by their environment. In the case of NGO staff, the pictures that the staff perceive in their minds are largely separated into two types – narrower views and broader views:

---

[17] In fact, Asians are not the only people who operate within a mode of communication that differs from the Western mode. An Ethiopian NGO staff member also articulates differences from the American mode: 'Americans want to put the problem on the table and resolve that right there, whereas Ethiopian culture doesn't want to confront a person directly, but we go around.'

One of the things I'm learning about working in a situation such as international headquarters, where I am now, [is that] you do get a big picture that you don't have in the field. Now, I think the difficulty is when I'm attempting to elicit co-operation from the field and support offices. I see how this contributes to the big picture, but they may not see that. And so I don't get the kind of co-operation that I need because I've got a whole world [view] and they've got a very narrow one.

Differences in perspective, according to this desk officer, have the potential to discourage staff members' co-operation and hence to divide the organization into fragmented pieces. The rest of this section of this chapter analyses how different perspectives work in four distinct ways to hinder the establishment of productive relationships among staff members.

'Where you stand depends on where you sit'

A country director describes how people's practices depend heavily upon the contexts in which they find themselves:

I learned a long time ago about very, very simple harmony. Where you stand depends on where you sit. It's just that they are different. Even with people who have experience in one side shifting to the other, that does not necessarily make the relationship between two much easier. At least you know the culture of the other but that does not necessarily make the work, or the relationships easier. Headquarters, with the job that I had, not only related to the field offices, but also related back to the larger organization. Once you are back in the United States [headquarters], a lot of times, you tend to forget about how it is to live and work overseas because it goes back [to] the whole issue of priorities. You are faced with a whole different set of pressures and priorities that you don't have overseas. They are just different.

The differences in people's positions are not merely differences in their tasks, roles and job titles. The differences are accompanied by contextual differences such as pressures, priorities and constraints.[18] Thus, having the technical ability to accomplish tasks does not guarantee one's actual working ability in a given context. Each context offers a set of different and unexpected issues that the person needs to deal with in addition to his or her tasks and roles. Even within the same organization, the director says, contextual differences between HQ and the field are so huge that one cannot always make use of one's experiences in the field when one goes back to HQ to work with the field.

NGO staff worry about the differences between HQ and FOs as a source of fragmenting forces rather than appreciating those differences as

---

[18] 'The people occupying particular locations will tend to develop models of organizational structure based on their peculiar priorities and problems – from a specific occupational or departmental standpoint' (Benson, 1977, 14).

a sign of diversity. One notable difference is that HQs tend to deal with broad policy matters while the field usually concentrates on day-to-day work.[19] As long as their tasks do not contradict each other, they can work co-operatively. But once they have a common task, on which they work not only differently but also oppositely, they can develop serious problems. Their differences are not only in their views,[20] but also in their responsibilities, their interests and the scope of their assignments.

Once a task is assigned to a staff member, she or he takes on responsibility for the task and treats it as high priority regardless of its importance within the organization overall. Thus, even if the task is not vital to the entire organization, the staff member prioritizes the assigned task over other important ones. A country director, who had work experience in HQ, describes his inevitable frustration due to positional differences:

> Thailand is one of the 11 or 12 country offices that headquarters has to deal with. Plus there is a whole other range of responsibilities. So the problems of this office don't always take priority in headquarters. Of course, they are my prime responsibility, so it can be upsetting or distressing when headquarters doesn't put the same value on my problems, my issues. And I dare say that, from their perspective, they might be upset and distressed that I might expect too much of them, that I'm not putting myself in their position, and so forth. I think that's going to continue to be the case. They've got a whole different set of pressures than I have.

While this account describes the gap from the field side, the following one presents an issue for HQ in its relationship to support offices. A desk officer in HQ remarks:

> We are trying to facilitate dialogue with senior management to get the systems defined. But most people don't care. They are just worried about getting along with their environment. We are trying to align our systems with strategies, but the problem is that this strategic document doesn't have a really good buy-in partnership. The participation of the leaders of fund-raising offices in creating this document is very weak. Very weak. They tend to do their own work and don't participate in the series of dialogues on this.

A couple of points can be drawn from these accounts to characterize the relationship between people's positions and their behaviour. First, differences in views cannot fully explain discord. A crucial reason would rather be found in the pressures that are attached to people's positions.

---

[19] Bryson (1988) discusses the nature of the tasks that individuals of a structured organization have. Because of confined information and assigned narrower tasks, they can only suboptimize within their narrower world. He suggests that they need to have opportunities to interact with others broadly to understand the overview of the organization's objectives.

[20] Needless to say, the two sides perceive a lot of difficulties in trying to understand each other's views. A country director points out that these difficulties are due, among other things, to the difficulty of encapsulating all of one's own activities, and those of the whole office, in a report. The flavour of what people are doing cannot easily be captured.

Assigning different responsibilities to the staff in the organization often decreases their sense of responsibility toward the organization's overall missions. They remain content with their own assignment at the risk of devaluing other issues, even if other issues are more important than theirs in light of broad missions. As the desk officer observes, 'people don't care' what others do. As a result, organizational missions are reduced to fragmented tasks.

The other reason that discord cannot be reduced to differences in views is the importance of hierarchical differences. Based on these two accounts, it can reasonably be argued that differences between support offices and HQ and between HQ and FOs are vertically distinguished. Each field office is one of many for which HQ is responsible, and is submerged under the broad interests of HQ. HQ, for its part, fails to influence support offices and does not take a strong stance toward them. In fact, hierarchy is expressed by staff members in different ways. When a desk officer at HQ characterizes HQ's relationship with the field, he confirms the sense of inability on the field side: 'If there is not openness in HQ, then you can have the best ideas in the world and little attention would be given to those ideas.' Their hierarchically assigned positional differences heavily affect their behaviours, and the behaviours themselves, in turn, confirm and reproduce the hierarchical differences.

'Superficial experts'

When a knowledge gap exists between what a staff member thinks he or she understands and what he or she actually does understand, this causes problems. In some cases, HQ and FOs each claim that they understand field situations better than the other. Field staff often feel that people from HQ do not understand the field as much as they do. On the other hand, staff in HQ sometimes feel that they can look at the field from a broader point of view and thus can understand the field more appropriately.[21] Because both sides have defensible reasons to rely on their own views, minimizing the gap is not an easy task. This gap then becomes a cause of arguments concerning the degree of HQ's involvement in the field. A case is described from a country director's point of view:

> There is an imperative for people in the headquarters to get involved in what's going on on a day-to-day basis in a country office. Not to control it, but to become involved at a level that may not be appropriate. There are too many decisions made based on a superficial understanding of the situations in the

---

[21] As an organization's size increases, its division of labour also increases. Moreover, not only labour but also human knowledge is divided and distributed in the process. Co-ordination becomes more difficult, more costly and more complex (Hayek, 1945; Zeleny, 1987). In the case of NGOs, because their missions are crucial in implementing projects, the broader view needs to be shared properly among the entire staff. However, this becomes difficult as the NGO develops, due to division and specialization.

country. Superficial in that they understand the top 2 per cent of what's going on; they don't understand the other 98 per cent. But they feel that they understand everything based on the 2 per cent. And they act too much on intuition. They may have visited here six months ago for three days. And then 'bun' (click), they are automatic experts on the situations. Perceptions and decisions are based on the superficial understanding plus this intuition based on some experience. Now, there is a possible contradiction there, because on the one hand, I want them to have a more in-depth understanding of what we are doing, and I want them to become involved in helping us to make plans, to make decisions, to develop strategies, and to support. But on the other hand, I'm saying that they should not be involved at the level of decision making, the detailed level that exhausts them and us.

His concern is not about a simple conceptual gap. He believes that the gap combines with the interests of HQ, with the unfortunate consequence that the HQ imposes these interests on the field. When he says, '[It's] imperative for people in the HQ to get involved in what's going on on a day-to-day basis in a country office. Not to control it, but to become involved at a level that may not be appropriate,' he is disappointed by the distrust of HQ and worried that the inappropriate involvement of HQ hinders work in the field.

Careless involvement of HQ leads the field staff to take a defensive stance. They become reluctant to welcome people from HQ. They may even act prejudicially, devaluing the suggestions of the staff from HQ, no matter what the suggestions are. A field officer candidly describes his case:

> When I was in the field reporting to headquarters, we complained to them all the time. All those guys came out here and screwed everything up. But in fact, they performed a useful function, we learned after a while. They did see the big picture, while we did not, because we are local. They really did perform a useful function even though we didn't like it.

The difficulty is that HQ's involvement is not always negative. Sometimes, though not always, HQ's involvement turns out to be positive, even though the field staff dislike it. The issue is, therefore, not whether HQ or the field understands the field better. Rather, the issue is how HQ should take advantage of its position and be involved in the field in a proper manner, and how the field should benefit from HQ without being hindered in its work. Such are the questions that confront NGOs. The strategy section of this chapter addresses these questions.

Antidiversity as part of diversity
Should the NGO staff value any and all different ideas as a way to embody diversity in the organization?[22] What if the idea itself negates the

---

[22] Cf. Fisher and Ury (1991, 161–5): 'Should I negotiate even with terrorists or someone like Hitler? When does it make sense not to negotiate?'

value of diversity? In this case, the idea would not be something that we can recognize without anxiety. In fact, being diverse can mean being open to any destructive concepts and forces, including fragmentation, homogenization, authoritarianism and so forth. To protect the organization from the undesirable influences of these forces, do we have to be selective about the types of differences that NGOs can accept? If so, some types of diversity are not welcome. In such cases, NGOs need to draw a line to keep their differences within an acceptable range. The following account identifies a discrepancy between diversity as an ideal and actual actions:

> Let's say that, in country A, our understanding of being Christian is that we only work with a particular kind of church. Now there are other people who, in that country, would be Christian. But we support projects and programmes that really would not accept the other types of Christians that we would find in the country. Then we have a very serious problem because we are carrying out our work in such a way as to sow division within a working community. We believe that true transformation is going to bring people together. It should contribute to building harmony and acceptance in that community regardless of the pluralism in that place. But what we do, in fact, is to create new élites, because of their relationships with the external funding agency, and we, in fact, are doing very imperial development work. Now, other country offices of the same NGO say, 'No, this is not our organization, this is not us. We don't do that.' But the fact is that country A, they are doing it . . . So what we discovered is that if each office is allowed to interpret the organization according to its own concepts it can have serious repercussions for other entities [within the organization].

The tensions between the concept of diversity and actual actions can be identified at two different levels. One is within country A where the organization's projects have had undesirable results. The other is found at the organizational level, where some types of differences in projects are not allowed.

The first discrepancy is straightforward. The field office faces the contradiction between what it practises and what it claims as its mission. The practices of the country office apparently distinguish it from people with different values, and excludes them. In contrast to what diversity requires, their criteria for selecting beneficiaries are specific and exclusive. They work not with all Christians, but with only a particular kind of Christian. As a result, they get contradictory results. Instead of prompting people to get together as a community, they end up increasing the gap between the rich and the poor in the same area. While they aim at promoting harmony and acceptance in the community, what they actually practise promotes the gap in the community.

The second issue is not so simple. If a country office engages in problematic practices, like country A in the quote above, how should the

NGO deal with the country office? Should it accept the practice in the name of diversity even if the practice of the country office appears to be authoritarian or exclusive? Or should the organization interfere and regulate the country office to prevent undesirable practices from being carried out, at the expense of diversity?

When other offices claim, 'No, this is not our organization. We don't do that', they imply that the organization has a set of values with which all offices ought to agree. This value system dictates which types of diversity they shall embrace. If a certain practice is not consistent with the range of diverse practices with which the organization needs to comply, then officers say, 'No, this is not our organization'. However, in practice, they cannot draw a clear distinction between acceptable differences and unacceptable ones. They work in many different cultures that may have totally different value systems. Hence, the same practice can be interpreted in totally different ways in different country offices. A certain practice in one country may comply with the organization's missions while the same practice in a different country may be unacceptable, due to contextual differences.

Even if the staff agree that diversity can be allowed within the range that complies with the organization's missions, asserting 'No, this is not us' with regard to certain practices in other country offices may be a thoughtless action with damaging consequences. The country office might hold totally different assumptions than those of which the staff members are aware. Nevertheless, avoiding instant judgement does not necessarily entail accepting any type of performance in another country simply because of its different context. In each specific context, the staff need to be accountable to their missions. The tendency, however, is that they either dismiss certain kinds of performance as unacceptable without serious examination, or they simply let staff members practise what they like without any judgement. NGOs, then, need to ask this question: what practices should the staff engage in so that they compromise neither diversity nor the organization's missions?

Before strategies are presented to address this question, another problem needs to be discussed.

Intentional ambiguity
The problem derived from differences in scope is ambiguity. Because the staff face multi-dimensional differences when they interact with each other, they cannot easily conceptualize cause-effect relationships for issues at hand. A desk officer in the field says:

> We have a lot of frustrating communication back and forth [between head-quarters and the field]. I don't know whether that's because of our own problem. I think if we knew what the problem was, it was basically solved.

One was suspicious . . . uh, I don't really know. . . . Maybe the key decision-makers are too busy with other things . . . it's really hard to say.

Ambiguity frustrates the officer. His frustration does not originate from some problem that HQ imposes on him. Rather, it derives from the fact that he cannot clarify the problem and therefore cannot take a clear stance *vis-à-vis* HQ. Because he is not sure whether there is a fault on the side of HQ, he hesitates to characterize HQ in one way or another. He just does not know if HQ is too busy or is just ignoring him. He does not want to complain, but at the same time he is not satisfied with the current situation. The ambiguous situation intensifies his frustration. If no clues are provided to understand the other office, one can take neither a positive nor a negative stance toward them. All one can do is either wait or keep asking until one receives a response.

The same can also happen for HQ. When a desk officer in HQ does not hear for some time from the field regarding his question, he just wonders:

> You don't want to go back with a second reminder. If they are dealing with it, you don't say anything very quickly. It may take them a few days to answer. When you are wondering what's going on, you can't plan strategies to deal with it unless you know what the reason is. Maybe it's difficult to find out. There could be an issue going on in the field. Maybe there is a funeral or someone has got malaria. I wouldn't necessarily hear about sickness, or personal problems, or problems in the field, the field director's diarrhoea or something. I mean, they are all humans and have their lives going on.

A field staff member describes his position, carefully avoiding any value judgement about the fact that he often does not receive responses from HQ:

> I don't have a clear idea but probably they are very busy. Nowadays, it has become rare that I get feedback on reports, for example. I'm asking and asking, but not knowing what they do there, like what kind of workload they have. . . . They may very well be overloaded. I don't really know what they do. Maybe they aren't too busy. I don't know. I can't say it's lack of willingness, either. Because that [would imply that their attitude is], 'No, I don't want to respond.' Maybe it's because they are out of town. . . . They have a lot of things to do, and maybe they don't have a chance to open my mail. So I don't know. I have to say, I don't know. I have no idea. If they say, 'Oh, this is not important,' then, it's not important for them to tell me that they are busy and will postpone for a week to answer while I say, 'It's important'. So there is no clue.

In contrast to the previous field staff member, this staff member does not show any sign of frustration and plainly explains the situation. It appears that he intentionally keeps himself in a position where he does not have enough information to criticize HQ. He tolerates his situation by being in an ambiguous position that does not explain why HQ does not respond.

For some reasons, besides his personality, he might want to keep the situation ambiguous deliberately.

Understanding his behaviour should start from his background. He was initially hired in his home country as a national staff member and was promoted to a senior manager post in a different field office. Thus, although he has assumed higher responsibility in the office, he would have had a historically developed mindset that may lead him to deprecate himself *vis-à-vis* HQ.[23]

In his mindset, keeping the situation ambiguous may have its own uses. First, it would save him from confronting HQ if the reality was that HQ did not care about the field so much.[24] Even if HQ intentionally does not write back, he would not want to clarify this fact for the sake of his responsibility because a confrontation resulting from the clarification may put him in a risky position. As a nationally-hired staff member, though he is currently international staff, he may not want to pursue the matter aggressively because he is highly dependent upon the organization in terms of benefits that he can enjoy in his current job, compared with those associated with other jobs in his home country.

Second, anybody, but especially someone with this staff member's background as a national hire, would be reluctant to pressure HQ to do something if they are actually working on it. People do not want to give an egoistic impression that they do not care about others, but they do want to get their own jobs done. Thus, unless a legitimate reason exists and allows one to prod HQ without appearing rude, one would probably wait for a response.

These two reasons may explain why this man elects a passive stance that maintains ambiguity. On the other hand, people in HQ can take advantage of his intentional ambiguity. They may be able to behave without many of the constraints enforced by the field as long as their behaviour appears ambiguous. Even if they do not write back because of their laziness, that is not questioned.

Staff members' efforts to maintain ambiguity can be regarded as a product of the mix of care and fear that field staff feel toward HQ. The care is valuable but the fear is unnecessary. However, because the two are intertwined, extracting only the fear is difficult.

Ambiguity as a product of a mix of care and fear has its own dynamic in influencing the organization. It is likely to prevent staff from engaging in open communication. It tempts HQ to reduce its work-load by ignoring the field – an act that rarely draws criticism from the field.[25] The tendency

---

[23] See *Encouraging top-down control* in the section on 'Constructing identity' (Chapter 5, pp. 116–17).

[24] Ambiguity may serve to soften disagreement or defer conflict (Schön and Rein, 1994, 168).

[25] Power can easily be applied when performance is more difficult to assess, and more uncertainty and disagreement exist. See Pfeffer (1992).

to discourage open communication perpetuates ambiguity and thereby fragments the organization. If the ambiguity is a product of care and fear, how can the organization free itself from fragmenting forces without losing a sense of care?

The Problem section of this chapter has discussed different types of problems that NGO staff face when they try to put the concept of diversity into practice. While the problems are divided into three categories for convenience, they all demonstrate that trying to embody diversity in the organization will result in fragmenting the organization into pieces. When the staff are more or less similar, they can easily relate to each other. But once their differences are emphasized their relationship becomes loose, if not totally delinked. To respond to this problem, the second half of the chapter presents strategies that NGO staff practise in the face of fragmenting forces.

Strategies: Building a sense of commonality

To respond to the problems of fragmentation, NGO staff employ several strategies to build a sense of commonality[26] based on their daily work. These strategies, described here through the staff members' personal accounts, fall into five categories: rituals, narratives, leadership integration, association of differences, and protection of time.

Rituals[27] as a mediator
Using ritual is a powerful strategy to play a mediating role and prevent the organization from fragmenting into pieces. Prayers and chats are analysed as strategic rituals.

---

[26] '[By losing] all sense of sharing in a common world, . . . [people] become increasingly dependent on administrative organizations to govern the world, and give up participation in voluntary associations, so that isolation, passivity and apathy displace their capacity for action' (Hill, 1979, 282).

[27] The difference between what ritual does and what conceptual language does is vividly expressed by Rappaport (1979), who argues that the work of language is to divide: 'The distinctions of language cut the world into bits – into categories, classes, oppositions, and contrasts. It is in this nature of language to search out all differences and to turn them into distinctions which then provide bases for boundaries and barriers' (194). In contrast, the work of ritual is quite different. 'It is . . . in the nature of liturgical orders to unite, or reunite, the psychic, social, natural, and cosmic orders which language and the exigencies of life pull apart. It is of importance in this regard that representations in ritual are often multimodal, employing at one and the same time words, music, noise, odors, objects, and substances. Part, though not the whole, of what is meant by ritual's establishment of order is the acceptance of that order by those who participate in it. Liturgical orders are public, and participation in them constitutes a public acceptance of a public order, regardless of the private state of belief. Acceptance is, thus, a fundamental social act, and it forms a basis for public orders, which unknowable and volatile belief or conviction cannot' (194).

Prayers

Prayers can be used as a strategy to get the staff to look at the same missions. A support office staff member of a religion-based NGO emphasizes the power of prayer. According to him, prayer plays a role for the staff who argue with each other, freeing them from unproductive arguments and inviting them to focus on their common issues together. I analyse the power of prayer with the help of his experience.

At an annual meeting where more than 20 leaders got together to discuss major organizational issues, they sometimes came to an impasse where their arguments were parallel and they could not draw any conclusion. They could not easily withdraw or concede their ideas, interests and agendas. Because they represented their offices, their ideas, interests and agendas were not personal, but rather involved a group of people in each office. The meeting tended to be a place where each staff pushed their points as much as possible to get them on the agenda and approved. As a result, their listening ability was minimized and they even criticized the positions of other staff in the hope of placing them at a disadvantage. He said:

> When we came to an impasse, the chairman of the meeting suggested we pray together. We stopped the discussion, closed our eyes and prayed together. After that, surprisingly, I cannot explain why, but for some reason, [afterward] we could come to an agreement on the issue after a short period of good discussion. The issue around which our arguments had been opposed for hours was resolved.[28]

Religion is not a theme here. However, his experience can provide a significant clue to understanding how fragmented arguments might be transformed into co-ordinated discussions. Analysing from the point of view of listening and speaking seems worthwhile.

When people bring different agendas, interests, issues and pressures to their interactions with each other, they identify their mission in terms of their own viewpoints. To do that, they tend to speak more than necessary and, as a result, listen less than necessary. They are so occupied with their own issues that they fail to understand what others suggest. They keep on advocating their points until others accept them. This obviously unbalances the speaking–listening relationship.

In this context, prayer can help restore balance to the speaking–listening relationship. Staff members may regain their listening ability when they close their eyes and listen to prayers. Prayer can also help them to reconfirm a sense of community; it interrupts instrumental argumentation and offers staff members quiet time to reflect on what they say and what others say.[29] The reflections provide staff with a chance to give

---

[28] Translated from an original language.

[29] 'One measure of healthy political talk is the amount of silence it permits and encourages, for silence is the precious medium in which reflection is nurtured and empathy can grow' (Barber, 1984, 175).

up their narrow pictures and to look at a broader picture of what they, as a community, are undertaking. Through prayer, they are able to look at the same goal together instead of instrumentally advancing their narrow agendas in competition with others.[30]

This experience provides useful insights. Prayers in this organizational context played roles in recovering listening ability, providing quiet time to reflect on past actions, and broadening participants' minds.[31] While prayers worked well in this organization, we do not need to treat this specific method as the only strategy. Even for non-religious NGOs, these three points provide a key to examining which strategies work to break impasses in different contexts.

Ritualized chatting

Ritualized chatting is another strategy for mediating conflict in an NGO. This strategy suggests that a ritually protected time during which staff can talk about their personal issues makes a significant contribution to their work. Conventional work ethics usually discourage staff from bringing their personal issues to the workplace except during breaks. However, this separation between job-related issues and personal issues is not necessarily wise.

Jobs cannot be worked out by themselves. In most NGO settings, many people are involved in a project. Thus, work situations are very complicated. The staff have to deal not only with their immediate tasks but also with other staff in order to co-ordinate. Getting the job done does not mean simply focusing on the job itself. A significant amount of work must be devoted to co-ordinating the job among staff. While co-ordination does not necessarily require that staff know about each other's personal issues, they can better co-ordinate if they know each other as persons. Two local managers in different countries reflect on how work and personal issues relate:

> If I had a vehicle accident just five minutes ago, I would not be in a very good mood to sit down and discuss work with you. Of course, I could say these things but I would miss things. There would be gaps in my communication with you. When you ask me something, I may be angry because I have something troubling me – not because I have anything against you, but that's

---

[30] On the occasion of a marriage ceremony, a pastor suggested to the marrying couple that they be one in a sense of looking up at the same star together rather than looking at each other. The suggestion has a significant meaning that may be applied in a meeting context. Although looking at each other seems to provide a basic mode of communication, we have to realize that we look at different things. Once you find something wrong in the other, your communication easily breaks down. Looking at the same star is an attitude that may help staff members work on the same issue together.

[31] Compare with Barber's (1984, 174) three general observations. 'First, strong democratic talk entails listening no less than speaking; second it is affective as well as cognitive; and third, its intentionalism draws it out of the domain of pure reflection into the world of action'.

human nature. So that's why knowing a person, his personality, his character, his background would help you.

Somebody might be having financial problems, and their children are out of school or something like that. So when you are dealing with such a situation, you have to know how the problem affects them, how it affects their work.

Both accounts vividly present concrete cases that explain how personal issues strongly influence work. This raises the question of how the staff can become aware of each other's personal issues while they are in a working context. In response to the question, the strategy suggests an informally defined, ritualized chatting time during office work. Here is an interesting observation from a desk officer at HQ:

You are dealing with a Western-oriented culture in which every second of the day counts and we watch the clock every minute. And we are trying to deal with colleagues who are in a culture in which personal interplay is the most important thing. You don't walk into a meeting and just immediately start talking business. You spend half an hour chatting about your kids, your grandkids and your family, and then you get the business done. For people from a Western-oriented, time-sensitive culture, this is like, 'My gosh, get off the subject, let's get to work here,' and yet we can get less done by doing that than if we just take half an hour to chat with people about what's important.

This people-centred strategy can be contrasted with the business-centred approach. The business-centred approach puts jobs before people. It requires the staff to focus their attention on their jobs and does not allow other issues such as personal ones to disturb them. The idea is that a staff member should write a project proposal without being influenced by his or her sick son, for example. This approach clearly separates person-at-work from person-as-human.

The people-centred approach looks at the issue from the point of view of people. As the two local managers explain, people cannot clearly separate their jobs from their personal issues. For them, the job is a part of their personal lives. Both taking care of a sick son and writing a project proposal are tasks which confront the person. Thus, writing a good project proposal may require that the person takes a couple of hours off to take the son to the hospital first. They can work better and live better at the same time.

But, this alternative can hardly be expected by the business-centred approach. They would get together to work right from the beginning regardless of serious problems they might face. However, when they chat, they can step back from a narrow focus on the job and look at it within a broader context. To allow chatting to happen in an NGO, the strategy suggests that spare time for ritualized greetings needs to be protected. Once spare time is protected in an NGO, it is legitimized to a certain extent, and therefore people are not afraid of talking about their personal concerns. Thanks to informal but ritualized chatting, they can co-ordinate work to select a better course of action from much broader alternatives when they work on a given issue.

Narratives[32]

Narratives are one of the most typical strategies used to develop a sense of commonality. As people narrate, they communicate what they have in mind and develop a sense of shared purpose. However, simply to talk without any attention, focus, implication, or plan is not a wise approach to building a sense of common purpose. NGO staff members demonstrate three different approaches to better using narrative for building a sense of shared purpose.

Coining organizational terms

Coining words to develop a unique language is another strategy for establishing a sense of commonality among the staff. As part of organizational culture, each organization develops and uses its own language either intentionally or unintentionally.[33] The language is usually developed by coining words that have specific meanings unique to the organizational context. Using coined words helps staff members contextualize themselves in the situations for which the words were coined and helps them to stand on common organizational ground. In addition, because the language of the coined words is specific to each organization, daily use of the language strengthens the sense of membership within an organization. A desk officer describes her organization's language:

> We have our own language. And most of the people who are into writing a proposal know our language by now.. We have a lot of nationalities in our organization, but we also speak HELP [the name of the organization], HELP-speak. We call it HELP-speak. Most of the people who write proposals are not very new. So we don't have too many problems with languages. Most people use HELP terms. That's another problem. We all speak HELP language but the donors don't speak HELP language. So we have to learn to speak human-

---

[32] Mumby (1993) argues that narrative works as a socially symbolic act. It interacts with the social not only to take on meaning in a social context but also to construct social context as a domain of meaning. In this sense, Mumby refers to society as an ongoing 'struggle over meaning'(5), and narrative works as a medium of struggle. In this line of argument, an organization, which can be a microcosm of society, can also be an arena where narrative acts as a 'struggle over meaning'. The struggle has multi-dimensional influences on the organization. It would construct certain kinds of social relations. It would also open for change, maintain and reproduce the prevailing system of power relations in the organization. These are just a few of the influences of this struggle. See Bruner (1990) for the characteristics of narratives.

[33] See Pettigrew (1979) for discussions about how symbols, language, ideology, belief, ritual and myth relate to the creation of organizational cultures.

speak. We have a lot of HELP terminology, languages, acronyms, and everything.

Developing a common organizational language is a powerful strategy for retaining a sense of commonality among staff members. Because they use the language every day as a means to communicate, they do not need to arrange special times outside work to use the language as a tool to develop a sense of commonality. Without spending time on such events as meetings, seminars and training, they produce and reproduce their commonality as they communicate in their organizational language.

Moreover, because language is strongly related to culture, the daily use of organizational language shapes organizational culture.[34] For example, an NGO coined a term, 'international office', to refer to what it used to call 'HQ'. The difference in naming the office had a great impact on staff members' mindsets and, in turn, influenced the organizational culture.[35] A desk officer describes how their identification as the 'international office' instead of 'HQ' marks their positional difference within the organization overall. A staff member in an office that used to be HQ but is now the international office says:

> We are a co-ordinating office, or international office. Headquarters is a dirty word because we don't dictate to the field. We are more of a client house. We have a fund raising office on one side, we have a ministry office on the other, and our work is to make sure that the field offices have the money they need – and that these support offices have the communication and information – as well as to maintain the quality of ministry.

Another desk officer in the same office briefly and slightly reluctantly characterizes how the change in the name of the office affected their power structure:

> Requests from here are no longer acted on as swiftly as perhaps they once would have been. In other words, this office has had a reduction in power in essence, because we are not headquarters, we are a co-ordinating body.

A few notable points can be drawn from this example to explain the impact of coined words. First, coining a term for a certain issue can play a vital role in establishing common feeling on the issue. In this case, coining the term 'international office' has succeeded in drawing the staff's attention to the power relationship between HQ and other offices.

Second, a coined term can powerfully symbolize the characteristics of what is described. Consider the statement, 'We are an international office. HQ is a dirty word because we don't dictate to the field'. The staff has become term-sensitive. When they say 'international office', they imply a

---

[34] As an example that illustrates the relationship between culture and language, Mazrui (1975, 48) purports that 'learning English is, to non-Westerners, a process of Westernization.'
[35] For a discussion of the relationship between language and status, see Liska (1991).

client house. When they hear 'HQ', they would imagine dictatorship. But they would not have felt that way unless the term 'international office' was introduced.

Third, the act of articulating coined terms can even influence the power structure of the organization. Again, as they articulated the term 'international office' instead of 'HQ', they remembered and identified that their authoritative power over other offices was lessened. The practice of calling an office by a different term changes its status within the organization. The articulation of a coined term is a powerful agent of change in the organization. However, whether an organization changes in a positive or negative way depends upon how this powerful tool is used.[36] In summary, by coining a term for a certain issue, the organization develops a sense of commonality around the issue, symbolizes the characteristics of the issue, and, finally, changes the issue itself as it is characterized by the term.

Envisioning and articulating

Envisioning and articulating common goals is not only valuable in itself but is also a wise strategy for developing a sense of commonality.[37] As envisioning and articulating processes go, a commonly-shared sense may be built even unintentionally. Building a commonly-shared sense is not a prime objective but a precious by-product of the processes. To understand how a sense of commonality is built, the contributions of envisioning and articulating are examined.

A country director's insight into shared vision is suggestive:

> Even though we have different contexts and different pressures, having a central agreed-upon statement like that has answered a lot of questions because over the years we got more and more entities and one statement is interpreted in many different ways. So this process of forming this identity has taken us back to a new starting point. There would always be opportunities for different interpretations. But we have come back to a new starting point where at least right now everybody has agreed that this is what this means. Those words over time would begin to get interpreted in different ways because new people would be coming in, changes would take place, etc. But it's been very healthy to go back to an agreed-upon starting point. And that would do an awful lot. I'm already seeing it's doing an awful lot to help us have the same priority. It's a very significant thing. So this identity has created and reaffirmed priorities.

---

[36] Feminists have pointed out that naming is political and have warned that labels of women's activities often contribute to the control and subordination of women. See Frye (1983).

[37] In the critical reflection tradition, the practice of imagining the future is one valuable practical method of learning as persons, as organizations and as societies. Through searching, listening, sharing and clarifying, participants generate concrete possibilities and options for choices for the future, and create new practices, new institutions and new ways of doing within their specific context (Deshler, 1993).

Envisioning may contribute to building a sense of commonality in several ways. First, the director describes the identification of commonly-shared visions as a result of envisioning. For example, when an NGO identifies transparency as one important vision, staff members all start to pay special attention to transparency and expect other staff members to treat it in the same manner. Envisioning helps the staff pay attention to the same issue (transparency, as in this example, or any other issue) and helps them to develop a sense of commonality around the matter.

Second, envisioning develops common interpretations among the staff. Without the envisioning process, staff members may interpret the same issue in different ways. If the staff are simply given transparency as their core value to follow, they would all have different interpretations in their minds. Going through the envisioning process together, they come to agree on what the term actually means.

Third, envisioning is a process of continuously reflecting on their starting point to produce and reproduce common visions. The visions that staff members agree on today may not be agreeable to them next month, due to changes in staffing, in the organization, and in their environments. Envisioning not only allows staff members to look to the future but also lets them reflect back to question if their visions are still relevant in changing contexts and if they are still commonly held among the staff members. Envisioning can reconstruct and reprioritize their visions to coincide with changing situations. As a result, even in changing environments, it can consistently work to reproduce a sense of commonality among the staff.

Articulation is the second half of the strategy after the staff go through the envisioning process. Articulation has dual roles in the organization: it legitimizes the visions of the organization, and it helps staff to reidentify themselves as members of the same organization. Both of these functions may assist in building a sense of commonality. To understand the relationship between the dual roles of articulation and the establishment of common feeling, we start by listening to a country director:

> We talked about what we want to become and ended up calling our identity, who we are. And some of the principles in there include words like transparency. We make mistakes as an organization, we do bad things. We do things that could be done better. But we want to learn from those mistakes, and we want others to learn from them, so we want to be open about them. We want to be honest. It's *very difficult*.[38] But it's something we got together and talked about. Because we believe it's important and we talked about it, it tends to happen more than it would if it wasn't addressed. That's another part of the dynamic to the extent that you get together and dialogue about these issues and then plan for them. They have a better chance of taking place than not taking place.

---

[38] Italics reflect the speaker's emphasis.

Articulation legitimizes the vision. After the staff members agree on their vision, they articulate it by writing it down and sharing it with the entire organization. Then the vision, such as transparency, for example, becomes an important concept for them not only because they identified and talked about it, but also because it has officially gained position in the organization. Whichever office you go to in the organization, you find the same vision written in their mission statement.

Once the vision is ingrained in the organization, it can easily be institutionalized as the written vision is read and the idea of the vision is articulated repeatedly by the staff. The term now has a life of its own and shapes the behaviour of the staff. The term plays a leading role in the organization. Everybody sees it and gets direction from it. Thus, articulation supports a sense of commonality by enabling the vision to be seen by everybody.

Second, articulating helps staff members re-identify themselves as members of the same organization. When the country director says, '[transparency] tends to happen more than it would be if it wasn't addressed', this very speech has dual roles. He not only identifies transparency as a valued and shared goal in the organization, he also re-identifies himself as a member of the organization by accepting the goal.

When a view or goal is legitimized in an organization, confirming the view is equivalent to re-affirming one's membership in the organization. When staff members speak of organizational views to each other, they reconfirm to each other that they are members of the same organization. They develop a shared sense of community by articulating that they are working toward the same valued visions.

This analysis of articulation does not aim to examine whether the organization is going to achieve its visions or goals, such as transparency. Rather, the point is that articulating develops a sense of commonality among the staff through the process of legitimization and re-identification. Legitimization and re-identification are related to each other. The more a vision is legitimized, the more staff re-identify themselves with the vision, which, in turn, enhances the vision's legitimacy, and so on.

Sharing experiences
Sharing experiences is an indisputable strategy for building a sense of commonality. This account from the field articulates the self-evident basis of the strategy:

> If we communicate more than one time, we recognize the name. But one day we meet: 'Oh, you are the one. Oh, OK. Can we go and have a meal?' We talk and share, we talk and share. 'Last time you sent photos, that's good, someone read about it and gave us more support.' So we feel that what we do is helping

them, and they are happy, they are able to express their appreciation to me. So we become friends. And after that, I can respond more quickly because I know what she is doing and how much she needs my help.

In an informal setting, staff members' sharing ranges broadly from job experiences to personal background and family. This helps them understand not only their job but also and more importantly themselves and each other. They may become friends from being colleagues as they develop multi-dimensional relationships. In addition to work, their relationships may incorporate their personal spheres such as families, hobbies, religion, culture, education, and so on. Needless to say, the contribution of these relationships to the development of a sense of togetherness is tremendous.

The use of narratives is one major strategy for building a sense of commonality among the staff. Coining organizational terms, envisioning and articulating visions, and sharing experiences have been examined as three types of narrative strategies.

Developing common understanding among leadership
This strategy aims to maintain diversity yet avoid fragmentation. Listening to the suggestion of a senior manager who is the force behind the strategy helps us begin to examine it:

> If all you have is diversity, we can spread apart. We are going to have twenty different organizations. We need to become unified around something that will allow us to be diverse. So what [we] have decided is that we want to become unified around this document [the identity statement]. It started with the staff in the field. It wasn't from the lowest staff persons but it was from country directors. Then the top leadership, about eight leaders, got together in a conference and did a first draft of this. So it started in the field and went into the leadership and went back down to the country directors to do the final edit. One of the issues was we would like to be a bottom-up organization. One of the leadership came here and said that it looks like we are now becoming top-down whereas we want to be bottom-up, because leadership got together here and are sending the document back down. We found we had to do it this way. Before, the leadership wasn't unified, we had to get the leadership unified in order to be able to bring others into the process.

Fragmentation is a pitfall of diversity. A new country director who brings a different philosophy of development confuses field staff.[39] Without consistency among the leadership, field staff cannot develop a sense of commonality, for they do not have clear visions that they can follow. Commonly-shared understanding among the leadership provides a solution to this problem. Once leaders are integrated by developing common understanding, the field staff can expect the same visions from any

---

[39] See *Dealing with consistency and changes* in Chapter 2.

country directors.[40] They do not need to worry about adjusting their practices to comply with a new country director. The consistency aids their continuous efforts to build a shared sense of purpose.

Another argument for developing common understanding among the leadership is based on the assumption that locals cannot initiate bottom-up processes but leadership can and should do so. Whether or not this assumption is correct, it provides sufficient grounds for NGOs to convince themselves that the strategy is relevant for the bottom-up approach and is worth attempting.

As the senior manager explains its discrepancy, however, a major challenge for this strategy is how integrated leadership can actually contribute to establishing a sense of commonality among locals and initiating the bottom-up approach. Integrating leadership may be a premise of initiating any organizational processes in a coherent manner. But, a premise is not enough to show clear directions that can lead the organization to develop a sense of commonality with the bottom-up approach. As far as this specific case is concerned, its results are still yet to be seen.

In fact, an NGO must take several issues into consideration when it attempts to integrate leadership. First, it should understand that integrated leadership can unintentionally widen the gap between the leadership and the local staff. It can empower the leadership *vis-à-vis* local staff and enhance centralization. Leadership can take much more organized action to influence local staff strongly. With forceful organized practices, leaders can contradictorily make locals initiate a bottom-up process by force regardless of local intentions. For the local staff, the process is simply top-down, although it may appear to be bottom-up.

Second, it may be that neither leadership nor local staff have a clear idea of how they can go about building common feeling among the staff from the bottom. Developing common understanding among the leadership can establish an objective of maintaining diversity yet avoiding fragmentation. However, a premise is a mere premise and not more than that. Leaders should carefully examine how integrated leadership can contribute to or detract from the bottom-up process of building a sense of commonality. As explained above,[41] the decent and honest intentions of leadership do not guarantee a better result. A country director discusses the issue in the context of an actual case:

> I have to be ready and willing to share information. But sometimes, I find it difficult. When you work at this level, you see a big picture, but when you work at a small agricultural project in a village, if that person wants to know the big picture, I am ready to tell them, but sometimes it only confuses them.

---

[40] See Brown (1993) for the importance of established norms and structures to organize and manage joint enquiry.
[41] See *Superficial experts* in Chapter 4, 'Differences in scope'.

Not because they are stupid but because their scale of influence is smaller. So you have to weigh, I don't know how to do that, the cost-benefit of sharing information all the way down to the local level.

He knows that sharing broad organizational visions with the local staff sometimes confuses them. Yet he still does not have a clear solution to this dilemma. He struggles to develop better sharing methods through trial and error.

Third, the leaders can be content with integrated leadership and have the illusion that they have accomplished their goal. Integrating leadership, which, by definition, builds common feeling among leaders, is still a means to initiate and achieve the broad process of building common feeling throughout the entire organization.

Lastly, integrated leadership may reduce diversity. As the first half of this chapter argued, taking an action to prevent fragmentation often reduces diversity. NGOs need to consider how they can maintain their diversity when they integrate leadership.

This is not to dismiss the integration strategy but to address key issues that need to be examined in order for the strategy to succeed. Without leadership's clear visions, NGOs lose their direction. NGOs can benefit considerably from integrated leadership. The key issues imply, however, that the strategy cannot succeed in accomplishing its goal without risk. Therefore, as part of the strategy, wise staff members carefully examine the issues to prepare a shelter against every storm.

Associating differences

Using any common ground to build a sense of commonality is a smart strategy when the staff are diverse in many respects. The strategy suggests that the staff first identify common ground and then develop mutual understanding on that ground. Any common ground may become an initial base on which to develop mutual understanding. The NGO staff show how cultural closeness, similar experiences and teamwork help them relate to each other.

First, in a typical situation in which FOs and HQ are geographically far apart, cultural closeness can help them overcome the problems of geographical distance. A country director says:

> For instance, 'Why are we not getting any budget increase for 1995?' These guys [local staff] would say, 'What?' I say, 'Wait, you have to understand the pressures these guys [staff in headquarters] are facing there'. So if they don't tell me, I have to go and find out. So the burden is on me to know both sides. In a sense, it may be a little bit easier to be an expatriate because even though I'm closer culturally to headquarters, at least here I have face-to-face time with the staff, whereas if I was a local person and close to the culture here, I have two things against me. I have not only the cultural distance but also geographical distance. So we can't always be clarifying things face-to-face.

The director makes an insightful point about the way NGOs may over-come the gap between HQ and FO. He plays a mediating role between HQ and the field office by taking advantage of the two common grounds that he has. One is with HQ in terms of his culture and the other is with the field in terms of his geographic location. He can easily relate to HQ, despite the geographical distance between them, because of his cultural closeness to the NGO leadership. In relation to the field office, he can have face-to-face contacts with staff there and share considerable time with them to have common ground. The strategy suggests that when the staff are culturally distant, they use physical closeness as their common ground to develop common sense, and vice versa.

Second, providing similar experiences is a strategy to build a sense of commonality. As a senior local staff member suggests, 'If you have a common experience, you can easily relate to that person'. When the staff have similar experiences, they can anticipate how people on the other side think. A desk officer says:

> All sides need to have people who've seen the other end of things so that you have much more understanding and you can say, 'Wait, I know why they are asking for that information'.

If one person shares another's experience, one can anticipate what the person needs, how the person wants to be treated, why the person behaves in a certain manner, and so forth. Similar experiences help them relate to each other and develop a sense of commonality. Some NGOs intentionally rotate staff from one place to another to provide them with many different experiences.[42] Consequently, staff can easily relate to others based on their common experiences.

Meetings, seminars and retreats offer excellent opportunities for the staff to develop common feeling among them. Virtually all NGOs hold annual meetings where key members of the organization gather to share their experiences, build relationships and reconstruct their identity. During the meetings, country directors can easily relate to each other because of the similar experiences they have in different countries:

> I was sharing examples at the international conference last month. I had been struggling with a personnel issue, and they spent about two hours talking with me, and [role-] playing with me, which was a great help to me, because no one else can understand my job. There are only 15 other people [country directors]

---

[42] Interviews with NGO staff revealed that the larger the NGO is, the more it systematically encourages staff rotation so that staff members can identify themselves more with the entire organization worldwide. When an NGO decided to move its headquarters, a convincing reason (besides financial issues) was that the move would enable the overseas staff to come back to headquarters more easily. However, this move turned out to have an additional positive twist for the staffing of the headquarters: the move managed to let what an interviewee called 'dead wood' in the organization leave.

in the world who face the same circumstances that I do. So that was a great fellowship of these people. Otherwise, we work in a vacuum. So every time we have these meetings, that enhances those relationships.

The country director is pleased not only because he can share his issues with other country directors but also because they can enhance their relationships based on their common experiences.

Third, teamwork develops common ground as its by-product. A regional accountant encounters a different culture and overcomes the difference through daily work:

> The accountant man, he is Muslim. So I dealt with him on a different level. I know a little about Muslim communities, and me going as a female, as relatively young, looking young, he is a lot older than I am, it's very, very stereotyped. So if I have to tell him something, I try to go about it a different way. At first, I think he thought of me as an auditor going there and trying to see everything he is doing wrong. But now I think he sees me more as trying to help him. I was there for three weeks. And during that time, I really tried to work on that and establish a personal-level [relationship], not as much as a friendship but just so he knows me and I know him and we could communicate a little bit better. And by the third week, he was opening up more, he was asking me questions which he wasn't doing before, and he wasn't so defensive when I asked him questions.

This accountant would not have established a good relationship with her co-worker if she had not had to teach him. Because they had to learn how to deal with their differences through the job, they could establish a sense of mutual understanding. Teamwork is a way to accomplish tasks and also a strategy to develop mutual understanding among the participants. The teamwork environment, in which people need to work together despite their differences, is a driving force in building a sense of commonality.

When the staff face differences, they try to find a common ground on which they can build common feeling. The strategy suggests that cultural closeness or similar experiences be drawn upon as a relevant common ground. The strategy also suggests that even if they do not have a common ground to begin with, the teamwork situation provides staff members with a valuable resource to build common ground and then common feeling.

Questioning what, how, when and who[43]
Without questioning, one may not even discern the difference between the enquirer and the respondent, let alone build a sense of commonality. Questioning is a fundamental initial step to developing common feeling,

---

[43] For the importance of the issues of what, how, when and who in planning, see Friedmann (1987, 271).

99

for several reasons.[44] First, it helps the respondent to clarify what the enquirer wants to know. Second, it induces the respondent to look at the same issues as the enquirer. Third, it conveys to the respondent what the enquirer cares about, worries about and is interested in.[45] Although questioning is a fundamental practice, practising high quality asking is not as easy a task as it may appear to be. To improve the quality of questioning, the enquirer must consider the following four dimensions strategically: what to question; how to question; when to question; and whom to question.

To begin with, the content of questioning must be considered carefully. Although what to question is obviously the core of questioning, this plain suggestion cannot easily be practised without intentional effort due to lack of information, knowledge, expertise and so forth. For example, as the previous chapter explains,[46] to ask the right questions to people in the field, one must gain a sense of what is going on in the field from a broad perspective. Asking the right question requires preparation, such as overviewing the situation and familiarizing oneself with the typical mistakes that might emerge from the situation.

Asking a specific question is another important point that the staff should keep in mind. When a desk officer in HQ wants the field staff to improve their reports, she has a way to do it:

> If you are just saying a general thing, they don't have time for that. If you just tell me to rewrite it, it's not good. That doesn't help me. If you are very specific, and if you also offer them a consultant to help them do it, or some other resources and guidelines, then they will do it, because they are very interested themselves in having a good project.

She does not negate the value of the report but rather encourages staff members to improve it by offering specific suggestions and help. In this way, she attempts to maintain good working relationships while improving the quality of the report at the same time.

How one asks a question is also important. The way in which questions are posed plays a crucial role in building the staff members' relationships. The following quotes from various NGO members all suggest that respect[47] is central to making questioning meaningful. While asking the right question in an improper way could undermine staff members' relationships, asking a nonsense question in a respectful manner could

---

[44] Forester (1989) offers insightful analyses of questioning as one major theme of planning. He carefully examines questioning as a vital process shaping action, educating, organizing, listening, and exploring possibilities, hope and concerns.

[45] Feminist studies can provide rich resources for understanding the implications of questioning. For example, see Belenky, *et al.* (1986).

[46] See *Broadening views to identify the right questions* in Chapter 3.

[47] Respect plays not only a specific role in making questioning meaningful but also vital roles in developing interpersonal relationships in general. For example, see Belenky, *et al.* (1986, 189), which links human development in maternal practice with respect.

increase the chances of developing mutual understanding. A country director judges the quality of questioning:

> I guess the tone is so important, how you deal with people. Deal with people in a respectful way. And in a way that underscores your respect for that individual, not constantly questioning, not being patronizing, but creating adult relationships, I think that's really important. You can be direct and respectful. I think being direct does not mean that you've been disrespectful or inconsiderate. I think that those are not mutually exclusive.

The director is not particularly concerned with either words or expressions. A good question, according to him, would be combined with the enquirer's respect of and care for the respondent. When a country director recognizes a problem in a programme, he adopts the following strategy:

> We tried to first acknowledge that there were good benefits to come out of the programme. People were helped, it was a good experience in terms of what it means to work. But we say, 'We think it can be improved by more experiential learning, and focusing on cross-cultural learning. Let's have them experience problems and learn from them about culture.'

He does not forget to respect the staff who handle the programme, and he asks questions strategically that can lead to change after he acknowledges the benefits of the programme. To demonstrate care through the practice of questioning, a field officer carefully situates herself in the respondents' positions to understand how they might feel about her question:

> 'Please do it immediately.' It's just like an order for Asian people. Western people say exactly what they want to say, 'Please do it quickly', but it doesn't mean anything negative. But you'd say, '*You told me* just do it *immediately.*[48] We are free not just to do your work'. I feel we should make it in such a way that people know that you are in a hurry but at the same time, instead of getting negative, we will think about it positively. It's the art of communication. Say what people would like to hear. When I contact someone and say, 'Hi, how are you?' I think you really relate before you work. [Don't just say,] 'Hey, I need your help'. No, no. Say something first. [It's not] necessarily Westerners, but those who are work-oriented, they just want to get work done. And they lose the human relations. They don't care if you feel good enough to get work done. You may be in bed. We've got to say, 'How are you doing? Oh, I'm sorry. How can I help you?'

This officer warns against drawing a line between work-related and non-work-related communication.[49] As she points out in a different part of her

---

[48] Italics reflect the speaker's emphasis.

[49] In Arendt's terms, business activities are included in either labour or work, but not in 'action', which involves activities that lead people to reveal their identities to each other. Thus, allowing work-related communication but disregarding non-work-related communication excludes 'action' and leads work-centred communication to become what Arendt calls 'the rule by nobody', in which 'nobody can be held responsible for what is done' (Hill, 1979, 282).

interview, 'People are not machines'. Her strategy suggests that the staff work better when they are treated like persons, not like machines.[50]

Third, when to question is another component that influences the quality of questioning. For example, a question like, 'Where shall we have lunch?' is relevant before having lunch but irrelevant afterwards. Asking and answering a question requires appropriate timing.[51] The relevance of a question is time-dependent. A desk officer approaches timing strategically in his daily work:

> One thing you have to do, if you are smart about it, is to test the waters. [You ask], 'Country directors, is this a felt need for you or not?' For example, in this case, their answer was 'Yes'. But if everybody is saying 'No', then I think the organization [needs to] reassess the whole process, 'Are we jumping into something that it isn't necessary to jump into?'

He tries to understand how country directors would feel about what he plans to implement before he actually initiates the plan on a large scale. The point is that the question has to be posed before significant effort is made so that he can still change the schedule or even cancel the plan.

How, then, do the staff know when to question? One thing that the staff should consider is the relationship between their timing and their capacity to accept different answers. A question with good timing enables respondents to express freely their real positions, opinions and suggestions without pressure and constraints. Although a question, by definition, can be responded to with answers, asking a question can often become another way of merely informing people about decisions already made, and, in practice, can block any critical feedback that would require some change in the decisions.

In particular, once considerable effort has gone into a plan's preparation and it is ready for implementation, asking whether to go ahead and proceed with it is not actually asking a question but is rather, in practical terms, making a statement to confirm it. Even though the respondent officially has a right to say anything, the fact that considerable effort has already been expended in preparation may put sufficient pressure on the respondent to accept it without feeling free to articulate his or her concerns.

---

[50] Cf. *Ritualized chatting* in 'Rituals as a mediator' above. Contrary to general expectations, chatting can improve the quality of work.

[51] Regarding the relationship between timing and making sense of new information, Schön's (1982, 164) concept of reflection-in-action is worth quoting at length: 'At the same time that the enquirer tries to shape the situation to his frame, he must hold himself open to the situation's back-talk. He must be willing to enter into new confusion and uncertainties. Hence, he must adopt a kind of double vision. He must act in accordance with the view he has adopted, but he must recognize that he can always break it open later, indeed, *must* break it open later in order to make new sense of his transaction with the situation. This becomes more difficult to do as the process continues. His choices become more committing; his moves, more nearly irreversible. As the risk of uncertainty increases, so does the temptation to treat the view as the reality.' (Italics in the original)

Thus, from the point of view of the enquirer, if one wants to ask a question that elicits the respondent's real opinions, worries and suggestions, one must ask it before the plan is developed in detail and its implementation is scheduled. A question that is well timed enables the enquirer to accept any possible answer and use it to reflect on the future plan. It also enables the respondent to raise concerns without feeling constrained.

Fourth and last, knowing whom to question is also important in improving the quality of questioning. Because every staff member works differently and in different contexts, the same question might make sense to one person but not to another. To address a question to the proper person, an enquirer needs to know who the person is, what work the person is responsible for, how the person would think about the question, and so forth. In addition to the person's job-related information, his or her personal situation is also important. If the person is sick in bed, one can ask, 'How are you?' but should not ask work-oriented questions at that time.

These four components of questioning – what, how, when and to whom – are all interwoven in actual situations. To practise high-quality enquiry, the practitioner requires skills to handle the interwoven components properly. Thus, although asking a question is a basic practice in relating to other people, it requires the staff to exert conscious effort to carry out the practice of enquiry for building a sense of commonality in a meaningful way.

Time is worth spending
Using time as carefully as using money is a wise practice even if NGOs do not like the proverb, 'time is money'. Time is limited and there is not enough of it to do everything. NGOs must prioritize activities so that they can better use time. Thus, the issue becomes whether or not it is worth investing time in building a sense of commonality compared with other activities. The arguments against doing so can be summarized succinctly. First, the concept of a sense of commonality may be so abstract that NGOs would not be able to clarify what it means to them. Second, NGOs may not perceive a convincing reason to make developing a sense of commonality a priority along with other core activities such as project implementation and fundraising. Third, its process is likely to be very slow, and it is difficult to identify concrete results over a short period of time.

In the face of these arguments against prioritizing the development of a sense of shared purpose, however, considerable numbers of NGO staff confirm its value and strategize to retain it as one of their major concerns. The following accounts reveal two strategic components that keep the process of building a sense of commonality alive. The first two accounts come from HQs of different NGOs and the last two from FOs:

103

We don't expect field staff to understand these issues immediately. We understand that it takes a long time. We've all worked here in developing countries. We all understand the process of developing consensus of looking, seeking agreement, strengthening their own values and their ownership of solutions. And anyone who has had experience with this would tell you it takes time, and time is well worth it.

When I came here, I was warned by a guy, 'Max, going into the office is very difficult. . . . People have mixed cultural backgrounds. Your assumptions about what's important can be all mixed up. So I would encourage you to be open and patient. Re-examine your own values, and listen to people, and plan on being frustrated by that. That's gonna slow you down.' But it's OK.

'This is how we understood what you said in your request.' And we go back and say, 'Right', or 'Wrong, this is what we actually meant'. It has to go back and forth, back and forth until both sides are so clear that they almost repeat the same phrase. [It requires] endless communication. [Question: How about if you are too busy to do it?] Then, we are working in the wrong place. It's better to take the time before than sort it out afterwards, because it takes a lot less time before when the others understand.

Building people. It's a lot slower than I had anticipated. But because of the nature of development, how can we ask our staff to be involved in promoting development with beneficiaries if we are not doing it with them? . . . So I think it's both/and. And I can't be either/or. People say, 'Oh, well, you are focusing too much on your staff.' If I don't focus on my staff, they can never do a good job with the beneficiaries. Now, I think there is a time when you do more or less. There's an art in finding the balance. . . . My first several years here, you are not going to see much difference with beneficiaries and that would probably disappoint [in the short term]. But it's not going to be the way I would like to see it because time has to be invested in the staff. I also have to take a long-term approach.

These four accounts all share two strategic components. First, all these staff had expected beforehand that building a sense of shared purpose would take a long time, and therefore expected to be frustrated rather than being taken by surprise by the frustration they would inevitably encounter. For example, the first respondent says, 'We don't expect field staff to understand these issues immediately'. The second one suggests that anyone undertaking this 'plan on being frustrated'. The third one suggests that it is better to 'take the time before than sort it out afterwards'. And the last one says that 'You are not going to see much difference with beneficiaries. . . . But it's not going to be the way I would like to see it.' Because they anticipated that the process would not always go as they expected it to, they prepared themselves to tolerate the process rather than abandoning it.

Second, they had clear visions for building common feeling and confidence that it is vital and worth pursuing. They all implied that building a sense of commonality among the staff is a valuable and necessary practice for projects in the long run. The last respondent explicitly states, 'If I don't focus on my staff, they never can do a good job with beneficiaries'.

The strategy suggests that, with clear visions and confidence, and with preparation to face frustrations, staff members overcome challenges associated with the endeavour of building common feeling.

Conclusion

This chapter started with the idea that managing diversity properly is vital for NGOs because they encounter diversity in their working environments, their target groups and their staffs. However, diversity can have an unfortunate tendency to fragment NGOs. Therefore the chapter has discussed the problems that arise when performance becomes fragmented in the name of diversity – decentralization, cultural differences, and differences in scope. It has also explored strategies for building a sense of commonality to address the fragmentation problems.

In the face of fragmenting forces, NGO staff members struggle to maintain the unity of the organization through various means. The second half of this chapter has explored rituals, narratives, developing common understanding among leadership, carefully associating differences, and protecting time as strategies that staff members employ to discourage fragmentation and encourage co-operative and effective relationships. Because all these strategies are practised by specific staff members in specific contexts, applying them to other situations without carefully examining their relevance may result in staff members failing to achieve their objectives. Nevertheless, the strategies provide us with valuable resources to improve our practices in the face of fragmenting forces.

CHAPTER 5

Similarity: Achieving Common Objectives

*We can either try to please everybody, which pleases no one, or we can say,
'Forget it, we are just going to do this whether they like or not.' Or we can
honestly look at the situation, sit down with somebody and say, 'How can I
help you?' It takes more time, it takes humility on our part to accept something that someone wants us to do instead of telling somebody to do what
we want to do. It takes patience and so it goes against the way the world
works. But I think it's the right way to do it.*

Assistant country director

Introduction

ACHIEVING SUFFICIENT SIMILARITY among staff members to attain their coherent integration is this chapter's theme. The chapter argues that staff
members should be similar in terms of their understanding and goals in
order for them to work coherently, regardless of their differences in other
respects. The chapter first identifies and discusses problems that NGO
staff face when they attempt to achieve similarity among staff members; it
then explores strategies to address these problems.

Similarity among the staff can become an important concern for an NGO
for several reasons that stem from the relationship between the organization and its staff members. For an NGO to function effectively, its members
should not be fragmented, as discussed in Chapter 4. Staff members need
to be similar enough to be united and to enhance their collective endeavour. Without enough similarity among the staff in understanding the objectives and identity of the organization, they may lack a common ground on
which to develop productive relationships. And without productive relationships, their diligent work cannot be expected to bring about desirable
outcomes. However, the issue is not simply whether relationships exist or
not. Not all relationships – not even all relationships that reduce fragmentation – necessarily contribute to an NGO's effectiveness. Some types of
relationships may even be destructive.[1]

This chapter focuses on two major types of relationships: homogenized
relationships and coherent relationships. Needless to say, neither type
is fragmented. However, the differences between the two are still
significant when one analyses them in the light of diversity: while

---

[1] This is especially true of relationships characterized by antagonism.

homogenized relationships do not involve diversity, coherent ones do.[2] When the staff members share organizational objectives and identity, their commonality helps them to cohere even as they maintain their diversity in other respects. However, homogenized relationships require more than similarity and do not allow the staff to be diverse even in other respects.

Although NGO staff have little difficulty understanding the theoretical differences between these types of relationships, understanding those differences is not the same as actually embodying them. In actual NGO situations, efforts to achieve similarity among the staff tend subtly to lead to homogeneity. Because developing a common ground is easier when the staff members share not only the identity and objectives of the organization but also the same interests, values, views and cultural backgrounds, an emphasis on developing relationships can easily undermine diversity.[3] The introduction of regulatory approaches to homogenize the staff members, whether intentional or unintentional, can induce them to build instant relationships. When NGOs attempt to develop similarity among the staff, they may be tempted to homogenize the staff by automatically excluding those whose characteristics are unfamiliar within the organization, even if these characteristics or differences would not actually cause any problems. Consequently, as the organization homogenizes its staff members, it suffers from the pathology of restricted performance in the name of similarity. With the lack of differences among the staff, the organization unreasonably excludes rich resources and minimizes its capacity to address problems.

This chapter discusses how some activities of NGO staff members may result in homogenizing the staff or excluding certain staff members, despite their intentions to the contrary. Rather than describing explicit regulatory practices, which are easy to criticize, the chapter focuses on honest and sincere practices that can none the less subtly influence the staff to subvert diversity and can thereby produce homogeneity or exclusion.

Problems: Restricted performance in the name of similarity[4]

When NGOs seek to develop similarity among their staff by sharing the objectives and identity of the organization, these efforts often result in the

---

[2] As indicated by Driver's (1991) statement that 'personal, societal and physical realities are not isolated from each other but participate together in a single field of divine power', some kinds of 'divine power' may help the parts of an organization get logically connected with each other. They might need something transcendent to which they look together, rather than looking at each other without any 'north star' to guide them.

[3] Perlmutter (1991) warns that global civilization imposes a homogenizing Westernization on the entire population on the globe.

[4] See Bryson (1988, 205) for a discussion of how groups enforce conformity, seek to minimize conflict and finally become homogeneous, with the result that they lose their ability to think strategically.

homogenization of the staff.[5] The organization loses valuable resources such as different ideas, values, views, skills and experiences that a more diverse staff embodies. In this case, restricted performance is the likely result. Recruitment and identity construction are two activities that can lead an organization to homogenize itself, exclude valuable people, and undermine its performance in the name of similarity.

Recruiting to homogenize the organization

When NGOs recruit people, they tend to exclude those with whom they are uncomfortable for one reason or another. Although NGOs do not intend to do so, they often homogenize their organizations by recruiting people with virtually the same values, cultural backgrounds and interests. This tendency is not always explicit or conscious, but it often predominates when recruiting to fill a key position gets underway. The more crucial the position is to the organization, the more likely it is that the position will be filled by a person whose values, cultural background and interests are identical to those of other leaders in the organization. Consequently, the recruitment exercise may become a target of criticism because it subverts the value of organizational diversity. Conversely, several factors exert pressure on staff members to follow the practice with little resistance. These factors include demands for organizational consistency, administrative efficiency and productive donor relations.

Organizational consistency

The goal of maintaining organizational consistency provides a legitimate reason to recruit a particular type of person, although doing so involves devaluing organizational diversity. It is easier to maintain organizational consistency by hiring a person whose culture and values are close, if not identical, to those of the organization's other members than by hiring a person with a different culture and values.[6] Especially when an NGO functions fairly well, its members do not want their consistency to be disturbed by bringing in people with discrepant values and interests. Rather, an NGO recruits people who can easily adjust to the organization rather than people who hold strong and discrepant values and interests and who try to change the organization instead of adjusting themselves to it.

NGOs recruit leadership positions carefully, for the impact of the leadership on the organization is enormous. When projects are implemented well on the basis of a certain philosophy of development,

---

[5] DiMaggio and Powell (1983) discuss homogenization from the point of view of institutional isomorphism in an organization.

[6] Recruiting a staff member from the same cultural background is also supported in a closed community context. Milofsky (1988a) argues that a community emphasizes closeness when it requires stable relationships to make claims on members to create and maintain values. For an NGO to maintain its oneness, a close community is more suitable than an open one.

maintaining that philosophy is crucial even if there needs to be a change in leadership. A country director says:

> [There were three country directors.] Every country director has a different philosophy of management, of work, and of development. So my field co-ordinator said, 'How much longer you will be here? Because you've asked us to do things in very different ways, which is OK, but if the next guy comes, will he allow us [to do it this way]?' If the organization wants to be effective in the long run, there has to be commitment. [Positions like mine] have to be seen as longer-term positions. Or there [should be the cultivation] of a deputy or assistant who may [be here] a long enough time that we share the same philosophy, so even if the people change, the philosophy is there.

Although the country director does not explicitly mention types of country directors to be recruited, he implies that country directors hold key influence over consistency in the field. The easiest and most reliable way to ensure organizational consistency is to conduct in-house recruitment to appoint an appropriate staff member from within the organization. Thus, only when the organization cannot find an appropriate candidate in-house does it go outside. A desk officer in HQ emphasizes the positive aspects of in-house recruitment as a strategy to maintain organizational coherence:

> Before they become a country director, they must work in this organization for many years. Directors are chosen carefully. They don't come from outside. They are always recruited from within. Usually they have had quite a lot of experience before they are appointed as director.

During interviews, a number of staff members indicated their support for in-house recruitment because it can help maintain organizational consistency. However, some criticized the practice because it excludes others as outsiders. A country director makes this case:

> [They believe the] country director should be an organization person. The person should be brought up in the organization. An arrogant outsider coming in and taking a key position is not the way they think it should happen.

He was new to the organization. But because he used to work with one of the major support offices, he could assume a country director's position with strong support from the office. However, despite his long work experience in the field of development, he received strong criticism from the other major support office due to his lack of work experience in the organization. This case exemplifies a general reluctance among NGOs to welcome a new, 'strange' person into a key position. Therefore, in the interests of consistency, in-house recruitment is legitimized and recruitment from outside is discouraged.

When outsiders are excluded in the name of consistency, an NGO loses a chance to absorb new ideas, values, visions, ways of doing things, etc.

As a result, it loses the capacity to change itself and adjust to changing situations, and tends to be content with the *status quo*.

Administrative efficiency: working language

NGOs cannot implement projects without administrative support. In fact, meeting administrative requirements comprises a significant portion of NGO activities. Thus, NGOs typically welcome any means to reduce their administrative burdens. Among many administrative issues, the selection of their working language is a major organizational concern. Once a working language is selected, it in turn determines the types of staff members who can be assigned to key positions. A country director speaks candidly about the preferred field leadership of an American NGO:

> The easier one for me is [to communicate with] headquarters because culturally I have that connection. If I were Thai, I would probably be more capable of communicating on this side [field], and struggling with that side [headquarters]. So from the organizational perspective, you have to decide what is more important. We are an international organization, but we are still very North American. Leadership is very North American. Then we have an American vice-president. So we admit that. That's no secret. To communicate, I think headquarters has an easier job communicating with countries where there are North Americans in leadership because we don't have cultural barriers. We don't have language barriers. Latin America is unique because they have a regional language. But you come to Asia, you've got Cambodian, Lao, Vietnamese, Thai, Filipino, Japanese, Korean, I mean there is no one that can relate to all of that. So in a way it's easier. I don't think this is intentional but it has been easier to keep people of the same culture at headquarters in the leadership position and let the point of difference be at a local level where this face-to-face contact takes place at a distance between headquarters and here.

English is the official working language of most international NGOs.[7] Local languages may be used in the field, but those languages cannot be the medium of communication between HQ and the field. HQ does not have the capacity to handle different local languages. As a result, reports written in local languages have to be translated into English in the field before they are submitted to HQ. This implies two things: an additional administrative burden (involving translation) on the field office, and the regulation of the field's culture to comply with that of HQ.

First, the administrative burden to translate falls solely on the field while HQ can avoid this arduous task. Staff at HQ can communicate with the field in their own language while the field staff must deal with the extra administrative task of translation on top of their project work. One

---

[7] Some notable exceptions include French and Japanese NGOs.

consequence of the language issue and the burden that translation represents is that relatively little input from locals in the field reaches HQ, in contrast to the much greater amount of input from HQ that reaches the field. Consequently, voices from the field are generally disregarded while voices from HQ may play a regulatory role in field activities. This unbalanced communication flow thus reduces diversity.

The second implication of this institutional reliance on English is that it requires that country directors have a good command of English, which in turn selects in favour of specific types of people to assume the position. Even if they are non-native English speakers, they should be fully exposed to and thus influenced by English-speaking cultures.[8] Hence, making English ability an important recruiting criterion requires the FOs to alter their cultures to comply with the cultures of English speakers, or of HQ. Even in the FOs, local cultures are disregarded and the cultures in HQ are valued as the cultures of the organization.[9] One major result of this is the homogenization of the organization.[10] The field starts to behave as an agent of HQ although the field is, according to a senior manager, 'the core place of experience in terms of who we [the NGO] are and how we define ourselves'.

Donor relations
Donors' preferences influence NGOs' in many ways.[11] NGOs cannot ignore donors' interests whether or not they agree with them, for funding is one of the most important requisites for NGOs to maintain themselves and implement projects. In fact, because donors are not only funding sources but are also key targets of development education to advocate to the public in general, NGOs have considerable investment in maintaining donors' interest and maintaining good working relationships with them. Donors are not mere funders. Thus, when donors' interests do not appear to disturb NGO activities, NGOs are willing to work to accommodate

---

[8] According to Mazrui (1975, 48), '[L]earning English is, to non-Westerners, a process of Westernization'. His argument implies that only those who have been Westernized can obtain privileged status and political control over the population. And the exercise of their policies have meant the spread of Western values that favour and support the political and economic status of Westerners and those Westernized.

[9] According to Laponce (1987), 96.4 per cent of world population speaks only 1–3 per cent of the total number of languages. More people are speaking fewer languages as a consequence of the strong influence of state policies, which, in turn, derives from a state's goals in the international environment. Moreover, he argues, fewer languages account for a large proportion of science communication, economic power, wealth and military expenditure. For example, English represents more than two-thirds of printed material. This means that the bulk of written knowledge is dominated by European and North American languages.

[10] '[A]n administration based upon the theories of social science will not take account of the individuality or the plurality of men' (Hill, 1979, 283).

[11] DiMaggio and Powell's research (1983, 154) has led them to the hypothesis that 'The greater the dependence of an organization on another organization, the more similar it will become to that organization in structure, climate, and behavioural focus'.

those interests. Nevertheless, donors' interests drive NGOs to homoge-nize the organizations. A deputy country director describes the trend:

> One of the ways they [headquarters] can feel more comfortable in transferring that trust is they send expatriate staff out to the field to work there. Donors, then, feel more comfortable with sending money over. You see it also in business relationships now, Japanese companies building up in Canada. Who is the head of the company? It's a Japanese, not a Canadian . . . And it's a comfortable feeling knowing that, 'Yes, someone from your culture is over there managing them', then you can delegate or give the trust factor more to the company, so that they can be more responsible.

Sending someone from the donor's culture narrows the gap between donors and the field. This benefits both the NGO and the donor. The NGO can communicate with the donor easily, and thus can not only gain trust from the donor, but also advocate with the donor easily. For its part, the donor feels close to the field and can trust the field in managing funds without much donor involvement. A desk officer points out, based on his experience, that once a good interpersonal relationship is established between a donor and an NGO, the donor is more understanding and co-operative, even if the NGO makes mistakes or fails to accomplish its goals in a project.

Their cultural closeness matters greatly. A person who may not be competent enough to manage projects in the field would still be regarded as trustworthy by a donor because of their shared culture. Because do-nors are usually not in a position to understand thoroughly the ability of leadership in the field, they tend to depend upon the communication ability of leaders as a major criterion to evaluate the leadership. Hence, donors rely on leaders from the same culture more than others who might even be superior in their working abilities. Realizing donors' attitudes in this area, NGOs take it into account when they recruit new staff for key positions in the field.

This arrangement, however, unreasonably excludes competent people because of their cultural distance from the dominant culture in an NGO, and it diminishes the diversity of the organization's staff. Many NGOs do not seriously consider the value of diversity when they initiate recruit-ment for a particular position.[12] NGOs, and organizations more generally, tend to prioritize the specific issue in front of them – recruitment in this case – over abstract and vague concepts such as diversity.

Therefore, donor relations take precedence over diversity, and NGOs identify recruitment as an issue of donor relations more than as an issue

---

[12] In contrast to closed communities, Milofsky's (1988a) concept of open communities may explain the diversity of an NGO, for it encourages people to have contacts with others who come from different cultural backgrounds and who have had sharply different personal experi-ences. NGOs need to take this aspect into account when they assess their working environ-ments, although diversity makes it difficult for an NGO to remain a single coherent entity.

of diversity. Because donor relations are a high priority, NGOs tend to sacrifice diversity in favour of donor relations without much difficulty. In the hope of better serving donors, NGOs fail to appoint a suitable person for a position based on the needs of the field, and instead hire a person who shares the cultural background of the donors.

Conclusion

Recruiting people with the similar values, cultural backgrounds and interests is an easy path to building coherent relationships in an organization. Organizational consistency, administrative efficiency and donor relations all indicate the positive contribution this practice makes. In the light of these contributions, diversity appears to lose its legitimacy within the organization and becomes a mere luxury. Consequently, the appreciation of similarity among the staff in sharing common objectives and the identity of the organization tends to be trivialized and reduced in the quest for homogeneity. Thus, the system excludes some types of people as a result. This subtle shift subverts diversity, although diversity is as important as similarity. When an organization homogenizes itself, it loses a rich variety of resources and its capacity to respond to changing situations.

Constructing identity

Strengthening organizational identity based on the staff's values and perspectives on development is vitally important to promote the effectiveness of NGOs.[13] However, constructing identity can be a means by which NGOs·are homogenized in the name of similarity.

> Obviously, one difficulty is when we did not have a common statement of who we are and what our mission is. That was a very major one, simply because we tended to look at our area of responsibility as being the entire organization, and we tended to lose sight of the larger picture. So with the development of the mission statement, and in a sense getting everyone to say, 'Yes, this is what we are to do', it helps each function within this partnership to understand and learn about these things.

As this senior manager in HQ notes, shared identity, which provides the staff with similarity, is crucial for the entire NGO staff to function in a coherent manner. Without it, staff members are dispersed and can neither stand on common ground nor look at a common goal. Identity provides them with a common language through which they can understand each other and produce and reproduce their common missions.

On the other hand, this process of identification can have a negative influence on NGO staff members. In fact, the local staff do not have enough opportunities and resources to share and develop their own

---

13 See Fowler (1991).

identity by themselves. Instead, their leadership typically constructs and provides the identity to the local staff in the name of the organization, with little participation from the field.[14] Consequently, the leadership may intentionally or unintentionally regulate the staff through the process of 'developing shared identity'.

Devaluing differences

The process of developing shared identity may discourage differences within the NGO. As workers in the organization, staff members' identification process takes place within the organizational framework. Thus, the process would probably induce individual staff members to passively identify themselves with the given organizational identity rather than creating a new identity for the organization. As a result, the diversity of the staff is reduced to fit within the range that the organizational framework can accommodate. Despite several benefits that diversity offers to the organization,[15] it appears to be – and is treated as – an obstacle to building organizational identity.

In an NGO context, the relationship between HQ and FOs shows how HQ subtly discourages these differences. Two accounts address how HQ constructs the identity of the field. The first account, in which a local staff member reacts against an insensitive question from HQ, provides an example of questioning as a form of constructing identity:

> They [headquarters] will come down very heavily, saying, 'This was the figure when you were applying. Inability to spend. Do you have capability to spend it?' That's the question asked us. But we know the situations better. So we have to tell them, 'Come on, this is what the situations of local countries are.' Probably it's easier to ask from headquarters why this money is not spent. In the local country situations, it takes anywhere between 12 to 18 months to get on land you want to purchase. Even if you get a title, there is a lot of political involvement that constrains this particular thing, and so on. So it takes time.

His explanation about the relationship between HQ and the field includes at least two dimensions. The first and straightforward implication is that

---

[14] Brown (1993) argues that collective reflections are vital to NGOs' effectiveness. However, while Brown's study discusses such important issues as the management of differences in values and ideology and the definition of participation, participants in the collective reflections he analyses were limited to organizations' leaders.

[15] Differences among the staff members can be rich resources for an NGO, especially because the organization works in a variety of field contexts. Diversity among the staff may enable the NGO to resolve different issues in different but proper ways. For example, local staff who are familiar with indigenous knowledge can apply that knowledge to address the field's needs much more appropriately than those expatriates who can only apply expert knowledge that may be unfamiliar to local people. Nevertheless, this does not mean that people with expert knowledge are less relevant than people with indigenous knowledge. Rather, each staff member's own skills, knowledge and background suit her or him to a specific area of concern within the NGO's operations.

he urges HQ to understand the field's position. For the field, informing HQ of field situations is significant in minimizing the gap between the two. The other aspect is that responding to HQ's question would itself serve the interests of HQ. By responding to the question, whether they take issue with it or not, the field staff supports the position of HQ as the agenda setter.

Consequently, the field is obliged in a subtle way to deal with the issue set by HQ, as the above account reflects. Many staff members implied, when they characterized the relationship between HQ and FOs, that HQ is an agenda setter while fields play a respondent role. Through this type of interaction, FOs are excluded from agenda-setting and are gradually absorbed into the framework of HQ. Thus they come to identify themselves as respondents to HQ's questions and implementors of HQ's agendas.

The second account expresses how the HQ's communication mode regulates the field activities in a tricky but coercive manner. A senior manager vividly displays her frustration:

> Too much paperwork is required from donors and the headquarters. It's a must. Because we receive funds from them, we have to do the reporting. Headquarters always asks about the projects, why we are delayed, why we are underspent. The other thing is timing. Suppose we write a project proposal now, we will get the confirmation of funding maybe a year later, or a year and half. It takes time, the situation has changed already by the time the project is approved. So strategies should be changed, objectives might be a bit different. We sometimes have to change some plan of action, or some activities, to suit the situation. We have to revise. But they don't understand. They say they signed a contract as it was written in the first proposal. But we cannot do what we first proposed, because of the timing. We cannot predict. We have to communicate by writing. You see, it creates more paperwork. We have to communicate. The reasons why we have to change the strategies and our plan of action, they need clarification.

This mode of communication strongly favours HQ. The administrative burdens on the field staff are not limited to the communication difficulty derived from the working language. This particular account identifies three problematic components of communication with HQs: English; in a written format; with HQ-centred communication. All three components place extra administrative burdens on the field while HQ enjoys its own communication style. The field invests effort in language translation so that HQ does not need to deal with other languages. The field spends a significant amount of time on writing papers to comply with the HQ's communication style. The field must revise its proposal due to changes in field situations during the time that HQ considers the proposal.

Even in the absence of direct guidance or intervention, the HQ's managerial style is enforced and disseminated to the field as they interact.

This process legitimizes HQ's mode of communication and results in identifying it as the communication mode for the entire organization. The field's different mode of communication is submerged by HQ's mode as the single acceptable mode.

By regulating the mode of communication, HQ places the field under its control, whether intentionally or not. The field staff face constraints in expressing their own agendas in their own ways. In this context, attempts to get staff to identify themselves with the organization are tantamount to disseminating and enforcing HQ's identity throughout the entire organization. Although doing so can facilitate maintaining coherent integration of the entire organization, it sacrifices the valuable and diverse views, ideas and experiences that the field staff possess.

Encouraging top-down control
The other negative influence of the identity-shaping process is that it intensifies organizational hierarchy. This stems from the combination of staff members' mindsets and the status of the organizational structure as an a priori fact. As staff members identify themselves to characterize who they are, this process provides an opportunity for their mindset and the organizational structure to interact and helps produce and reproduce the hierarchy.

This tendency can be observed clearly in the ways HQ and FOs identify themselves. Rather than identifying themselves as members of the entire organization, they are more likely to identify themselves as the members of one of the two subgroups: HQ and FOs. By separating themselves from each other, both HQ and FOs maintain and enhance organizational hierarchy.[16] A desk officer in HQ describes the position of HQ:

> There are two parts. One is that, like a child in some way, they like guidance from the parents. They want to know that the parent is concerned. But on the other hand, they don't want the parent to know. They send documents to us. Then if they don't get feedback, it's not wonderful. But if the feedback is, 'Well, it's good, but change this and this,' then they don't want to hear.

She characterizes the relationship between HQ and FO as a parent–child relationship, but this characterization is not simply a product of her observation. Rather, it shapes the way she looks at and treats the field office. Once she perceives the relationship as a parent–child relationship, she is likely to observe only those aspects of field office behaviour that are consistent with her view. Consequently, as she analyses the behaviour of

---

[16] In his discussion (based on an analysis of Fieldhouse, 1982) of the durability of hierarchical structures, Said (1993,11) argues that 'the durability of empire was sustained on both sides, that of the rules and that of the distance ruled, and in turn each had a set of interpretations of their common history with its own perspective, historical sense, emotions, and traditions'.

the field based on the parent–child relationship, she may reconfirm, re-define and re-identify the top-down characteristic of the HQ–field office relationship. It can be implanted in the mindset of the HQ staff such that it informs not only the way they characterize the relationship between HQ and FO, but the way they shape that relationship as well.

The top-down relationship is also augmented by the mindset of local staff in the field. Their mindset has been developed through their own experiences within the broader relationship between industrialized countries and the Third World. As they understand the top-down characteristics of that broad relationship, they perceive the top-down relationship in the organization in a similar manner. They thus perceive themselves to be in the lower echelons of the organization, with an attendant self-deprecatory mindset *vis-à-vis* HQ.[17]

> First of all, [there's] the mindset of the individuals. People believe that anything that comes from funding agencies is good. That's probably a role mindset that we have to do everything that they say. Everything is supplied from the top. Everything that office says, people believe.

Moreover, the self-deprecatory mindset of the local staff members is amplified due to their employee status *vis-à-vis* the employer status of the staff in HQ.[18] HQ and FOs identify themselves separately and clarify their differences from each other. From the organizational point of view, the process of identifying themselves ought to break the barriers between HQ and the FOs to develop an integrated identity of the entire organization. Ironically, however, rather than sharing and developing their common missions, both HQ and FOs emphasize their differences in terms of their identities.

Once the differences between HQ and FOs are verbalized in terms of their identities, these differences influence their perspectives and shape their behaviour.[19] The HQ staff behave as parents while the field staff behave as children. As the staff identify themselves, they shape their behaviour to fit their self-images. When they identify themselves as parents or children, they behave as parents or children. Consequently, their identities not only divide the organization but also reduce their diversity by framing them to play symbolic and confining roles.

---

[17] Cf. Fanon (1967), who provides insight into the issue of identity problems that face black men.

[18] 'Whatever is real about the executive's power as far as control of resources, rewards, penalties, approval, and so on, are concerned, there is much about it that need not be real at all but require only staff members' perceptions of, and responses to it to make it work to the executive's advantage and to their disadvantage' (Levy, 1982, 123).

[19] 'Each person has an image of his or her own identity. An identity is closely related to some group, cluster, or organization in society with which the individual identifies' (Boulding, 1989, 114).

Given identity

The other undesirable way in which the identity formation process works to regulate the staff involves the fact that local staff members do not really have ownership of the process because the core process usually takes place at HQ. The field staff are often content to receive 'identity', whatever it is, from HQ. Their identity comes from outside rather than emerging from within themselves. The lack of local staff members' participation in the identity formation process is a function not necessarily of intentions but rather of administrative considerations.

When the entire staff develops, adopts and shares an identity, it is not something handed to the staff as a static concept[20] but is rather a dynamic expression. Identity is not something to be discovered; rather, it continuously emerges from within. In practice, however, interactions among all staff members are virtually impossible in an NGO. Hence, developing identity becomes a process that includes some staff while excluding others, due to two types of constraints: the limitations of administrative capacity and structural constraints.

Considering NGOs' administrative capacity, its members are usually too many and too dispersed geographically to get together to share visions and develop a group identity. Practically, an Ethiopian local staff member working at a remote project site, for example, can hardly relate to a Thai local staff member working in the field. A small number of representatives is selected to get together and develop the identity of the members of the larger organization. As has been quoted in Chapter 4, a senior manager describes a problem derived from the participation of representatives:

> One of the issues was we would like to be a bottom-up organization. One of the leadership came here and said that it looks like we are now becoming top-down whereas we want to be bottom-up, because leadership got together here and are sending the document back down. We found we had to do it this way. Before, the leadership wasn't unified, we had to get the leadership unified in order to be able to bring others into the process.

He understands that unified leaders are crucial to introducing the interaction process at local levels.[21] According to him, without a common understanding among the leadership, local staff would never have an opportunity to take part in the process of organizing themselves. How, then, does the leadership relate to the local staff after they are unified? A desk officer in the same organization says:

> This sheet of paper [memo on organizational identity] is being presented to every field office, to all staff, whether they are drivers, or a kitchen helper, or a

---

[20] Said, in his talk with Oe, argues for the importance of mobility in identity (Said and Oe, 1995), in contrast to Erikson's (1959) concept of identity as a static definition.
[21] See Uphoff (1988).

118

cook. Everyone that is on the payroll worldwide, this will be communicated to them and altered for cultural context. That is one way to bridge the gap between headquarters and the field. Because we are all in this organization, that's what we stand for. And the headquarters is trying to bridge the gap in communicating to our project manager in Kenya, 'Hey, our vision of organization is this'. And then they are going to say how we do that. We are going to sit together and work together.

The field staff members may have an opportunity to interpret the identity in their own ways to contextualize it in their work situations. But apart from this opportunity to interpret it, they cannot alter the organizational identity that the leadership has developed. The opportunity for the local staff to influence the development of identity is minimal, except for indirect influence through their country directors, who participate in the process as their representatives.

The other type of constraint is structural. The structure of most NGOs prevents the local staff from having any voice in HQ. Because HQ and FOs are linked by a small number of leaders such as country directors and senior managers, most local staff cannot directly influence the ongoing discussion in HQ.[22] Even an assistant director in a field office cannot have direct contact with HQ.

> We depend on a line of relationship quite a lot. According to the structure of the organization, there is only one person here who is able to communicate what is what in headquarters. I'm not allowed to communicate from here.

When this kind of organizational structure is already in place, local staff cannot express their visions to HQ. Hence, they can only accept the organizational identity as given. Their identity is framed by the bifurcation of HQ and FO, rather than their identity framing the organizational structure. In a large organization, socializing oneself to accept the structure is easier than attempting to change it. Therefore, unless the local staff have strong investments in making their work for the organization conform to their values, they are tempted to accept an organizational identity as given without attempting to contribute to that identity.

Through constructing identity, an NGO tries to achieve sufficient similarity among the staff to develop coherent integration. However, as the three dilemmas discussed above indicate, this effort tends to devalue differences among staff members, encourage hierarchy in the organization, and assign identity from outside. The result is the unreasonable exclusion of some types of people, the devaluation of diversity within the organization, and the organization's ultimate homogenization.[23]

---

[22] From the point of view of network analysis, Hage and Harary (1983) explain how the information centre (the country director's position in this case) gains centralized power.
[23] See DiMaggio and Powell (1983) for a discussion of how an organization becomes homogenized as it deals rationally with uncertainty and constraint.

As mentioned earlier, reducing diversity results in a loss of valuable resources such as different ideas, experiences and skills. Therefore, the lack of diversity reduces the organization's capacity to respond to changing situations and changing needs.

Strategies: Interacting with staff with distinctive skills, values, and views[24]

The first half of this chapter has identified and discussed problems that NGO staff members face when they try to achieve coherent integration through emphasizing their similarities. Restricted performance due to exclusion and homogenization within the organization in the name of coherence has been identified as the main problem. The problem is most pronounced on two occasions: when the staff recruit new members and when the staff construct their identity.

The second half of this chapter presents and discusses strategies for avoiding the restricted performance that results from exclusion and homogenization, while maintaining similarity among the staff. The findings of the study reveal two broad types of strategies: dealing with differences, and taking charge of processes. In the face of differences, the strategies present various ways to make better use of the differences as valuable resources instead of devaluing or suppressing them. Taking charge of processes is another strategy through which the staff members can demonstrate their distinctive skills, values, views and so forth within organizational contexts.

Dealing with differences[25]

The unique ideas, experiences and views that staff members bring to an organization are invaluable resources for the organization. At the same time, however, these same resources might also hinder efforts to build organizational coherence through emphasizing similarity among the staff members. In day-to-day work, the staff members need to analyse both the advantages and disadvantages of their differences. The three strategies discussed below offer ways in which organizations can take advantage of the differences among their staff without suffering a lot of negative consequences.

---

[24] Because each person has different abilities, which are unique and distinctive, those abilities become rich resources that enable people working together to perform great deeds and create incredible things. See Arendt (1958).

[25] See Hirschman (1967, 13): 'Creativity always comes as a surprise to us; therefore we can never count on it and we dare not believe in it until it has happened. In other words, we would not consciously engage upon tasks whose success clearly requires that creativity be forthcoming. Hence, the only way in which we can bring our creative resources fully into play is by misjudging the nature of the task, by presenting it to ourselves as more routine, simple, undemanding of genuine creativity than it will turn out to be.'

Consistently focusing on merit but not on the people involved
One strategy to deal better with the staff members' differences in interests, ideas and values is for the staff to focus on merits and not on the people involved.[26] When you decide to agree or disagree with an idea, you tend to be influenced by the person who presents the idea rather than solely by the idea itself. In an organizational context, the confusion of issues with people originates not simply from interpersonal relationships. People's positional differences, power differences, interests, agendas and so forth all influence their attitudes toward an issue at hand. Different contexts would lead the same person to behave differently with regard to the same issue.

The following account describes a problem that exists between issues and people, and then a strategy to address the problem. A country director struggles to serve in two leadership positions – at HQ as the head of administration, and at a support office as a source of funds:

> We have a different financial computer system for the support office. It's a fact of life. We've changed our financial system to suit their way. We run two financial systems. One to look after the support office, and one to [communicate our financial situation to] headquarters. But I think there is a style at headquarters that says, 'No, this is our mission'. Our headquarters is extremely critical of the support office because of the systemic problems and differences in philosophy, differences in personality. I'm not critical of either side. Absolutely frank. For example, this mission has not yet developed a long-range strategic plan. I think the long-range strategic plan developed by the support office is brilliantly structured. It's well thought-out. It's valuable. So I said to our headquarters in my mission statement, 'I think the model developed by this support office is the one I'm going to use, and I'm looking for extremely strong support from both the support office and headquarters in the development of this strategy'. I should be honest. This is the way I think it should be done. You have to be very open and frank.

Despite his understanding that his administrative boss (HQ) is critical of his financial boss (the support office), he still decides to introduce a plan developed by the support office. He seems deliberately not to take into account the conflicting relationship between the two offices. He does not favour one office over the other in a general sense. He decides to use the plan purely for the sake of its merit for the project.

Taking neither side might confuse both offices at the beginning. But as he consistently makes decisions based on the merits of projects rather than the people involved, he demonstrates how fairly he judges issues based on consistent criteria. Once his decision-making style is shared by both offices, neither of them will see his decisions as a product of betrayal or co-optation, even if he supports an idea of one office and disapproves of an idea of the other.

---

[26] See Fisher and Ury (1991, 17–39).

He strategically presents his stance to both sides even though it means to agree with one side as a consequence. He frankly communicates with both ends to encourage their support. Although he decides to use a plan developed by the support office, he shares the decision and its rationale with HQ, and by doing so, he lets them take part in the decision together with him. His strategy suggests that one can maintain respectful relationships with others even if one critically examines others' ideas and issues. Presenting and sharing one's own thinking with others in a respectable manner maintains diversity and also develops respectful relationships.

Anticipating differences •

Anticipating differences that staff may not realize exist beforehand is another wise strategy. The anticipation leads them critically to question their own understanding of others and encourages them to ask questions in the hope of clarifying others' points of view. Through the cyclic process of asking questions and getting reflections from others, one may maintain the process of reconstructing one's own understanding. A field officer describes the characteristics of this strategy:

> We expect people to do things in our way because this is the only way we know. Those things fight against each other inside ourselves. We can either try to please everybody, which pleases no one, or we can say, 'Forget it, we are just going to do this whether they like or not', or we can honestly look at the situation, sit down with somebody and say, 'How can I help you?' It takes more time, it takes humility on our part to accept something that someone wants us to do instead of telling somebody to do what we want them to do. It takes patience and so it goes against the way the world works. But I think it's the right way to do it.

This strategy shifts the issue from a choice of 'either my stance or your stance' to a question of 'how can I help you?' It sets aside established options and aims at developing a new alternative through a co-operative enquiry process. The process does not negate either party's perspective but rather attempts to build new understanding out of those perspectives.

This strategy is grounded in the assumption that significant differences in interests, values and ideas exist among staff members. The differences do not need to be reconciled in order to build unity. Rather, the strategy implies that differences should be identified, shared and understood among the staff members in the hope of creating new alternatives. Staff members' differences are as important as their similarities that enhance coherent relationships. Individual differences are a rich resource for improving co-operative endeavours, as long as those differences are used to augment, rather than undermine, organizational coherence. For example, balancing staff skills can improve a field office's capacity to remain flexible, adaptive and responsive to diverse local problems.

122

Going into others' spheres[27]

Using the other's communication mode. Going into others' spheres is a strategy for identifying ways in which the staff may identify, understand and benefit from their differences. When the staff try to identify their differences, the strategy suggests that they enter each other's spheres. A local desk officer presents his strategy for communicating cultural differences to other staff:

> I have three Westerners reporting to me. We Asians tend to look at feelings. And sometimes I feel that there is a certain personal problem, certain issues. But I finally find that it's not. It's just the way they say it, the way they do it. I have one staff member who takes a very Western approach. So I had to talk with him in a way that he would understand. So I started with the right brain-left brain theory, because he would understand it. If I had started culturally he wouldn't understand. So I said, 'Your approach is this, this, this'. I try to communicate in a way that they understand to explain the differences in human relations, culture and everything.[28]

The differences derived from cultures are multi-dimensional, and include not only simple differences in behaviours and expression of the same issues, but also differences in ways in which staff members identify their very differences. For example, this Asian officer would tend to read more implications into the way people speak than this particular Westerner, who would rather read implications more from the content.[29]

Thus, because they have different ways of identifying their differences, they will not be able to discuss those differences if they continue to express their positions in their own styles. So, if an Asian staff member tries to convey his concern to the Westerner by the way he speaks rather than by the content of what he says, he will be less effective in conveying his message. By taking into account the complexity involved in communicating, this strategy encourages staff members to go into each others' domains to explain what they think in a way the other staff members can clearly understand.

Listening attentively to others. Another way to go into others' domains to deal better with differences is to try to listen attentively to others to understand the frameworks within which they operate. A country director explains how his boss has gained a better sense of field situations:

---

[27] See Casse and Deol (1985).

[28] The importance of trying to understand how others think so as to discover the meanings they attach to one's own actions may also have a negative aspect. If all participants were to practise such reflection, the result would be mutual paralysis (Schön and Rein, 1994, 39).

[29] The point here is not to generalize about differences between Westerners and Asians, but is rather to use this specific account to identify multi-dimensional differences and to explain the complexity of mutual understanding.

123

[When] my boss comes to visit, he spends most of his time with people. He comes to build relationships, to make sure that communication is going on, [to see if there] are any problems, personnel problems or organizational problems. He takes a lot of time to go down and works at the village level to meet village people. I have 25 staff members. He remembers every one of their names. 'Tom, how are you doing? How is your son?' He works on people's skills. He doesn't stay in a hotel, he stays in our home, so he gets to know my family. So spending time with my wife, talking frankly, encouraging her, how she is doing, becoming aware of the issues that I face in my daily life. . . . So when I tell him things, he has a framework to understand. That makes country directors feel . . . there is trust there. They care about you, not just as an employee but as a person.

The boss tries to understand the circumstances his staff face. Instead of telling them what to do, he listens to them. He understands their concerns, worries, anger, interests and so forth. Moreover, his area of concern is not restricted to job-related issues. Rather, he tries to understand their daily lives as people. Interestingly enough, these non-directive and non-job-related interactions with staff lead this country director to conclude that 'there is trust there, they care about you not just as an employee but as a person'.

The country director feels fulfilled, not because the boss manages staff to implement projects in a proper manner, but because the boss cares about the staff members as individuals. The boss's strategy is to break the framework of job-related interactions and relate with the staff on a personal level. How does this relationship help their work in practice? In fact, its contribution to their practice is enormous. Because he has a framework to understand situations in the field, he has the capacity to respond flexibly to the field situation in a coherent manner without directing from the top what field staff should do. By interacting with each staff member at the personal level, he can understand, appreciate and learn from their distinctive skills, knowledge, experiences and so forth, and can apply these diverse resources to projects in proper ways.[30]

Supporting the other person's position. The last approach to going into another's sphere to deal with differences is to support the other person's position. A desk officer in HQ tries to support the field by offering what the field needs instead of what she thinks the field needs:

To find out not only the things that I want from him that he doesn't give to me, but other things that he is looking for from me, you know, I try to focus my energy and my time more on the things that he is looking for, basically funding. And I'm not supposed to be here as a fund-raiser, but what he really likes from me is funding. Funding and maybe some technical support.

---

[30] Compare with the human resource model that would regard the staff as a mere factor of production, and not as persons. See, for example, Carr (1990, 52–53).

When many different opinions exist concerning the ways in which a certain issue should be resolved, this strategy suggests that the staff support the person who takes responsibility for the issue. The strategy is based on two assumptions: the person knows the situation more than anybody, and the person can make a wise decision when he or she is supported by other staff members. A country director explains how his boss's support helps his work:

> We have some staff problems here. Some staff said that I should solve [the problems] in that way. Some other staff said to kick them out. They are different. And there are people in the headquarters with their own ideas about how to solve this. But he (my boss) said, 'Tom, I support you. You make your decision and you have me 100 per cent behind you.' And when I made the decision, I told him that I made the decision based on this, and that. And he said, 'OK, I trust that that's right. I support you'. I have found moral support from my headquarters which is not very common in this world. If they don't trust you, then you feel very insecure. You wonder, 'Do I dare to make a decision like this? Do I dare to take a step in that direction? But maybe they don't trust me'. That's really discouraging. So trust is very important.

At a glance, this strategy seems to contradict the merit-centred approach described above.[31] The strategy appears to focus on the person involved instead of carefully judging which idea is wise. However, this strategy and the merit-centred strategy do not, in fact, necessarily contradict each other. From the country director's point of view, the strategies are totally different.

The two strategies try to answer different questions. The merit-centred strategy attempts to answer the question, 'Which idea has more merit for the project?' But the strategy to support the director tries to respond to the question, 'How can the boss draw fully on the potential of the director to enable him to act as best as he can?' When the director says, 'If they don't trust you, then you feel very insecure. You wonder "do I dare to make a decision like this?" ' the director implies how much the support from his boss helps him feel confident in making decisions.

This strategy offers security and confidence to the staff when they feel overwhelmed by different ideas, opinions and suggestions. Yet, the strategy does not coercively direct the staff to take a certain course of action. Rather, it appreciates and relies on the potential of the staff. As a result, the staff are encouraged to employ their abilities to take action.

The strategy of going into others' spheres anticipates that other staff members have distinctive skills, knowledge and experiences that can be better applied to their work when the staff understand, appreciate and learn from their differences. When the staff take steps to communicate in each other's mode, to listen to other people carefully, and to support

---

[31] See *Consistently focusing on merit but not on the people involved* above.

other staff members, their differences become rich resources for the organization, the projects and themselves.

Taking charge of processes

Taking charge of the processes of activities is another strategy for the staff to make better use of their distinctive skills, values, views and so forth, for the organization as well as projects. The findings of the study have identified two different approaches to serve this strategy.

Questioning to probe

Questioning to probe and develop understandings is a strategy to maintain one's distinctiveness in the organization, yet at the same time maintain similarity and build coherent integration among the staff. In other words, questioning is a way to avoid both restricted and fragmented performance. A desk officer emphatically argues that questioning to probe is vital for the staff:

> They should be not afraid to ask questions. Never be afraid to ask questions: some people are more accessible than others, but you have to be a bit breezy about it. Say, 'Look, I don't understand this. And I can't do this until I understand it. So you've got to explain it to me.' And you have to be very determined to get the answers to your questions so that you don't end up with more problems in the long run.

When a staff member questions, she or he can become the owner of the process. The staff member initiates the process by questioning and thus brings it to the attention of other staff members. The staff member concludes the process by receiving answers from others. Through the process, the staff can manage coherent integration without losing their diversity. This process yields the following results.

First, questioning itself creates a sense of ownership on the part of the person who develops the question. Questioning can play a role in bringing issues into one's domain. The person's concern is shared with others from his or her point of view, for questioning shapes ways in which an issue is addressed.[32] Thus, questioning not only maintains staff diversity but also develops a commonly-shared sphere of concern that can easily lead to coherent integration of the staff.

Second, getting an answer to a question confirms that one's question is shared, listened to, legitimized and processed by others. Getting an answer is crucial, not only for the sake of getting relevant information. More importantly, it completes the circle of interactions between the person asking and another staff member. Through this cyclic process, a person who raises a question integrates with other staff members without

---

[32] For the relationship between questioning and organizing attention, see Forester (1993).

devaluing their distinctiveness. Once a staff member gets a response from another staff member about his or her question concerning a certain issue, the staff member is more confident in taking actions regarding the issue because she or he can anticipate how other staff members will react to the action.

'Don't ask my permission but do it'

This strategy strongly encourages the staff to own activities and take responsibility for them. The account of a development director introduced in Chapter 3 is worth quoting again here for its insightful strategy:

> I'm trying to create an environment where they don't ask me. If they feel that they need to go to the office, they should go to the office. 'If you feel that you need it, I trust you.' Maybe somebody is flying abroad. It's expensive. But I would be saying, 'OK. Don't ask me permission for that, you know it, do it.' That's where trust begins. Otherwise, say, 'OK, I value you that you are not going to waste money or whatever on an air flight, just go and have a break.' . . . people [are] not impotent like oxen. I'm going into this person's territory saying, 'We know what's there. But do it. And if there are problems, I live with problems. If it creates problems, then I deal with problems, but I'm not going to stop the process'. I think these are the kinds of informal ways that we can develop concepts of what we are. They must be part of decision making. Otherwise, it's not a decision. It's something handed down.

This may appear to contradict completely the previous discussion. While that discussion encourages asking questions as a valuable strategy, this account says, 'I'm trying to create an environment where they don't ask me'. How can we make sense of these two apparently discrepant strategies? Can the development director's strategy keep similarity and develop coherent integration without sacrificing diversity?

When the director says, 'Don't ask me', he tries to convey the message that you can make a decision, for you are competent, not like oxen. He shows his appreciation of the distinctive skills, values and judgement that each staff member possesses. Thus, at least his strategy embodies the appreciation of diversity. But then, can his strategy lead staff members to share ideas and develop coherent integration as suggested in the previous section? The answer would be yes and no. One may conclude 'yes' from his account that he wants to trust and rely on the staff. He even says, 'If there are problems, I live with problems'. This sentence reflects his bottom line, that he is ready to support them when necessary as a member in the same boat. His 'no' relates to his concerns about the ways in which the staff tend to use their relationships. He worries that the staff will depend upon his decisions and approval too much and give up their own judgement if he, as their boss, is always involved in their activities.

Therefore, the strategy of asking questions and the strategy of 'don't ask' are not totally contradictory. Their differences are identified in the ways the staff take into account the possibility of dependency when asking questions. The former strategy uses asking questions as a creative tool to develop one's unique performance, while the latter strategy warns that asking tends to become another form of mere approval-seeking.

When the director feels that asking is used as a way to give up one's own judgement and responsibility, he deliberately discourages his staff from asking permission from him. However, he does not thereby give up his responsibility as a boss. The strategy rather originates from his strong belief that 'people are not impotent like oxen'. This reflects not only his high expectations of the staff's potential but also his commitment to the staff.

Although they appear on the surface to contradict each other, the two accounts both indicate that the ownership of the processes plays a considerable role in enhancing similarity and achieving coherent integration without sacrificing diversity. Asking questions is a relevant strategy for staff members who try to make use of their own distinctive expertise. On the other hand, the strategy of urging people to 'do it' provides the leadership of NGOs with valuable insights into what they need to pay attention to and how they can better draw out staff members' potential.

Conclusion

This chapter has discussed problems of restricted performance due to exclusion that an NGO faces when the organization loses its diversity and homogenizes its staff members. Without diversity, the organization cannot maintain its capacity to address a variety of needs that arise from changing situations. Losing diversity means losing rich resources that enable the organization to deal with unexpected complex issues in responsive, flexible and adaptive manners. With this concern in mind, the first half of the chapter has identified and discussed how an NGO systematically excludes some types of people, loses its diversity, and ends up restricting its performance. The second half of the chapter has discussed the strategies that NGO staff members employ to address these problems.

As the central cause of the problem, the study has identified NGOs' temptation to achieve the similarity of their staff members without careful examination of the potential side effects of that effort. When an NGO emphasizes the similarity of the staff and, by doing so, develops coherent integration among them, it may sacrifice diversity in the process. The findings have revealed that recruiting and identity-constructing processes play considerable roles in unreasonably excluding particular types of people, diminishing organizational diversity by homogenizing the staff members in the name of similarity, whether intentionally or not. When an NGO deals with recruiting and with constructing organizational identity, similarity plays a more important role than diversity. Therefore, NGOs' activities in these areas tend to promote similarity at the expense of diversity. Consequently, NGOs suffer from restricted performance.

In the second half of the chapter, two distinctive types of strategies to address the problems of staff members' homogenization have been presented and discussed. Both types of strategies try to encourage staff members to make good use of their distinctive skills, values and views in their day-to-day work. The first type is to respond to the problem by carefully managing the ways the staff deal with differences. The three main variations of this strategy include: focusing on merit but not the people involved; anticipating different, or even opposing, ideas, views and values; and actively entering each other's spheres.

The second type of strategy involves maintaining the staff members' distinctiveness by letting them own the processes and activities in which they participate. Two distinctive approaches have been addressed. For the staff in general, the first approach suggests that questioning to probe and develop understandings is essential to gaining ownership of the activities at hand. The second approach suggests that NGO leaders should carefully avoid inappropriate intervention into the work of their staff so that the staff can fully own the processes of their activities with a proper balance of authority and responsibility.

PART III

Flexibility vs. Consistency

An NGO deals with a variety of organizational activities to carry out projects. These include not only operational activities, such as assessing needs, planning projects, negotiating with local governments and implementing projects, but also administrative activities, such as opening bank accounts, procuring necessary goods, maintaining offices, paying salaries and so on. Because organizational co-ordination and consistency are crucial to dealing with these activities, an NGO develops systems to facilitate them. For example, an NGO develops systematic procedures to ensure that the salaries of the staff are paid in a manner consistent with their contracts. Even this simple activity requires a system so that the NGO avoids problems such as paying some staff members but not others, or failing to pay on payday due to lack of advance planning. Systems are effective co-ordination tools that facilitate organizational consistency and help to avert opportunism.

While systems assist in maintaining organizational consistency, they can also tend to minimize the organization's capacity to respond flexibly to diverse and dynamic field situations. For example, once a periodic reporting system is in place, staff members must write reports regularly even if they are fully occupied with an emergency relief operation in the field. As reporting becomes highly systematized, it begins to serve itself instead of supporting the staff.

Table 3. Tension in Organizational Response

Pathology		Area of Tension		Pathology
Opportunism	Flexibility	◄──────►	Consistency	Unresponsive-ness

When NGO staff members pay more attention to flexibility, they tend to value responsiveness more than consistency, with opportunism the likely result (see Table 3). But when staff members concern themselves with opportunism, they then emphasize consistency over responsiveness and introduce increasingly formal and rigid systems. In this case, unresponsiveness is the likely result. In both cases, the organization suffers from pathology: opportunism in the former case, unresponsiveness in the latter.

This part of the book addresses the question of how to maintain both flexibility and consistency simultaneously. Although they are not mutually exclusive, their coexistence requires a combination appropriate to each specific context. A slight shift in emphasis of either of the two characteristics can easily disrupt any equilibrium between them. While two opposite types of pathology threaten NGOs, they are more likely to suffer from unresponsiveness than from opportunism because of the systems they introduce in the hope of developing consistency, standards, co-ordination capacity and so forth. Therefore, Part III focuses specifically on systems in order to examine the tensions between flexibility and consistency.

Chapter 6 identifies and discusses how NGOs struggle amidst the tensions in the face of the pathologies of opportunism and unresponsiveness. The first half of the chapter describes the rationale for employing systems as a major means of maintaining consistency and then presents the problems they cause. As strategies to address these problems, several methods of developing informal reflections are introduced and discussed.

Chapter 7 identifies and discusses how systems gain autonomy, perpetuate themselves and bring about undesirable consequences for the organization. The chapter first discusses how systems create their own paradigms/languages and contribute to the reproduction of hierarchy within the organization, with the result that the organization becomes inflexible, and thus unresponsive. The rest of the chapter presents strategies that address these problems in practical terms.

CHAPTER 6

Flexibility

My challenge . . . is that things are constantly changing.

Desk officer

Systems always lag behind the reality.[1]

Senior field manager

Introduction

THIS CHAPTER IDENTIFIES and analyses problems that NGO staff members encounter when they employ systems to handle the issues that face them. It then examines strategies that the staff employ to address these problems. The term 'system' in this chapter refers to rules, regulations and policies. But, in addition to this narrow interpretation of the term, 'systems' as used here also includes widely shared resources and tools, such as money and languages.[2]

The main theme of this chapter is succinctly reflected in a desk officer's question:

How can organizations be flexible enough to be able to adjust to fluctuating environments and yet meet the needs of people?

NGOs need to be flexible and responsive enough to be able to adapt themselves to changing environments. Yet, at the same time, their flexibility and responsiveness should not lead them to sacrifice their consistency and core values.[3] NGOs need to maintain two features simultaneously, as they operate in a changing world: flexibility in adapting to dynamic environments, and consistency in their mission objectives and core values.

The first half of this chapter focuses on the tensions that emerge between an organization's interest in employing systems and the undesirable impact those systems can have on the organization. The analysis of these tensions clarifies problems derived from gaps between the circumstances that systems anticipate and actual circumstances. The second half

---

[1] Decisions need to be made in ambiguous situations (March and Olsen, 1988).

[2] Giddens (1979, 33–4) refers to Wittgenstein to argue that language is 'a system of differences in the sense that the meanings of words are not constituted through the nature of utterances or marks as isolated items, but only through the ways in which they acquire an identity through their differentiation as elements of language-games'.

[3] That is, it is important to avoid rigidity and opportunism at the same time. See Sager (1994).

of the chapter explores several strategies to address these problems. The strategies involve developing informal reflections among the staff and thus minimizing the gaps between systems and reality by easing constraints that arise from rigidly formal systems. Broadening views and prioritizing the staff over systems are the two major types of strategies.

Problems: Gaps between the systems and reality[4]

A typical feature of problems derived from organizational systems is clearly addressed by a field manager:

> If you are in an organization, things change more often than systems must change. And I don't think that a change in systems will be [sufficient] to cope with a change in the operations. So what I'm saying is no matter how efficient you are, systems always lag behind you. And there would always be some problems in the process. Systems are behind. We are not getting reports on time, and those kinds of things.

An NGO develops many systems to support its activities, such as financial systems, recruiting procedures, job descriptions, procurement procedures, reporting systems, line management systems and performance management systems, to name but a few. To identify the problems derived from systems, this section first discusses the rationale for instituting systems, and then explores systems' undesirable contributions to organizations.

Rationale for seeking systems
When an NGO introduces a certain system, it has a specific objective that the system is designed to accomplish. This section's examination, through four case studies, of the rationales behind systems suggests that systems cannot easily be abandoned by NGOs, despite their negative consequences for the organizations.

Systems as efficient learning mechanisms
Systems can be efficient learning tools, helping the staff figure out what to do. Staff members new to an organization may be glad to find established systems – such as a manual, for example – that help them understand what their jobs entail and how to accomplish the necessary tasks. This benefit is especially welcomed by staff whose jobs require more systematic processes. For instance, systems are important to those who deal with financial resources, such as accountants, financial controllers and procurement officers. A procurement officer in a field office articulates how an established procurement procedure helps him in his work:

---

[4] Bryson (1988, 206) argues, 'Structures and systems exist primarily to protect current practices – which in the longer run may not best serve the interests of the organization or its shareholders.'

The system is in place [so anyone] could take over from me. You can understand what's going on easily because the system is there. So when any purchase comes, the procedure is there, everything goes smoothly. I tried to make the structure more clear so people are in place, the reporting system is in place, the controlling system is there, the approval authority system is there. So I think it's running well. I think it all depends on how the mechanisms go, in every mission, how things are processed. Once you learn how these things [work], you can do something better to change things.

Repetitive daily work that involves clearly defined tasks and few uncertainties can benefit significantly from systems, as this officer points out. In this case, systems can provide guidelines that facilitate organizational consistency. Repetitive work can be incorporated into organizational systems.[5] Once systems are in place, the organization acquires the capacity to maintain its consistency even through staff changes, because the systems retain the necessary information and processes to enable new staff members to perform their duties in the same way they were performed previously.[6]

Going beyond opportunism
Flexibility is the capacity of an NGO to address diverse and changing problems. However, flexibility without any systems tends to result in case-by-case decisions without organizational direction and consistency. A desk officer warns:

Flexibility can be a very positive thing. But it can be a negative thing, too. Sometimes you can be pulled in all different directions. You have to be insistent in saying, 'Look, you are asking me to do too many things, where is the priority?' So I think you have to prioritize, and not get panicked.

When the degree of flexibility exceeds its appropriate range, staff members may fail to prioritize issues and thus may not handle the issues properly. If one is responding to every issue that comes along without prioritizing, one tends to be trapped by opportunism[7] and to give up

---

[5] Starbuck (1965, 480) identifies as one characteristic of organizational learning that 'organizations try to perpetuate the fruits of their learning by formalizing them'. For a discussion of the relationship between formalization and organizational learning, see, also Levitt and March (1988).
[6] However, an NGO also faces the negative effects of systems. Because systems are crucial to maintaining organizational consistency, changing systems to accommodate diverse needs undermines their purpose and utility. Systems may be a good foundation on which an organization and its staff members act. But precisely because they are so fundamental, it is very difficult to change them. The second half of this chapter explores these problems.
[7] Faludi (1987, 206) distinguishes opportunism from flexibility, 'By accepting uncertainty and applying forethought to how to cope with it, flexibility helps in achieving as much certainty as is possible in a world in flux. Opportunism, on the other hand, merely reacts to uncertainty wherever and whenever it hits. Though seemingly pragmatic, it is not a rational response to uncertainty, because erratic reactions to uncertainty form an additional source of turbulence, over and above existing uncertanties.'

one's own judgement. To avoid opportunism, an NGO can employ a system that sorts out demands issuing from various directions and suggests a possible and reasonable course of action that will be consistent with organizational missions.

Nevertheless, employing a system is different from treating the system as non-negotiable. Rather, a desirable system should play a role in co-ordinating the missions and issues at hand, in indicating desirable approaches to and priorities among the issues. Despite the risk of rigidity that systems carry, they are attractive to NGOs as valuable resources for avoiding opportunism.

To be more accountable

Accountability is another vital reason that NGOs develop systems to regulate their staff members' activities. A senior field staff member explains:

> Whenever you launch in a new country, you get some accountability problems. So you tend to tighten and control from the top level. Because we have seen evidence of people not being accountable, we created a structure by which we make sure that the accountability standard is met.

When an NGO faces an accountability problem, a straightforward, effective and efficient way to enhance accountability is to institute a system to regulate the practices of the staff members. Even if the staff members value informal work styles, they cannot ignore the fact that formal systems are better equipped to deal with some issues in an accountable manner than are informal ones. A field staff member advocates a formal system to resolve accountability problems:

> A criticism of this organization could be that too much of it is done on an informal basis. I think that a lot has to be achieved by doing things formally. Having decisions made right at a meeting where we promptly discuss this, this, this, and this. So you have accountability, and a more formalized style of meeting that accommodates more accountability. This organization had been such a small organization based on certain individuals who could put a lot of time, effort, years into the organization. But times are changing, the organization is getting bigger. An informal style of communication and reporting can still be maintained. There is a lot to gain from it. But we also must have a more formal level of communication. It's too easy for people to forget things. No accountability. Did we not decide what is supposed to be done three months ago? How can we decide and write a memory?

Compared with the formal systems, the informal styles of work, according to him, lack accountability because the work depends totally on individuals. Informal styles of work impede the organization's ability to organize, co-ordinate, disseminate and retain information. Informal work usually takes place at a personal level and cannot become an organizational activity. An NGO as an organization is not involved in the informal,

136

personal level of work, and thus fails to follow up what the staff members are doing. As a result, responsibility for the work falls on individual staff members without organizational backup.

Moreover, informal working methods rely solely on individuals' memories to keep track of work, whereas formal systems retain information not only at the individual level but also at the organizational level. In the case of informal work, no organizational mechanisms exist to create institutional memory. Thus, lack of accountability is the likely result once staff members fail to retain information, which is likely to happen because, as the staff member quoted above says, it is 'too easy for people to forget things'.

Managing quality
Managing the quality of organizational activities is another rationale for instituting systems. Systems help to ensure greater coherence between policies and projects, to control NGOs' output, and to manage the flow of information.

Coherence between policies and projects. NGOs work to carry out projects that embody their policies without contradicting them. However, NGOs' working situations are so complex and diverse that developing and implementing organizational policies at the project level, with no higher co-ordinating authority, would exceed the capacity of individual projects to co-ordinate with each other. Hence, NGO staff would be tempted to conclude that establishing and maintaining coherent relationships between the policies and projects without any regulatory mechanisms would be unrealistic. A country director says:

> Field directors have an obligation to work with the organization's policy. And if there is too much autonomy in the field, and no control, particularly no budget control, I think it is possible for a country to take off in different directions that would be outside of the policy, which I wouldn't agree with. I think budgetary control is one way of maintaining that. I don't have a problem with it. It's not a big deal to contact headquarters and say, 'All right, we are receiving a donation, we would recommend that we spend it in the following ways', and headquarters would usually approve if it is within our policy.

Note that, in this account, the director herself acknowledges a need for HQ to exercise budgetary control over her office. When she refers to budgetary control, she does not expect HQ to play a coercive regulatory role, shaping field activities by force. Rather, she understands budgetary control as a guideline system through which the field can confirm that its activities fall within organizational policy.

Controlling NGOs' output. The need to control the quality of an NGO's output to its constituencies is another incentive for the organization to employ systems.[8] We can understand how this type of quality can be managed through organizational systems by looking at the example of reporting to donors. In this case, an NGO tries to ensure that only reports of acceptable quality go out to donors. A desk officer explains an organizational structure that can systematically screen the quality of reports:

> If you are saying something completely crazy, or emotional or whatever, your department head should stop that. I think that's dead wise. I think that's a function of the department. One of the functions of the department head is to make sure that whatever is coming from me is representative of the division's general view. I should be aware of that first. But because I'm human I would make mistakes. I might be in bad humour someday.

Although the officer works as a desk officer under a department head, she does not claim absolute autonomy. Instead, she expresses her consent to a structurally ordered system for the sake of organizational accountability *vis-à-vis* other constituencies. Why is she content with the system that hierarchically situates her under the department head? Does she consider only the organizational point of view?

The introduction of regulatory systems might be expected to be an unwelcome development for staff members. However, it can be wise not only for the organization but also for individuals. Because systems take responsibility for quality control, individuals are not obliged to take full responsibility for their performance *vis-à-vis* other parties, such as donors and governments.[9]

Even if a report submitted to a donor is poorly written, the report writer does not need to take full responsibility as a representative of the organization. The writer takes responsibility within the range of her or his own job description and might be required to rewrite the report. But individual writers in the organization do not receive pressure from donors directly, because the organization systematically manages the quality of reports.

Managing information flow. A need to manage the information flow in an NGO legitimizes the introduction of systems. A 'donor relations officer' in HQ, who plays a mediating role between the donors and the FOs, feels strongly that the organization needs some system to control information flows among the staff members in different offices:

> It is through the division head that donors contact the field. You have to have a controlled procedure. Otherwise, everybody is shouting, trying to contact

---

8 'Finding the balance between being flexible and open while staying focused and in control is essential' (Kelleher and McLaren, 1996, xiii).
9 'Routines are independent of the individual actors who execute them and are capable of surviving considerable turnover in individuals' (March and Olsen, 1989, 22).

different staff in the field. So there is a central control at all times to make sure that all the information flows to one person, and to make sure that information is distributed toward people who need that information.

She claims that a messy situation in which 'everybody is shouting' is avoided by instituting an information flow system. Whether or not a centralized structure promises more desirable results than does a messy structure in which 'everybody is shouting',[10] a request to manage information flows between HQ and FOs seeks a response in systematic control.

These accounts reveal the rational bases on which NGOs claim the importance of systems. The accounts all suggest positive impacts of systems. Without systems, NGOs may suffer from less than optimal learning and coherence, lack of accountability and low-quality performance. On the other hand, some undesirable influences of systems are also apparent. Systems can easily become strategic tools to serve the interests of particular people in an NGO at the cost of imposing negative influences on the others. Moreover, once systems gain legitimacy in the organization, they can gain autonomy and move beyond the staff's control. The next subsection discusses problems that result from imposed systems.

Systems' undesirable impacts

While operating systems confer benefits, they also impose unavoidable, negative side effects on the organization and the staff. Systems often do not have the capacity to adapt to changing situations.

Employment terms: consistent, but staff suffer

Problems emerge when systems fail to respond to changes in situations. As a typical example, two accounts (from different organizations) depict how rigidity and lack of responsiveness cause tensions among staff members when the organization tries to recruit new staff.[11] A field officer describes the impact of organizational change on the NGO's recruitment practices:

> We are paying some people and not paying some other people. We are paying some people who have never worked. So I'm saying, 'You could be finding a lot of disharmony in certain lines of the organization. You find that a lot of jobs are decided between two individuals as opposed to a policy deciding it. And that isn't good. If you have a policy, stick to it. If you are a

---

[10] See *Given identity* in Chapter 5, 'Constructing identity', to consider the negative effects of having too few links between HQ and FOs.

[11] Here, the practice of recruitment is analysed in light of the tensions between flexibility and consistency, while the discussions about recruitment in Chapter 2 analyse it in relation to organizational means and ends.

volunteer, you stick to it. You don't start to pay some people and then not pay other people.'[12]

This account was expressed in the midst of rapid organizational expansion. Previously, virtually all staff members had given several years of unpaid volunteer work to the organization, through which they not only developed their skills and experiences but also learned how the organization functioned. Because they all had the same unpaid work experiences prior to becoming paid staff, the difference between paid and unpaid staff was not a matter of inconsistency. However, once the organization started to expand and newcomers with some experience outside the organization began to take paid staff positions, the rationale for having paid and unpaid staff dissolved. As a result, the terms of employment became inconsistent.

This inconsistency originates in the gap between the established employment policy and the change in situation. The assumption underlying the system of employment terms, although not formally articulated, was that skilled and experienced staff went through several years of unpaid work within the organization to gain their skills and experience. But when the situation changed in ways that broke with this assumption, the employment policy revealed inconsistencies and became the target of criticism. This problem resulted from a recruitment practice that was unresponsive to changing situations.

Problems in recruitment originate not only from the failure to adapt to changing situations, or from the inconsistent application of systems and policies. The problem is also caused by a lack of responsiveness to the field staff who suffer from lack of financial support. A country director addresses the problem behind the differences between paid and unpaid staff:

One of the things I feel uncomfortable with in this organization is that some people receive salaries and some people raise their own support. Is it inconsistent? Yes and no. It is not inconsistent in a sense that there have always been paid and unpaid staff and when someone chooses to do that they understand up front that's what they are doing. It is not a secret. If you choose to do it, you choose to do it. So in that way it is not inconsistent. But the reality in the field is that it actually depends on if their support is consistent or not. If they are short of support, then it becomes awkward for me.

Even if there is consistency between what the system says and what the practice actually is, the system does not make sense if the field staff suffer under it. The director points out that the issue is not whether the system is

---

[12] Here, I focus on expatriate employment terms as a case to demonstrate the need for systems in an NGO. Needless to say, the gap in employment terms between expatriates and locals is much larger and more systematically structured. However, this case is irrelevant to the rationale for promoting systems in an NGO under discussion here.

consistent, but whether all the staff receive enough support, regardless of their employment terms. The danger of the system is that it tends to discourage an understanding of how it influences those who have been recruited under its terms. Once a recruitment system (even an informal one) is set up, staff members tend to be concerned only about its internal consistency (i.e., the relationship between what the system says and what it does), and they disregard the system's purpose. The staff begin to serve the system instead of the system serving the staff.

Money: a powerful regulatory system

A country director says:

> Even if there is the most gripping, intellectually stimulating, and exciting thing, unless you get somebody to pay for it, it's not going to be done. That is *the singular* most important reality.[13]

Money functions as a powerful system that regulates the behaviour of NGOs.[14] As much development literature points out, the donor–NGO relationship is one of the major issues facing NGOs.[15] Without sufficient financial resources, NGOs cannot even sustain themselves, let alone implement projects. Thus, to secure funding, NGOs expend significant effort, time and money that would otherwise be directed to project implementation.[16]

The issue of funding is not simply a matter of investing NGOs' resources. The attractive power of funding may often lead NGOs to alter or abandon their original missions.[17] If you understand the funding status of an NGO, you can predict the behaviour of the organization to a great extent. When funding increases, most NGOs expand the scale of their operations even if they can predict facing adverse times in the near future, as budgets shrink and the over-grown organization must contract. A regional officer admits the mistake that the organization made:

> Between 1986 and 1991, there was tremendous growth, a lot of demand from new projects, and a lot of demand from new sponsors, so, in order to meet the demand, we established this office especially [to have a] structure to meet this

---

[13] Italics reflect the speaker's emphasis.

[14] See, for example, Antrobus (1987), Fowler (1992b), and Smith (1987, 1990).

[15] See, for example, Brown and Korten (1989), Lissner (1977) and Smith (1990).

[16] While there are many kinds of resources that organizations require to start and maintain their activities, financial resources are among the most important ones on which they rely. Private volunteer organizations (PVOs), in particular, do not usually generate income out of their activities and must rely heavily on external financial sources.

[17] Constantino-David (1992), Edwards and Hulme (1992a, 1992b), Hashemi (1996) and Van Der Heijden (1987) discuss how funding concerns can distort the missions of NGOs. See *Organizational issues over operational issues* in Chapter 7, 'Systems as a catalyst to reproduce hierarchy,' for a discussion of how NGOs fail to maintain their missions. *Donor relations* in Chapter 5, 'Recruiting to homogenize the organization', discusses NGOs' strong interests in donors.

demand. But what happened is, unfortunately, [the organization] did not grow but the structure continued to endure.

He cannot justify the presence of his own office, which would have played a useful role if the growth had continued. A contraction in funding rendered the office superfluous. In NGO contexts, budget change is drastic, uncertain and unpredictable. Thus, NGOs must strategically take into account the possibility of a sudden budget decrease even as their budgets expand. In contrast with this strategic planning, however, the following account exemplifies how an opportunity for budget expansion enchants NGOs and nullifies their planning:

> In 1982 and '83, we had such a huge income because of boat people out of Vietnam and because of Cambodia opening up. We were flooded by it. We had tons of money flowing in, tons of opportunities, and no people, no infrastructure. We had 30 per cent income growth in one year. So we said, 'We are not gonna make that mistake again'. We did a five-year plan. We built into that five-year plan 30 per cent growth every single year. Of course the following year, all the donors forgot about the boat people, about Cambodia, and our income, instead of going up 30 per cent, dropped by a large amount. We were devastated. It was a very tight time. We finally recovered from that and income was growing again when Ethiopia hit. You would think that we would not make the same mistake again, we would not plan for all this growth, hire tons of new people, buy all kinds of new equipment. But we did. Then people lost interest in Ethiopia and famine in Africa. Suddenly, we had all kinds of people that we couldn't afford, and all kinds of equipment. We suffered. We haven't learned the lesson.

This account vividly depicts how an NGO fails to learn[18] a lesson and ends up making the same mistake again. The account offers critical insight into the way NGOs may deal with money. Maintaining a strategic stance of being prepared for a sudden budget drop in the context of budget expansion is much more difficult than an NGO expects. Even if the organization made the same mistake previously, the attractive force of the expansion opportunity can exceed the power of the lesson learned. Despite changing environments in which NGOs work, staff members can lose their critical stance when an opportunity presents itself, and can convince themselves to treat a short-term budget increase as if it will last for a long time.

The account implies that the most critical issue is not exactly the lack of learning from previous mistakes, though this is certainly a problem. Rather, it is the failure of NGOs to understand that lessons learned are all vulnerable in the face of money's power. Had the organization taken into account the vulnerability of the lessons it had learned or had it

---

[18] Handy (1990) suggests that learning is not finding out what other people already know, but is solving our own problems for our own purposes, by questioning, thinking and testing until the solution is integrated into our understanding and approach.

understood the power of money, it would have developed different strategic plans. The real lesson is that a lesson learned from a mistake is fragile in the face of systematic financial forces. Money talks by itself and regulates NGOs like a system.

Language: not a mere medium but a regulatory system
As has been discussed elsewhere,[19] working languages systematically regulate, distort and shape the behaviour of staff members. Based on the discussions in previous chapters, three aspects of the systematic roles that language plays in the organization are summarized briefly here.

First, an organization's working language is not selected by the organization, but is already in place by the time the organization is founded. The working language has been deeply embedded as one major component of the organization since the beginning. Thus, selecting a working language does not make much sense once the organization is founded.

In the case of most NGOs, founders' languages become their organizations' languages. As founders use their own languages during the founding process, the languages gain legitimacy within the organization. As a result, the languages spoken in HQ become the working languages imposed on the field. Therefore, the field staff face structural disadvantages in communicating with HQ.

Second, once the language spoken in HQ becomes the organization's working language, communication between HQ and the field systematically places extra burdens on the field. The issue is not the language selection but ways in which non-native speakers of the working language are treated. Besides language training offered to non-native speakers, most NGOs do not have any systematic support to reduce the burdens on non-native speakers.

Rather than facilitating communication among the staff members, the working language – and its command as a major criterion for membership on the organization's staff – can threaten non-native speakers. If the staff members are to work in the organization, they are expected to handle the language in the same way that native speakers do. Consequently, the extra efforts required of non-native speakers are systematically discounted in the name of the working language. The suffering of non-native speakers neither emerges explicitly as a problem nor becomes an organizational concern.

Third, the working language is not merely a communication medium. It regulates and shapes the behaviour of the staff members.[20] A country

---

[19] See *Local language vs. working language* in Chapter 3, 'Locals vs. expatriates', *Coining organizational terms* in Chapter 4, 'Narratives', and *Administrative efficiency: Working language* in Chapter 5, 'Recruiting to homogenize the organization'.
[20] See Burbules and Rice (1991) for a discussion of how language relates to different parties in power relationships.

director applies it as one recruiting criterion: 'That person should be someone who speaks and writes English very, very well.'

Once English is recognized as the organization's working language, command of it, in turn, becomes a major criterion for recruiting new local staff. As a result, only those who are exposed to English are hired by the organization. Instead of serving simply to facilitate staff members' mutual understanding, language can become a tool for screening candidates in the recruitment process. For non-native speakers, the working language is neither from themselves nor for themselves, but is rather a scale against which their abilities are measured. While native speakers enjoy their advantages, non-native speakers suffer. For non-native speakers, the working language is a matter of being hired or fired.

Modus operandi: *a device to control field offices*

Modus operandi is another device that systematically regulates the behaviour of FOs. Although each field office has an indigenous *modus operandi* derived from the local context, the organizational demand to improve administrative effectiveness and efficiency usually conflicts with the local *modus operandi* due to its inefficiency. FOs face tensions between an indigenous but inefficient *modus operandi* and externally derived but efficient ones.

Two accounts demonstrate how an ill-suited *modus operandi* is subtly imposed on FOs to subvert local value systems. A field staff member expresses her frustration with the meddlesome intervention of HQ:

> Westerners [pointing to headquarters] expect us not only to implement but also to do it in a theoretical way. If we are Thai, we are doing like Thai do. But they expect us to do it in a theoretical way to be up to their standards. If we don't do it one, two, three, four, five, six, like this, they expect that it is not the standard they want. But we sometimes have to do step one, step four, step two, step three, something like that. Different ways. But Westerners say, 'You must do like this, this, this, this, this.' If not they don't accept us as standard. They don't change because they are brought up in that way.

In this case, the gap between HQ and the field office is unambiguous. Thus, the officer can easily identify the problem and challenge it. However, a more subtle and tricky way of imposing *modus operandi* exists. An executive officer in the field says:

> In the socio-economic setting in Africa, you live in the family, you care for people much more than paper. So if you can personally meet, my priority is to talk to you, not a fax machine. That [pointing to the fax machine] is the worst. Unless you have an appointment, it's unlikely that you will be able to see the people you want. As a result, people in the Western countries easily respond to any request, or meet deadlines of communication. But on this side, many people now have influence over my daily production component. . . . We are

144

being forced to compromise without somebody telling me to change. I'm closing myself off and asking visitors not to disturb me. Otherwise I would have an endless number of people coming to visit us. I have to say, 'No', and minimize. I must discipline myself to learn how to use the computer, how to prepare fax message, how to send faxes, and how to use the computer to send out or receive e-mail.

As he says, 'We are being forced to compromise without somebody telling me to change'. Even without the HQ's intentional interference, the field is strongly influenced and forced to change its *modus operandi* in a novel way.[21] Through day-to-day work, the field is systematically subordinated to the HQ's style of work. Three points illustrate the process of HQ systematically imposing order on FOs.

First, whether one is imposing or being imposed upon is strongly related to whether one is questioning or responding to questions. As HQ asks questions to FOs, it disseminates not only the content of the question but also its *modus operandi* through its particular framework of questioning. Then, FOs are expected to respond in the same *modus operandi*, regardless of its content. When the officer says, '. . . without somebody telling me to change. I'm closing myself off and asking visitors not to disturb me', he sacrifices his style of work to meet the needs of HQ.

Second, a *modus operandi* internalizes its own value system. Hence, accepting the HQ's *modus operandi* means accepting the HQ's value system by disregarding the field's own value system. As the above case shows, when paperwork becomes the style of work in the field, the field staff lose their *modus operandi* that values caring for people. Without explicitly devaluing personal relationships, the *modus operandi* can discourage an emphasis on them.

Third, the field has double difficulties in overcoming the imposed regulatory devices. It is taken for granted that the field represents the lower part of the organizational structure. Moreover, the local style of work, which, compared with HQ, generally depends more on face-to-face interactions than on paperwork, is less efficient and effective in disseminating the *modus operandi* itself than the goal-oriented, paperwork-centred style of work in HQ. Therefore, the field is more likely to be influenced by HQ's style than to influence HQ.

The field has few defences against HQ's work style. In the name of efficiency and effectiveness, the field adopts the HQ's style. At the same

---

[21] 'There is a tendency for large, powerful actors to be able to specify their environments, thus forcing other actors to adapt to them. Dominant groups create environments to which others must respond, without themselves attending to the others. This is a fairly standard characterization of the position of dominant ethnic or gender groups, of persons in authority in totalitarian regimes, or of leading firms in a concentrated industry.' (March and Olsen, 1989, 47).

time, however, this shift also means a shift in the field's attention from 'caring for people' to 'not accepting visitors'.

The first half of this chapter has discussed the rationales for employing systems, as well as some problems that can be observed in virtually all NGOs. The findings of the study have shown that systems are beneficial for facilitating learning, avoiding opportunism, enhancing accountability and managing performance quality. Problems in employment terms, money, working languages, and *modus operandi* have been examined to illuminate their systematic roles in imposing undesirable, negative conditions on the organization.

Although the problems identified do not stem from the rationales for seeking systems, this section has identified both positive and negative features associated with systems. Each system has both positive and negative aspects. For example, although money strongly drives NGOs in undesirable directions, money is still necessary for the organizations to carry out their missions. The second half of the chapter discusses some strategies to address these · kinds of problems concerning systems.

Strategies: Developing informal reflections

NGOs' systems exist for particular reasons and confer particular benefits to the organizations that institute them. Thus, strategies should aim not at devaluing systems *per se*, but at maintaining organizational flexibility, adaptability, and responsiveness together with systems. Doing so requires different strategies for different situations. In some situations, the staff try to change systems to enhance flexibility, adaptability and responsiveness. But in some cases, the staff can make use of systems as a strategic tool to develop flexibility, adaptability and responsiveness. Strategies themselves need to be flexible enough to be able to respond to different issues in different ways.

The second half of this chapter discusses informal reflections as the main focus of the strategies. Compared with formal reflections, informal ones are vulnerable, fragile and unpredictable, and thus more difficult to manage, plan or control. But, at the same time, they are flexible, adaptable and responsive. For example, when the staff meet with each other informally to discuss their issues, they may more flexibly respond to the issues, although the response is fragile because there is no systematic support to ensure it. Through informal reflections, staff can keep up with dynamic environments as well as changing organizations. The strategies indicate that the influences of informal reflections are not nominal, despite the lack of formality. They play significant roles in deconstructing the rigidity of formal activities. Broadening views and putting people first are the two broad categories of strategies.

146

Broadening views

Broadening views encourages informal reflections by challenging the task orientation of staff members' interactions. Broadening views helps staff members in different positions share a common understanding concerning their activities; it also facilitates their informal reflections. Strategies to broaden views work against the tendency of specific, assigned tasks to narrow people's views and discourage broad interactions. The strategies present practical ways to go beyond assigned tasks, enhance the diversity of interactions and activate informal reflections. The findings suggest six variations as alternative strategies.

Sharing information

Sharing relevant information with other staff members is a strategy to build relationships and broaden the staff members' views. Through building relationships and broadening their views, the strategy aims at questioning formalized daily routines and developing informal interactions among the staff through which they can flexibly address diverse problems. A senior staff member at HQ describes how he applies information in his strategy to develop informal relationships:

> When you don't have the authority of line managers, then you have to go with building relationships where you can influence them. It's an informal line and that is very important. Strategically, because I have visited several African countries, I will frequently send little notes. I try to keep my eyes open for information that would be useful. Because I'm looking at [the situation] more globally, I can pick up a lot of information that would have local value, so I will track this type of information and send it to them.

The strategy is valuable in several ways. First, with relevant information from a global point of view, the local staff are better equipped to judge their practices in a broad context rather than simply following their daily routines.[22] Second, as he says, the strategy helps them build informal relationships. Assisted by both formal and informal relationships, the staff can increase their capacity to understand situations from multiple perspectives and respond to them more appropriately than if they had only formal relationships. Third, their positional differences are valued as the precious resources of the strategy. Because all staff members assume different positions, they have different information, views and ideas that can be of help to each other.

Questioning for reflections

In Chapter 5, asking questions was introduced as a strategy to own processes and make better use of staff members' distinctive skills and

---

[22] In this sense, NGO staff members can be considered planners who are concerned with making non-routine decisions (Friedmann, 1987, 7).

experiences. Another valuable contribution of asking questions is to break away from confining frameworks[23] and develop learning environments for staff members. It releases the staff from system-bounded views and plants seeds of new views that grow from within themselves. Questioning is responded to by answering. While answering can be a process of taking a particular stance on an issue, questioning can be a process of exploring new insights into an issue.

Questioning and answering form a cyclic learning process of action and reflection.[24] A question leads to an answer, and the answer then develops a question, and the process continues. The combination of questioning and answering is a dynamic process as opposed to static nouns: questions and answers. Because the process is exploratory, it is not satisfied with particular questions and answers. The purpose of questioning is not achieved by finding the right answer because exploring different ways of looking at the issue is its vital objective.[25] Similarly, the purpose of answering is not to resolve the issue because taking part in the exploratory process by judging and responding[26] is a critical objective of answering.

The process links actions and reflections and develops responsiveness and flexibility. To remain responsive and flexible, staff members keep the issue alive by continuing the exploratory process instead of drawing the final answer to conclude it. The cyclic process of questioning and answering strategically frees the staff from the formalized, goal-oriented question-answer relationship. An evaluation director describes how to put this strategy into practice in a real working situation:

> My job is to facilitate their thinking about evaluation. In my view, the best way you facilitate someone's thinking about something is, first of all, you understand what they really think, and even why. So when I'm talking with them, I'm asking them to explain how they go about evaluation work, how it's useful to them. Then if they ask me to help them with the evaluation, again it's the same kind of approach, together we decide what we are going to do. The things I might do differently that they might not have done if I hadn't been

---

[23] The type of questioning discussed here differs from questioning as a means of imposition as discussed in the section '*Modus operandi*'. Instead of imposing different views, this questioning hopes to encourage staff members to explore different insights and new ways of looking at things. In contrast to questioning as a means to impose, this type of questioning does not demand answers, for its purpose is to encourage exploration. Questioning is used as an initial push to help staff members take an exploratory approach, as opposed to a question that imposes a framework.

[24] See Schön (1982, 1987).

[25] '[Enacting organizations] do not assume that there is an ineluctable structure, a "right" answer, or a universal view to be discovered; rather, they continually look for innovative ways to impose new structure, ask new questions, develop a new view, become new organizations. By asking different questions, by seeking different sorts of explanations, and by looking from different points of view, different answers emerge . . .' (Brown and Duguid, 1996, 75).

[26] Compare with practical wisdom that is praxis and judgement. See Beiner (1983).

148

there is that I ask them to process what's happening as we go about doing this survey. Ask them to think about, for example, 'While you are interviewing these families that we selected, what do you think their impressions were of you? What was the value of the information? How do you think they felt during the whole experience?' It's not a question that you ordinarily ask within the traditional approach to the evaluation. 'Are you comfortable with how you think they respond?' And then I might ask a question about the way we went about doing this survey. 'Is that consistent with the way you plan and work with the community on development activity?' I don't give them answers. I raise questions. So in that sense, I'm still, I believe, playing a facilitator's role.

His questions are all open-ended. He is not requesting particular answers to his questions. He questions to motivate the staff to think about issues differently.[27] His questions are virtually all about the staff's own practices rather than objective issues outside them. Through questioning, he lets the staff reflect on their own practices from different perspectives. The continuous process of questioning and asking develops informal interactions among the staff and provides them with opportunities to learn from each other.

Missions as a base for critical enquiries

To challenge the meanings of the staff's daily activities, a senior manager in HQ poses a provocative question: 'What business are we in? A fundamental question. Unless you know what you are doing, everything else is irrelevant.'

Among various questions, the relationship between the staff's practices and their missions is one of the most critical questions that they need to contemplate. Because the missions are the fundamental reason for the organization's existence, they can be used as a starting point from which staff members can critically examine their activities and alter them if necessary. The manager continues:

The crucial thing is that we focus on the poorest. All organizations have to constantly remind themselves that that's why they are set up. The poor are very, very difficult to work with. The aid you bring to some people seems wasted, because there is no way we get return. So what people tend to do is, or what NGOs tend to do, is they move up. We work with farmers, because we can increase the aid as we go along, because we can measure [results]. We can write a report about it and get more funding because it's tangible. How about farmers with no land? They have greater problems. It's much more difficult to deal with farmers with no land than deal with farmers that have land. All our focus is to remember that and keep looking backwards.

---

[27] 'The political future belongs to those who have the courage and vision to form new alliances based on ways of thinking that cannot be defined by the old categories' (Korten, 1995, 328).

Here, the point is not the quality of this specific mission. Instead, the point is to look at how the missions may direct staff members' attention. First, considering staff members' activities in light of the missions broadens their views. It helps them step back from their day-to-day work and understand it from an organizational point of view. Identifying their tasks in relation to the organization's missions changes the way the staff members perform their daily work.

Second, considering practices in light of the missions facilitates critical analysis of the meaning of the staff's activities in NGOs. For example, in light of the organization's missions, fund-raisers are challenged by the tensions between their fund-raising activities and organizational missions. While writing an attractive report is necessary to securing funds from donors, this practice does not necessarily reflect the NGOs' missions; in some cases, it may even disturb them.[28] Although invoking the missions *per se* does not resolve the issue of funding, it helps keep the tensions between the missions and fund-raising alive. Without keeping the missions in mind, the staff can easily become mere fund-raising technocrats who systematically focus only on maximizing their funds. Missions are a legitimate resource for their reflections to reconsider the meanings of their activities in dynamic working environments.

Setting aside time for developing broader understandings
In order to broaden views, it is necessary to set aside time for the staff to reach an understanding of what the NGO is all about. Because the staff's day-to-day work – such as procurement, report writing, translation, meetings with government officers and accounting – does not relate directly to the organization's missions, staff members do not feel any need to sacrifice their valuable time for the missions unless they are given time specifically assigned for the purpose. For example, once a staff member works as an accountant, he or she can manage the job without keeping organizational views in mind. However, working only at one's specialized job tends to lead one to disregard the fundamental missions that are the ostensible reasons for the organization's existence. A field accountant who cares about development warns:

> We look at accounting and project work as one thing. The field accountant should understand more about development work and also more about what goes on in the field rather than trying to say that we need to put figures into

28 A desk officer says, 'The best way to raise money is to show starving children on television, what I would call development pornography, but it works.' Although the organization recognizes that this method does not fit with its mission, making a change is difficult due to the need for funding. Billis and MacKeith (1992) have also identified the tension between raising money and raising awareness as one major organizational issue facing NGOs. Duffield (1991) and Korten (1990a) warn that NGOs may redirect their projects to donor-led activities – a practice known as 'public service contracting' – due to financial flow from donors.

the computer. As an accountant, the person can do accounting, but at the same time, I think he or she is not just locked up in a little corner typing numbers, but being a part of a larger [undertaking].

This strategy suggests that, in order to avoid becoming locked into a narrowly specialized task, and instead to become part of the organization's overall mission, staff members should consciously protect time for understanding organizational activities. To put this concept into practice, he says:

> I would rather take two hours off even if it is necessary for me to take work home to finish. I feel it is important to marry the two together. Accounting, I can take the computer home, it's a laptop, and then work a couple of hours. I would create time to understand what project managers require, or to explain to a project manager why something is needed, so that, in the future, we have good understanding among staff members. I even take work home to do rather than just inputting into the computer in the office.

Three key conditions support this strategy. The first is the accountant's belief that he is there to serve the organization, not simply to do its accounting. Thus, he organizes his schedule based on the benefits to the organization, not just to his own position within it. A second point is the institutionalization of the practice. He protects time for understanding the entire organization regardless of his accounting workload. The third point is the support of his boss concerning his style of work. He understands that his boss, according to him, 'gives me a lot of room to work on my own'. The boss creates a culture that encourages the staff members to serve projects according to their individual capacity, without constraints derived from their positions in the organization.[29]

When the staff are occupied with work on narrowly specialized assignments, protecting time is a strategy to ensure that they maintain a broad view of the entire organization. By broadening their views and adopting the perspective of the organization as a whole, they can better serve the organization's missions.

Protecting informal time
This strategy is based on the premiss that formalization works to protect informal time. As the previous subsection explains, sparing time for something that is not directly related to staff members' immediate tasks is practically difficult, given their workloads. The more business-minded they are, the more occupied they are with their immediate tasks, and the

---

[29] For a discussion of how the culture of the top management is contextualized at the lower level, see Rose (1988, 147): 'Contextualization is assumed to occur through a hierarchical arrangement of several levels of meaning such that meanings at lower levels of the hierarchy are reflexively contextualized by those at higher levels.'

less willing they are to take time for ambiguous tasks such as under-standing the entire organization. As a result, they tend to work only on formalized tasks in a systematic manner. The following account de-scribes a strategy that attempts to counteract this tendency by sparing time for informal reflection that can offer beneficial insights to the staff members:

> The annual meetings have been an excellent place where they bring us all together. It's the only time I talk to somebody who faces the same pressures I do. I meet other country directors that have the same job description as me. 'Oh, you got that problem, too, in your country?' So we can talk. But it's also when there's a relaxed enough atmosphere. We have enough time. We don't try to [cover everything] in five days. It's usually 10 to 14 days. There is plenty of time for social time, for talking, sightseeing, whatever you want to do to build those relationships. So the thing that really impresses me is that I [meet] other people who I actually have a personal relationship with. We write letters back and forth. This week I got letters from Uganda and Bolivia, a phone call from Laos. It's up to me to take the initiative to follow up or not. But there is a fellowship and that meeting has created that.

This strategy attempts to legitimize informal reflections within a formal setting in several ways. First, the strategy involves holding personal, infor-mal reflections within the formal organizational setting. One might argue that informal reflections undermine formal systems and are therefore incompatible with formal systems. However, the account suggests other-wise – i.e., the formal setting does not necessarily diminish the oppor-tunity for informal reflections; nor do the informal reflections undermine the formal organizational structure and functions.[30]

Second, the strategy can effectively convey the impact of informal, personal interactions on the organization because the informal inter-actions are embedded in and processed through a formalized system. The strategy does not devalue formal interactions, but rather attempts to make good use of the formalized system. In this sense, this strategy is effective and wise compared with informal interactions that take place outside the formal setting.

Third, the strategy institutionalizes informal reflection within the NGO. Once the annual meeting is institutionalized as an organizational event, time during the meeting is officially protected. Because the meeting is an official annual event, attending the meeting takes priority over daily tasks. Nevertheless, the meeting itself does not necessarily preclude staff mem-bers from interacting informally with each other. As the account suggests, formally protected time helps to encourage informal interactions. A coun-try director appreciates the function of structure:

---

[30] 'Structure . . . is not to be conceptualized as a barrier to action, but as essentially involved in its production' (Giddens, 1979, 70).

The beauty was that even though there was misunderstanding, the structure [allowed] the time to work it out and the process increased the level of trust.

In his case, misunderstanding between a support office and his country office could be resolved because of the opportunities for interaction that are structurally organized, such as annual meetings. His colleague explains:

As they [talked and] developed personal relationships, they found that there was a lack of communication that resulted in misunderstanding. They came to understand that both of them thought [the same thing].

Compared with formalized informal interactions, informal interactions that take place outside of any formal framework would be more difficult to practise because they are not protected from the demands of staff members' daily, arduous tasks. Formality builds in room for protected informal activities. The strategy actively seeks to normalize, and thus facilitate, informal interactions.

This strategy can be a powerful tool when an NGO tries to improve its capacity to remain flexible, adaptive and responsive by encouraging informal interactions among the staff. However, because it slows down the staff's immediate daily work, it is not cost-effective in the short term. For the strategy to be successful, the organization must look beyond the short term to the benefits it can confer over the long term to the organization's capacity for flexibility, adaptability and responsiveness. However, this strategy and the long-term focus it requires should not be interpreted as devaluing staff members' daily tasks. The staff can plan in advance to have protected informal time and can organize their work schedules accordingly to minimize its negative impact on their daily work.

A structural change after people change
Routinized, systematic daily work is not the only factor that makes NGOs resist change. Staff members themselves are also so accustomed to routinized work that they find it difficult to alter their practices even if a different approach appears to be more promising than their present course of action. When the staff work in a systematic manner, responding to a changing situation is not a matter of deciding which course of action is preferable. Rather, it is a matter of understanding how an alternative course of action can be introduced into an existing system. Rather than focusing on goals, the strategy emphasizes the importance of planning processes through which desirable change can emerge. A planning director at a regional office carefully plans changing processes:

You start from this [grassroots] level and ask if this [project] is effective or not. They say, 'No, all the projects are lasting for twenty years'. So we ask them, 'Is it an appropriate strategy?' And they themselves come and say, 'No, we have probably several alternatives'. So we deliberately started from the grassroots level. And number two, what we have done is we have encouraged cross-functional teams to get a wider perspective. . . . We have to bridge the gap. All the level of the staff in the field understand what is the mission statement that they have, what are the key elements of the country strategies. We deliberately and consciously put anything to do with structural changes at the end. Because we felt that they probably create some sort of instability in the mindset of the people. We don't want to put pressure on to get this done in six months' time. So we are looking at a three-year plan. And then we sent that information to every office of the partnership, and support office, and told them, 'Come on guys, we are working on this, it's going to take two or three years' time, we are moving in this direction. We are sending this to you so that you will have a better understanding of this process and handle this issue carefully.'

The processes for instituting change can be divided into several distinct and ordered activities. To begin with, change begins at the grassroots level, and the change is planned in such a way that it comes from within the organization rather than being enforced by outsiders. Outsiders may take part in the process by questioning and challenging the field staff. As a result, the field staff are motivated to begin considering the quality of their practices.

Second, wider perspectives are introduced by developing cross-functional teams. This helps staff members to step back from their daily activities and gain a broader view of their work. They can then reconsider their specific missions in light of these broader perspectives.

Third, the strategy ensures that a structural change is the end result. Because structures tend to regulate the behaviours of the staff, the change can kill the seeds of individual, voluntary changes, which are more sustainable than externally-enforced change. To ensure an internal, organically-emerging change, ample time must be allowed so that time pressure does not bring about enforcement from the top.

Fourth and finally, to ensure that the processes unfold in an appropriate order, the purpose and goals of the processes should be understood, accepted and promoted by support offices within the organization (see Figure 1 in Chapter 1). This sharing is targeted to allow the field staff enough time to develop themselves without insensitive intervention from the outside. The changing process is like sowing a seed. When you sow a seed in soil, you should not dig it up to check whether it is growing or not. Insensitive intervention will kill the seed, which would otherwise grow and bear fruit in the future. You can only help it grow by providing it with an accommodating environment.

While several accounts have been introduced and discussed as practical alternatives to broaden views, broadening views is a strategy to develop the organization's capacity to remain flexible, adaptive and responsive without totally negating the value of systems and the structure they confer. By broadening views, the staff can identify alternative courses of action that may better serve their needs. Instead of subverting formal, systematic processes, it can supplement them by trying to make better use of them.

Prioritizing the staff over systems[31]

This strategy not only pleases the staff (because it appreciates their values); it also, and more importantly in a practical sense, results in improving the quality of their work as they develop informal reflections. Prioritizing the staff over systems in a working context is difficult to do for two reasons. First, it can often distract the staff from their work. It can lead the staff to disregard formalities, forget their jobs and squander their work time chatting. Second, it requires extra effort for those staff who are preoccupied with immediate tasks. While staff members need to interact with each other to get information, work toward a common goal and negotiate decisions, they do not need to personalize communication to get their jobs done. Even in the face of these discouraging factors, the strategy's expected impact on the practices of the staff and organizational activities can appear to be significant enough to consider seriously. The following accounts present different ways to prioritize the staff over systems. Each account reflects not only the ethical value of the strategy, but also its contribution to the organization and the staff in a practical sense.

Developing multi-dimensional relationships

Contacting face-to-face. Contacting face-to-face is a strategy which contributes not only to building relationships but also to deepening the understanding of the issues concerned. A field officer says:

> If you know the name and the face of the person you are communicating with, you feel at ease, and positive about understanding whether that fellow has a problem or not. It's power. At least the knowledge and the experience would give you good power and a good established relationship, and will also help you tolerate and work with each other.

Face-to-face contact allows the staff to have multi-dimensional and contextually rich interactions. Ways of speaking, listening, looking and acting can all convey a person's message and help other staff members understand the person's concerns, worries, cares, feelings and so forth. Understanding these personal dimensions leads staff members to sympathize with the person and helps to develop the staff's capacity for tolerance.

---

[31] 'Personal initiative plays an ever smaller role in comparison to the plans of those in authority.' Max Horkheimer (1974, 94) quoted in Giddens (1990, 116).

Practically speaking, this type of contact contributes significantly to staff members' judgement,[32] because they can understand issues in a specific context and address them accordingly, instead of simply following abstract guidelines without taking context into account.

Relating as a person. Relating to each other as persons enriches staff members' personal relationships and discourages them from following systems for systems' sake. For example, a senior staff member uses the telephone to relate to other staff members:

> Calling them up. That encourages them. To have somebody talk with them. It is important to me, how they are doing personally. Family life, your wife and kids. I am genuinely interested in that. Usually they have personal problems that they deal with. Sometimes, staff tell me about it. Give them some advice. I hope I can talk with them at least once every couple of months. Just to talk. Just to have a relationship. I also send them personal letters. Maybe sharing things that I am learning. Modelling as opposed to saying you should do this and that. Trying more models by example.

For him, supporting and encouraging his staff members is not an instrumental tool to enable him to work better. Although he identifies this practice as his major task, his genuine interest in his staff makes his interactions quite different from task-oriented interactions. How does this practice affect his staff and benefit the organization? Accounts of two staff members who work under him provide answers to this question:

> I agree with so many things that he says. I'm happy to work with the organization. I'm committed to it.

> [It is] very much servant leadership. I think this is one of the reasons I've stayed with the organization. Because my boss has really modelled servant leadership. I have always felt as though he was in that position as a service to others, and he is trying to do what is best for other people and the organization as a whole as opposed to himself.

The two accounts suggest that these staff members' relationships with their boss are much more than a formal subordinate–boss relationship in several respects. First, the relationships elicit the staff's commitment to serve the organization rather than making them content with systematically getting their jobs done for their own sake. Second, in contrast to conventional subordinate–boss relationships, the boss practises what the staff member calls 'servant leadership' to serve the staff by providing them with a favourable work environment. And 'once . . . you create a quality and enabling environment for the people to work', a field administrator suggests, 'then you do not need to stand behind my back every

---

[32] '[T]o judge is to understand, to understand is to sympathize, and to sympathize is to be able to forgive' (Beiner, 1983, 76).

moment [to supervise me].' Third, as the boss models servant leadership, staff members learn how to serve others in the field. Fourth, because staff members learn servant leadership voluntarily, their consequent practices are sustainable, as opposed to practices imposed by regulatory forces from the top. The less the boss employs formal relationships to regulate his staff to accomplish tasks, achieve goals and promote effectiveness, and the more he cares about the staff as persons, the more success he will have.

This strategy can also be used when NGO staff contact donor staff or government officers. A senior manager explains how the organization got financial support from a government:

> We didn't do a big lobbying campaign. But in an informal setting, we asked the foreign minister. But it's not aggressive, because they are human beings. They are caught within their own bureaucracy. They are caught within their own politics. You don't have to do a protest or a lot of lobbying, if you can get in and talk directly to the Minister. I think we have got a lot of respect from government circles, because we don't try and beat them with a stick. We knew that the foreign minister didn't have a budget for Somalia. There was no point in telling terrible things to him, because that makes him more defensive. So we say, 'Why don't you visit our projects, why don't you see what's happening?' And he did. The foreign minister went to Mogadishu. He came back and fought for the budget.[33]

This is a strategy of neither 'beat [the government] up with a stick' nor show loyalty to the government. While the NGO staff maintain the tensions between the NGO and the government regarding their interests, the NGO staff try to relate to the minister as a person who faces his own set of constraints, pressures and limitations. The strategy demonstrates that informal personal contacts may, at least sometimes, work better than yelling, shouting and protesting.

Valuing emotions[34]

Expressing emotions. Expressing emotions is one of the least formal types of interaction and thus offers significant clues to understanding a person's

---

[33] This, however, is not always a viable scenario. One must consider the contextual advantages in the situation. First, the organization enjoys a favourable reputation and solid public support. Second, the head of the organization is a well-known Catholic father. In a country where most of the population is Catholic, he is not simply the head of the organization but may be viewed as a representative of the population. Third, it was a disaster case for which they appealed for government support. Knowing that disasters can arouse public opinion easily, the government could not ignore it, or to be more precise, it was an opportunity for the government to look good in the eyes of the public by acting in a proper manner. Lastly, this organization is the largest and the most popular one in the country. These factors facilitated their actions. Nevertheless, these advantages do not nullify the value of their approach.

[34] Fineman (1993) offers valuable insights into the considerable roles emotions play in organizations.

concerns, worries and feelings. We learn about each other through emotions.[35] Emotions also reveal how the person relates to others. A desk officer uses her emotional expression in a nice way not only to get her job done but also to sustain her friendships with her colleagues:

> I know the people personally. In this case, I say, 'Send me the information.' If I didn't know them, it would be a different story. It would be a case of, 'Hi, could you please forward information as soon as possible?' And my guess is [it would take] four or five days' time, because people have their own agendas. But I know these people and I can get on the phone and scream, 'Send the bloody information now', and they will. They want to come out here on holiday at some stage. Blackmail people and give me the information.

Whether she strategically uses this communication style or not, it has several advantages. First, she successfully conveys what she needs and, as a consequence, quickly gets what she wants. Emotional expression effectively conveys the urgency of her need for information.

Second, being able to express her emotions demonstrates to others that she is open to them. She also assumes that others can accept her ways of asking as an expression of friendship. When she says 'blackmail people . . .' she does not really mean to scare them. On the contrary, because she feels that she is a friend of theirs, she can say that. This interpretation can be defended when one considers her formal enquiry to a stranger as narrated above.

Third, informal interactions can be supported and enhanced by formal structures.[36] When she asks another staff member a question, the question takes place within the formal framework. But the way she asks the question is informal. Thus she asks a question in an informal fashion within a formal framework. Nevertheless, she gets her job done more quickly than if she had asked in a formal manner.

If she asks a question informally in an informal structure, she might not expect an answer due to the lack of accountability that the informality entails. On the other hand, if she formally asks a question in a formal structure, she might expect that it takes a long time to process it. Her strategy combines the formal and informal interactions properly to get the job done quickly without sacrificing friendship.

Smiling is another way of expressing emotions. Several staff members identified smiling as a major strategy for expressing one's respect for another person. A Thai field staff member cares about ways that people communicate with and respect each other.

> Human beings want to be respected. When you see people, smile even if you can't speak Thai. You smile, they feel warm, and feel that you are friends.

---

[35] Plato's proverb reads, 'All learning has an emotional base.'
[36] Compare with *Protecting informal time* in 'Broadening views' above.

The power of smiling overcomes a language barrier and even breaks through differences in opinions and interests. A senior manager of an NGO explains:

> You have a strategy to let them listen to your opinions, despite the fact that yours are opposed to theirs. When you oppose someone's idea, that person tends to regard you as an enemy. But if you smile and, at the same time, tell the person about your positions and opinions, then you convey a sense of respect to the person despite the difference in opinions. Only in that manner, they get to listen to you and understand the difference. Unless they feel respected, they do not listen to you.[37]

Smiling shows respect and enables staff members to listen to each other. Smiling also enables one to oppose the ideas of another without showing disrespect. If you do not respect the other person, they will not want to listen to you regardless of the formality or content of what you say. Then, because no listening means no reflection and learning, the organization is likely to be set back because learning opportunities have been lost.

When staff members have diverse opinions, views, interests and concerns, smiling is a vital resource for moderating their differences. With smiling, people relate to and learn from each other in the context of respecting differences rather than trying to argue with and convince others.

Protecting room for emotions. Expressing emotions is not always easy. Some environments enable us to express emotion easily while others do not. Constructing suitable environments for expressing emotions is one major goal when the staff value emotions as rich interaction resources.[38]

Several staff members pay attention to the language that they use to encourage personal feelings to come out. The following accounts indicate that expressing emotions, feelings and concerns can best be done in staff members' native languages.

> When I am speaking on the telephone or visiting, I am always speaking in Spanish basically. I think that's important because that allows them to express themselves freely. When I go to the field and communicate with staff, I do my best to try to make opportunities available for staff to talk with me, their personal issues, problems. And that is mostly done in their local language. Some of the staff who I talk to are not able to express themselves fully in English, so I would do my best to listen to them and advise them in their language.

---

[37] Translated from Japanese.
[38] Forester (1989) discusses the relationship between emotion and substance in dealing with negotiation. Van Maanen and Kunda (1989) and Rafaeli and Sutton (1989) offer insights into the relationships between emotional expressions and organizational culture.

Constructing suitable environments is not limited to the language issue. More broadly, it includes ways the staff interact with each other. A field officer presents his communication strategy:

> My communication is that I must speak in the way they can understand me. . . . To me, systems can mean a lot. But the person-to-person contact makes a lot of difference. One has to be open-minded, open to criticism or misunderstanding and open to solving misunderstandings. Nobody told me this, I learned this through experience.

Preparing room for expressing emotion requires care and sensitivity in both speaking and listening. The strategy suggests that one should speak in a way that makes sense to others and listen with an open mind to accept different, contradictory or critical suggestions. If the staff understand that you have a positive attitude toward different, contradictory or critical comments, they can feel free to show their concerns, worries and ideas. On the other hand, if you do not accept critical comments, staff members will not dare to express their real concerns, but rather will concentrate on flattery.

In summary, desirable environments may be developed through sensitive and caring actions undertaken with an open mind. When staff members show their acceptance and respect to other staff as they speak with and listen to each other, they can protect room for real concerns, worries and feelings to emerge. To encourage the staff members to develop this kind of relationship with each other, an organization should try to develop non-threatening communication environments in which all staff members can express their interests, concerns, feelings and worries without feeling much pressure from others. As the above quotes can imply, one way to develop better communication environments is to employ a communication system where higher-ups in the organizational hierarchy adjust themselves to the communication modes of the field staff lower in the hierarchy. For example, in an environment where local languages are used as the medium of communication, the field staff can express themselves much better than if they had to use their second, third or fourth language.

Caring for personal concerns before relying on systems
Informal discussions are more likely to elicit accurate reflections regarding staff members' concerns and interests and their perceptions of each other. This mode of communication works especially well if they deal with sensitive or important issues. A field officer describes a typical case:

> If I have such an important issue that I have to deal with and don't know how people perceive it, in the past, I would normally write it down and get a response from them. Now, I do it differently. It will cost a little bit more. I ring them up over the phone, give my view, ask them how they see it. Once it

comes to an agreement, I write it. Because English is my second language, I may not be able to express it quite well. But if I talk over the phone, I say, 'This is my concern, how do you see it from your end? Is this OK?' So I need to support him so that he can support me as well. I can't win if he loses. I'm not saying that I have to please him. If what I'm doing is good, it must be good for him as well. It can't be good for me and bad for him. I'm writing more with approval rather than asking and then returning and asking more questions, and they answer. It will enhance communication.

Although he does not totally devalue systematic, formal interactions, he strategically distinguishes the time to use formal, systematic interactions from the time to use informal interactions. Employing informal interactions before formalizing an issue benefits the staff in several ways.

First, informal communication is suitable for sharing ideas and developing consensus. He can get informal reflections from his colleague while simultaneously explaining his ideas to them. In contrast with formal communication that needs to go through formal, time-consuming channels, informal ones can go back and forth without lengthy procedures.

Second, because informal communication tends to become a sharing process, both staff members involved try to achieve a both-gain solution[39] rather than competing to beat each other. The informal communication allows a staff member to say, 'If what I'm doing is good, it must be good for him as well. It can't be good for me and bad for him.'

Third, informal communication over the phone or face-to-face can easily convey not only this person's idea but also his feelings, interests, worries and concerns. He can express himself more accurately by changing tone and speed, emphasizing words and so forth as he speaks. This feature is especially beneficial for non-native speakers like him.

Lastly, the lack of accountability in informal communication enables staff members to speak more freely. It releases them from the constraints imposed by their positions in the organization. The less formal the interaction, the less the people involved need to take responsibility for what they say, and the more freely they can express their real feelings, concerns and interests.

Strategies of putting people first before systems, developing multidimensional relationships, valuing emotions and caring for personal concerns have been discussed. Although these strategies are all informal and cannot be formally instituted by the organization, they can be promoted by the organization. This section has descriptively presented strategic practices employed by NGO staff in their day-to-day work, instead of systematically describing the strategies in a formal manner.

The strategic practices are fragile and have rather weak rational bases because of their informality and non-task oriented nature. However, a

---

[39] See Susskind and Cruikshank (1987).

number of NGO staff members identify informal reflections as a vital means for an organization to remain flexible, adaptable and responsive.

Conclusion

This chapter has treated a broad range of commonly-shared functions as systems. Systems include not only rules, regulations and policies, but also money, languages and *modus operandi*. These systems, or commonly shared functions, are all important for NGOs to function properly. However, the systems are often accompanied by undesirable side effects. Systems tend to decrease an organization's capacity to remain flexible, adaptable and responsive, despite this capacity's vital importance in addressing diverse and changing problems in the field.

This chapter began by discussing the rationales for systems and then examined the undesirable effects that the NGO staff experience when they apply systems. The relationship between the rationale for systems and their undesirable impact illuminates the gaps between the systems and reality. Employment terms, money, languages and *modus operandi* have been introduced as examples of systems to examine the gaps between their expected functions and their real impact on the organization.

Addressing problems that derive from the tensions between the rationale and the negative impact, the second half of this chapter has explored strategic practices that are employed by NGO staff members. The strategies, instead of addressing the identified problems directly, attempt to judge the characteristics of systems, supplementing them in some cases and making better use of them in others. The findings of this study indicate that, to make wise judgements and take appropriate actions, staff members must have the opportunity to engage in informal reflection. The two main approaches to developing informal reflection are broadening views and prioritizing the staff over systems.

CHAPTER 7

Going Beyond Systems

*There are a lot of requirements, unnecessary requirements and rules that
they have to follow, that make them busy. Everything goes into a circle.
They want to prevent something happening by creating rules and regulations. Changing rules means more rules.*

Former field officer

'Yes, it's good to write a manual, but don't forget why you wrote it.'

Senior officer

Introduction

THE PREVIOUS CHAPTER discussed the ways in which systems such as rules,
regulation and policies impair NGOs' responsiveness and flexibility; it
then introduced and analysed strategies that staff members use to address
these problems without subverting the important functionality of systems.
However, this study's findings reveal that systems not only play regulatory roles in NGOs, as explained in the previous chapter, but they also
establish an autonomously perpetuated sphere for systems' own sake.
Systems are human-made. But once they are ingrained and legitimized in
an organization, they can sustain themselves independently and tend to
become separate from the staff who created them.

This chapter argues that systems gain autonomy, perpetuate themselves, and shape the behaviour of the staff to comply with them. The
first half of the chapter identifies and analyses two broadly divergent
mechanisms by which systems perpetuate their control: systems' construction of their own autonomous worlds, for example by developing
rules that in turn lead to the development of more rules for their own
sake; and systems' function as catalysts to perpetuate hierarchical differences, for example through the systematic employment of rules,
which results in clarifying, reinforcing and perpetuating the hierarchy of
those rules.

The second half of the chapter introduces strategies that the staff members use in practice to address the problems that arise from self-
perpetuated systems. Judging systems, using tensions, and using ambiguity are discussed as three general strategies, each of which has several
variations.

Problems: Perpetuated control mechanisms

Constructing their own worlds

NGOs' systems such as rules, regulations and policies do not simply serve the purposes for which they were defined. In addition, they construct their own closed worlds and perpetuate themselves in unexpected ways. This section describes three self-regulating mechanisms that are observed in NGOs. First, the way administration and operation relate to each other systematically augments their differences and dichotomizes the organization. Second, once a rule is introduced, it leads to another rule, which requires still another rule, and so on, to perpetuate the rule-making process for the rules' sake. Third, the more the staff 'participate' in a collective activity, the more they have opportunities to clarify their differences in interests, intentions, and positions, and, thus, the more they demand 'participation', which they treat as opportunities to persuade others. These cases all demonstrate the self-perpetuating mechanisms embedded in the systems that organizations employ.[1]

Systematic gap between administration and operation

The differences between administration and operation are not merely functional differences in the organization. The way administration and operation relate to each other systematically augments their differences and dichotomizes the organization. In NGOs, the differences are deeply embedded in the organization at both the organizational and the individual levels. Organizationally, HQs usually play administrative roles while FOs perform operational roles. At the individual level, each staff member works for either administration or operation.

Functionally, administration is supposed to support operations, while operations carry out projects. But this functional difference does not describe their real relationships. They both identify their differences, but in different ways. The voices of a field officer and a financial controller offer a clue to understanding the gap, for the financial aspects of administration reveal distinctive differences from operations. The field officer vividly describes the tensions she feels between the two:

> Finance people don't get out to see what field conditions are like. So they don't really know what it's like out in these remote places. And the other thing is that finance people think like finance people whether it's people in headquarters, or whether it's people in a country office, or even someone in a project site. They look at figures more than looking at people and that's where the real problem is. For them, at the end, everything has to balance, but in some of these conditions, things just don't.

---

[1] See DiMaggio and Powell (1983), to compare with the irreversible momentum of bureaucratization.

A dedicated financial controller provides a different view concerning the administration-operation issue:

> If they want to construct a dam, I will know beforehand how much money they require. I transfer 50 per cent of it, and ask them how much they spent. They send the vouchers, I check it, satisfy myself, and transfer the rest of the money. Concerning finance, everything is in the manual. There is written guidance there. Everything is there. When you [establish] a good system, people work well. If your system is bad, people work poorly. We really do check the system. Otherwise, we can change a person for another person. So long as the system is there, anybody would be able to do [the work].

The two views clarify the gap between HQ and the field in different ways. First, the staff of HQ and the field staff locate the cause of the discrepancy between them in different places. The field officer attributes the gap to accounting people whose mindsets are too narrow to consider the reality of the field. On the other hand, the financial controller regards the gap as a function of their systems. Hence, their suggested solutions are also different. The field officer proposes that accounting people need to widen their views to understand the field, while the financial controller would close the gap by improving the organization's financial systems. Because the suggested approaches to closing the gap differ substantially, the gap is augmented by the very attempts to close it in conflicting ways.

Second, financial issues and operational issues have different frameworks. Finance-related tasks have a clear framework in which they can be performed. The line between financial and other tasks is clear and unambiguous. Financial officers can identify what they need in input from the field and what they are supposed to produce as output. They have a clear time schedule to follow. They do not need to take into account environmental changes, for those changes have little impact on their day-to-day work.

In contrast, the framework for operation is not clear. Those who are engaged in operation-related tasks deal with 'development', which, for a number of reasons, cannot be categorized into a set of mechanistic processes. First, development deals with people who cannot simply be reduced to numbers. Second, operation deals with a variety of issues that people face in different socio-economic environments and at different times. Third, operation takes place in unstable environments because social, political and economic environments in the Third World are highly erratic and unpredictable.[2] Because administration and operation work within totally different frameworks, the staff on the one side fail even to

---

[2] For a discussion of the ways that specialization filters perception and influences behaviour, see Lawrence and Lorsch (1967).

understand how the staff on the other side identify the gap differently. The efforts of both sides, hence, lack a common ground on which to develop mutual understanding.

Third, systems such as rules and regulations distract administration and operation from interacting with each other to resolve the gap between the two. A field officer critically observes this tendency in HQ:

> People in the headquarters have their own problems, bureaucracy that they have to deal with. They are divided into different offices: the finance office, the project office, etc., and sometimes these departments do not talk to each other. These departments have their own rules and regulations that require this and that. They are not really looking at the reality. People in the headquarters are more concerned about the accomplishments of the papers. Papers should be good. But that is not what development is all about.

Rules and regulations separate one department from other departments.[3] Ironically, rules and regulations, which are supposed to improve departments' and organizations' effectiveness and efficiency, tend to fragment them into pieces and diminish their effectiveness and efficiency as a whole.[4]

Both administration and operations develop their own rules and regulations that fit their specific needs. However, the more they try to meet specific requirements by doing so, the more narrow-minded they become. As a result, each side may concentrate on its immediate needs, even if doing so has a negative impact on the other and on the organizational missions as a whole.

These three differences – perspectives, frameworks, and rules and regulations – all pull administration and operations apart. The staff not only work on either administrative issues or operational ones but also augment the differences as they work in the different spheres. Ultimately, this situation dichotomizes the organization.

Rules lead to more rules

When an NGO develops systems, staff members need to analyse carefully not only their positive but also their negative impacts on the organization. Systems often possess internal reproduction mechanisms to perpetuate and multiply themselves. Rules encourage the staff to make more rules. Although rules provide the staff with benefits such as standardization, guidance and consistency, they are not panaceas. They can indicate general guidelines and directions but they do not necessarily provide concrete answers to specific questions. Rules are helpful tools but cannot

---

[3] Co-ordination between different departments is problematic. See Billis and MacKeith (1992).
[4] For an overview of critiques of the nature of bureaucracy, see, for example, Fischer and Sirianni (1984).

make judgements by themselves.[5] The staff are the ones who apply systems to make sense in a given context. Hence, ambiguity always exists in the interaction between the staff and systems because staff members cannot mechanically apply a system to a specific context without using their judgement:

> There are a lot of requirements, unnecessary requirements and rules that they have to follow, that make them busy. Everything goes into a circle. They want to prevent something happening by creating rules and regulations. But then they are so busy following rules and requirements that they do not have time. Changing rules means more rules.

This field staff member realizes that no rules and regulations can cover all possible situations. There will always be some issue or situation which is not anticipated by existing rules and regulations. When the staff members face such an issue, they either unreasonably continue to apply existing rules and regulations, or they modify them to make sense of the issue at hand. These two approaches embody different tensions respectively.

The staff can easily follow the first course of action unless they intentionally try to make a change. Once rules and regulations are in place, changing them goes against the natural dynamic of the organization.[6] In fact, rules and regulations make sense only when they are fairly stable, even under changing circumstances. If they change often, they cannot set standards. Despite the need for stability in rules and regulations, however, rigidity is also problematic. If rules and regulations are not flexible in the face of changing situations, they move totally beyond staff members' control. Rules and regulations can regulate the staff in undesirable ways.

For example, once a financial system is developed and gains legitimacy within an organization, the staff may follow it without critically considering its relevance to their situations. Following the system is an easier and safer practice than analysing it critically because the staff are protected from criticism insofar as they comply with the system, even if it does not make sense. This risk-averse practice maintains the *status quo* in the organization. A country director vividly describes this situation:

> There is a big discrepancy between the reality and theory. There is a theory that we have this wonderful financial budget system. But in fact it is very rigid, and the reality is that we've treated it as being very flexible. And nobody shouts. It looks like they put a lot of effort into something very sophisticated.

---

[5] Dewey and Tufts (1910, 333) distinguish rules from principles, 'Rules are practical; they are habitual ways of doing things. But principles are intellectual; they are useful methods of judging things.'

[6] Pfeffer (1982, 234) argues that rules are likely to remain in existence for a long time, 'in part, because no individual knows enough about all the organization's operations really to question the fundamental premises underlying the decision rule'.

Changing systems to make sense is a courageous and challenging practice. The danger is that once the staff members begin making new rules, regulations or policies to respond to new issues, they are tempted to become involved in endless system development. They may start making rules for rules' sake.

When the staff rely on systems too much, they can get caught in either of two traps: strictly following the existing systems with little reflection, or perpetually developing new systems. When systems are too rigid, they control the staff more than necessary. On the other hand, when systems change frequently, they fail to set consistent standards for the staff. In either case, systems have a detrimental impact on the staff and perpetuate themselves for their own sake.

Battlefield called 'participation'[7]

Participation, a concept that enjoys broad support among people who value democracy,[8] is not problem-free. Too little or too much participation are both problematic in an NGO. The former tends to lead to the development of an authoritarian, top-down organization, while the latter tends to make co-ordination among the staff unwieldy.

NGO staff members generally do not disagree with broad staff participation in decision-making processes. However, in day-to-day work, the practices of participation do not always bring about what NGOs value or seek.[9] Broad participation of the entire staff in making decisions is too idealistic and naive a goal in practice. A field officer describes a case in which 'participation' in an NGO was systematically distorted to produce and reproduce a top-down structure in the organization:

> Field offices were asked to submit plans. But in terms of being a part of the decision-making process, they had only a minimum influence. It was these headquarters and support offices that tended to make decisions about what systems were needed, whereas field offices were seen primarily as respondents.

Two different types of participation are involved in this account. While FOs' participation takes the form of responding to HQ's requests, HQ's participation takes the form of developing a framework in which FOs'

---

[7] Ritualized meetings may have positive and negative influences (Gutmann 1993).

[8] Fishkin (1991) presents three conditions for democracy: political equity, the absence of tyranny and deliberation. Carr (1990, 62) points out the danger of common knowledge, i.e., that '[it] may assume . . . [that] democracy is reduced to elections. . . . It confuses cause with structural cause, such as the belief that poor health is caused by lack of adequate food but that the latter has nothing to do with land ownership. Common knowledge does not view the whole, the structure, only isolated elements.'

[9] While much literature emphasizes the relevance of people-centred approaches – see, for example, Brown (1985), Daley and Angulo (1990), Friedmann (1992), Korten (1990a), and Lovell (1992) – Dichter (1989) cautions that the 'people centred' approach devalues other forms of projects without careful consideration.

participation takes place.[10] For the field, participation means the implementation of HQ's plans.[11] But for HQ, participation means crucial decision-making[12] on organizational policies, missions and systems.[13]

These assigned, unequal types of participation cause tensions between the staff at HQ and at FOs. The field staff challenge the unequal participation by advocating consensus decision-making, in which all different entities within an NGO participate in the process so that the decisions reflect their views. This solution, however, causes another kind of problem. A staff member in HQ worries about the consequences of this approach:

> There has been an increased emphasis on consensus decision-making almost to the point where it's impossible to do anything without getting the consensus of nearly everyone in the partnership. They wanted representatives and the meeting became so unwieldy. We had 40 people sitting in the room all talking at once. It became impossible.

While this staff member emphasizes the difficulty of co-ordination among the staff, the issue is not solely a matter of co-ordination ability. The issue is that the various members compete for their interests and rights rather than co-operating in shared endeavours. Participants try to maximize and protect their own offices' benefits, if not their personal benefits.[14] Consequently, participation simply fuels internal conflicts and competition. The same staff member describes how the field staff understand the meaning of participation in their given contexts:

> A lot of people would no longer accept the final design because they did not have a say in it. You can argue that that's democracy. But it's unwieldy. You end up with decision-making that takes months if not literally years for anything significant to be decided on and changed. We can't get a decision made without checking with everyone. No one is willing to give up some of the autonomy of their offices. They are not willing to allow task forces to simply do their job and be done with it without having a say in what's going on. So, it's become a very unwieldy process.

This unwieldy situation in the name of participation can be intolerable for those staff who suffer from it. The sufferers address the problem by

---

[10] Forester (1989, 67–71) examines how organizations systematically discourage certain interest groups from participation in important decision-making processes.

[11] Chambers (1996) argues that submissive participation – ' "they" participate in "our" project' (246) – is a result of top-down planning.

[12] March (1981, 232) suggests the importance of the decision-making process: 'Decision-making is, in part, a performance designed to reassure decision-makers and others that things are being done appropriately'.

[13] See Cohen and Uphoff (1980) for different types of participation.

[14] Barber (1984, 174) warns that talk can easily be confused with speech and speech is reduced to the articulation of interest: 'It is far easier for representatives to speak for us than to listen for us.'

raising the fundamental question of what participation can do for NGO activities. After serving many years as a country director, this staff member has found consensus decision-making in HQ hard to appreciate:

> How much value does it add if 10 or 15 people [participate] in the decisions versus five who know the subject? It's much more efficient, and we are not that efficient. We made a decision, and someone says, 'No I don't agree'. Then you start over again. I find that is really hard. I don't have a final say because I have bosses above me.

NGO staff face a continually unresolved tension between the top-down participation format with fewer participants versus the horizontal participation format with many participants.[15] Several components that fuel tensions and conflicts among the staff can be drawn from the above accounts.

Number of participants. The number of participants is the easiest, yet least useful, criterion by which to judge participation. Should the value of participation be measured solely by the number of participants? By reducing the value of participation to the sheer number of participants, NGO staff lose an opportunity to take other valuable aspects of participation into consideration.[16] Dealing only with the number of participants trivializes participation and encourages an unsophisticated view of the meaning of participation.

Ambiguity of the term 'participation'. This abstract term leaves a lot of room for interpretation. For example, some staff may consider it to mean taking part in decision-making processes while other staff may consider it to mean taking part in project implementation.

Because NGO staff members take the term 'participation' for granted, so long as they use 'participation', they think they are speaking the same language regardless of what their use of the term is meant to imply. However, when the staff clarify what they mean by 'participation', they reveal differences in the meaning of the word, which throws into question the value of their common language. Hence, instead of clarifying 'participation', keeping the term's meaning ambiguous is wise if the staff members want to conceal their real intentions.

Participation justifying personal interests. The staff members can use the ambiguity of the concept of participation in their own interests.[17]

---

15 Milofsky (1988b) analyses the tensions between leaders and members of an organization with respect to their participation in decision-making processes.
16 See Rahnema (1990).
17 Ambiguity is one major tool to address problems derived from systems (see 'Using ambiguity' in the strategy part of this chapter, pp. 186–90). However, ambiguity, like other tools, can also be abused in the pursuit of personal interests.

Especially when they do not trust each other, invoking 'participation' can become a strategic tool to protect their own rights or even maximize their benefits. They 'participate' to assert their rights, interests, benefits and so forth. In the name of participation, fighting for the benefits of each office or individual can be legitimized. Even if some staff members use 'participation' as the battle field on which they fight for their personal benefits, other staff members cannot easily criticize their 'participation', for the concept is a broadly shared and highly-valued one.

Institutionalized participation. Once consensus decision-making based on the participation of the entire staff becomes a legitimate participation style, the style tends to be institutionalized and embedded in the organization, and becomes a rule. This rule, then, starts to regulate and shape the behaviour of the staff, and comes to be seen as the only way to make decisions, even if it is 'a very unwieldy process'.

In the name of participation, the staff in HQ can compel the field staff to carry out what the HQ wants them to do. On the other hand, the field staff members challenge this distorted demand by vigorously asserting their rights to participate in all decision-making processes. 'Participation' can easily become a strategic tool for both of them to pursue and protect their own interests rather than to share ideas and develop coordinated practices. Through 'participation', the staff of both sides separate themselves from each other to construct two exclusive worlds: HQ and FOs.

Systems as a catalyst to reproduce hierarchy

Systems are closely related to hierarchy. A desk officer succinctly addresses their relationship:

> In the system, you need some standards. To have one system, you've got to agree on definitions, terms like data items. You almost need some hierarchy in order to get to an agreement.

This account advances the argument that maintaining order in an NGO requires some degree of hierarchy.[18] This section goes farther to argue that hierarchy is not simply the product of systems; rather, the two are symbiotic, such that systems and hierarchies reinforce and perpetuate each other. Six hierarchically structured components – perspectives, issues, staff members' positions, credibility, the value of experience and job titles – are discussed to show how each of them reproduces and perpetuates the hierarchical structure in different ways.

---

[18] For a detailed discussion of the relationships between systems and hierarchy, see 'Decentralization and loss of order' in Chapter 4.

Different perspectives

A senior regional officer explains the gap in frameworks between HQ and the field. His vivid account is worth quoting at length.

> The field offices are working under the framework of well-defined objectives and mission statements. They have immediate needs to meet. The way they think is in terms of defined boundaries. They do not properly visualize or understand the vision. But these people in headquarters are operating under the notion that the field staff have the same type of understanding. Enhancing the quality of life of these people living in this particular village by providing so and so. That is the goal at the top level. But if you go and ask the people who are working at the grassroots level, they would never see their activities in terms of enhancing the quality of life, for it will be giving shots to 200 children, immunizing 15 expectant mothers. The higher perspective, they are not able to visualize that. Headquarters cannot feel what it means to carry out this programme and put it in statement for implementation.

The account shows, with an example, that each side fails to understand the other due to the difference in the scale of frameworks.[19] While the field staff fail to view broad organizational missions in their day-to-day work, the HQ staff not only fail to understand field staff members' views but also mistakenly believe that the field staff's view is the same as their own.[20] HQ and the field are on a par with each other as far as the lack of understanding is concerned. However, this account does not only address the gap as a product of hierarchy. He continues:

> But they [headquarters] are the decision-makers. So they eventually end up making decisions which do not take problems into consideration, and anything that comes from headquarters is viewed in the fields as less relevant or as bureaucratic, and as evidence that they [headquarters] want to control the field staff. Headquarters teaches what they may call the systems or procedures in order for this project to come out with flying colours to the donors, and so on.

HQ's superior position over the field makes its negative influences on the field more serious than those of the field on HQ. To be accountable to donors, HQ needs to ask the field to do what donors request. Hence, in the name of organizational accountability, HQ makes irrelevant or insensitive demands on the field due to lack of understanding of the field situations. But the field is expected to respond to the requests because of

---

[19] Linking the 'micro' with the 'macro' is one major issue that faces NGOs (Edwards, 1994).

[20] The lack of understanding is not confined to the relationship between headquarters and field offices. A desk officer who is at the lower ladder within headquarters claims, 'The head of the division doesn't have an appreciation of detailed problems, because obviously they can't get involved in the detailed problems'. This implies that the lack of understanding – the gap – between people at higher levels in the organization and those at lower levels is more generally observed by the former.

its subordinate position, despite the irrelevance of the requests. HQ demonstrates its superiority over the field in that, as this officer says, '[headquarters] wants to control the fields'. If the field does not respond properly to HQ's demands, HQ perceives that the field has failed, because HQ does not see the irrelevance of its demands.

As HQ interacts with the field, it repeatedly exercises its control over the field in a top-down relationship. When, as the officer noted, 'Headquarters teaches what they may call the systems, procedures in order for this project to come out with flying colours to the donors', HQ enhances the top-down relationship. The difference in frameworks between HQ and the field not only is a result of the hierarchical structure but is also a cause of hierarchy at the same time.

Organizational issues over operational issues
In an NGO, organizational issues and operational issues often conflict with each other to create tensions. Operationally, an NGO has a set of missions. The missions of most NGOs include neither profit making nor organizational maintenance, but rather facilitating the efforts of those in need to support themselves. But organizationally, an NGO must deal with another set of issues. For example, it needs to obtain resources from its environments for its organizational survival and maintenance.[21] Because neither operational issues nor organizational issues can be ignored in NGO activities,[22] tensions emerge whenever the two aspects of the organization conflict.

Nevertheless, the tensions *per se* are not the issue here. The issue is the impact of the tensions on the organization. An operations director characterizes the tensions:

> I'm dealing with operational issues. The president and the vice-presidents are dealing with political issues. So political issues of the organization come here and you always have some tensions here. Although operationally it's correct, politically it may not be correct in terms of our relationships with some of our donors, and our relationship with the US public.

Although the director does not complain about organizational issues *per se*, he does not like the way organizational issues are treated *vis-à-vis* operational issues. The director would want the two types of issues treated equally. Because the organization is structured hierarchically, organizational issues, dealt with by the top leadership, are always prioritized over operational issues, which are dealt with mainly by the field

---

[21] See Hunter and Staggenborg (1988).
[22] Weisbrod (1988) discusses the relationship between funds and activities, arguing that NGOs must make joint decisions on funding and project activities. For a study of the relationship between resources and organizations, see Pfeffer and Salancik (1978).

staff.[23] Organizational issues would be likely to shape operations to a great extent, but not vice versa.[24] The combination of resource acquisition needs and hierarchically structured job divisions contributes to this one-way relationship between organizational issues and operational issues. In the one-way relationship, as organizational issues systematically redirect and alter the nature of operations to serve the interests of organizational maintenance, the top-down structure is reproduced and strengthened.

Apathy and fears of raising voices

Vertical classifications in an NGO are not only functionally ordered differences. The apathy[25] and fears of the local staff also contribute to vertical differences. In NGO contexts, the local staff often feel subordinated[26] and are not at ease with expressing their own ideas. When they are interviewed, they rarely express their feelings toward their bosses, with the exception of one courageous local.[27] This exceptional voice is invaluable for gaining insight into the mindsets of the local staff:

> It's difficult to tell that to our boss. I don't feel good about that. I mean it's his private business. I feel that he doesn't work 100 per cent. But I shouldn't say anything because I don't think I should criticize the boss. He is doing it anyway.

His boss works on a personal agenda in conjunction with development projects, and he does not like that. Among more than 30 local staff, he is the only exceptional person who could point this out. But even in this person's case, he did not raise the point to his boss because of his mixed

---

[23] See Handy (1990), Hughes (1991), Jackall (1983), Mizrahi and Rosenthal (1993), Mumby and Putnam (1992), Scott (1992), Silverman (1971) and Tsoukas (1992) on tensions between organizational means and ends. Billis and MacKeith (1992) point out that the board lacks members who know the field situation better and directs the organization based on its members' different backgrounds and priorities.

[24] NGOs try to promote their values and raise the awareness of donors regarding development. However, their advocacy is always secondary due to the importance of fundraising. As far as NGOs get funding from donors, they can hardly play a critical role in educating donors (Billis, 1992; Edwards and Hulme, 1992a).

[25] Handy (1990, 75) argues, 'The apathy and disillusion of many people in organizations, the indifference and apparent indolence of the unemployed is often due to the fact that there is no room for their purposes or goals in our scheme of things.' Hill (1979, 282) also critically analyses how people lose their capacity for action in an organization setting, 'Defined as jobholders, men become isolated into their discrete functions in the economy and lose all sense of sharing in a common world, let alone the sense of their capacity to take common initiatives in order to affect the course of affairs. They become increasingly dependent on administrative organizations to govern the world, and give up participation in voluntary associations, so that isolation, passivity and apathy displace their capacity for action.'

[26] In the study of organizational behaviour, the subordination of an organization to its leadership is sometimes referred to as the 'iron law of oligarchy'. See, for example, Fischer and Sirianni (1984) and Perrow (1972).

[27] Taking care of emotion is the same as taking care of substance, as 'emotion and substance are interwoven' (Forester, 1989, 94).

feeling of apathy (the boss does not listen to him) and fear (the boss may treat him coldly).[28]

The issue here is not whether the boss can work on his agendas or not, but whether the local staff can express their feelings, concerns and views to their bosses.[29] In situations in which the local staff fail to communicate with their bosses due to their apathy or fear, the distorted interactions between the local staff and their bosses intensify vertical differences.

Hierarchically ordered credibility

A senior field officer observes a contradictory implication regarding the credibility of the staff's speech:

> If you say, 'This is how we do it', they may be open to it. But it may not always be easy. You should have the credibility to say it. It's the person who says it that matters.

He understands that bosses can listen to their subordinate staff, if the staff have credibility for what they say. But their credibility is usually low for the very reason that they are in subordinate positions. The higher the staff members are on the NGO's hierarchical ladder, the more responsibility they have and thus the more credibility they are regarded as having.

People in lower positions, therefore, are inclined to feel that their views do not have credibility *vis-à-vis* their bosses and HQ. Organizational hierarchy develops differences in credibility levels accordingly. The less seniority the staff have in the organization, the less their ideas are taken into account. Hence, the lower-level staff remain at a lower level because vertically ordered credibility reinforces hierarchy.[30]

Less field input results in still less concern about the field

After working in the field for years as a country director and gaining a lot of valuable experience through projects, this staff member came back to HQ to find himself at the bottom of the organizational ladder:

> You have people with a lot of work, with a lot of experience, but suddenly back here [at headquarters] there is no room to express that. And they get very frustrated.

At least as far as this NGO is concerned, a country director position, which is at the top in the field, would still be equivalent to the bottom of

---

[28] Boulding (1989, 43) suggests the difficulty of conveying information from the bottom to the top: 'By the time it reaches the top it may produce images of the world that are quite unrealistic. This is particularly true of bad news. Nobody wants to convey bad news to a superior.'

[29] For the quality of enquiry in the context of organization, see Argyris and Schön (1974, 1978) and Schön (1983).

[30] Becker (1970, 18) states, 'We are . . . morally bound to accept the definition imposed on reality by a superordinate group in preference to the definitions espoused by subordinates. Thus, credibility and the right to be heard are differentially distributed through the ranks of the system.'

the hierarchical ladder in HQ. His job does not draw much on his field experiences, his skills developed in the field, and his knowledge about the field. Moreover, his responsibility and autonomy are quite limited, so his valuable comments or suggestions derived from his experiences are not taken seriously by other staff in HQ, as discussed above. In the hierarchy, the field situations would not easily reach the leadership at HQ. Then, because the leaders do not grasp the situations in the field, they can only apply their own framework to regulate the field. Here again, hierarchy is systematically maintained.

Titles: fueling hierarchy

Lastly, job titles are another source for the maintenance of organizational hierarchy.[31] Job titles and descriptions are given to the staff to clarify their areas of responsibility, tasks and roles. Although the titles are given as functional conveniences, they can often work subtly to maintain and reproduce organizational hierarchy. A senior field manager in a Christian NGO worries about the negative impact of titles on the organization:

> The structure is set up just to make people know where they are, what their responsibility is. I can say that even Christians sometimes forget, [and act] like 'Oh, I'm director, I'm bigger than you, manager'.

In day-to-day work, each time the staff members come across their titles, they are reminded of their positions in the structure of the organization. As the staff members remember their positions, they can easily project their titles on to the organizational hierarchy and compare their positional differences vertically rather than simply identifying their areas of responsibility, tasks and roles. Consequently, the titles become a source of vertical comparisons that can fuel competition among the staff instead of enhancing co-operative work. When a competitive atmosphere dominates the organization, the staff can easily be tempted to seek their own promotion rather than to achieve organizational missions. Thus, the titles can work to reproduce hierarchy in the organization.

Strategies: Living with dilemmas[32]

The first half of this chapter has argued that self-perpetuating systems create contradictory problems in many cases. For example, while a rule itself may be convenient, the rule can initiate endless rule making. In the face of the contradictory problems, staff members need to be equipped with strategies to come to terms with contradictory situations. Judging

---

[31] Axelrod (1984, 149) argues that '[Labels] can support status hierarchies'.
[32] The importance of maintaining a contradictory situation rather than trying to resolve it is one major theme in the current multicultural world. See Said (1993).

systems, using tensions and using ambiguity are alternative practices to address the problems.

Judging systems[33]

NGO staff members are expected to follow rules and regulations so that they can work in a coherent manner. However, at the same time, they are in charge of systems. They not only follow but also manage the systems simultaneously. The following strategies provide insight into the ways the staff balance the tensions between following and managing the systems. The strategies do not involve disregarding the systems altogether. Rather, they try to spare room for the staff to judge and make better use of the systems as powerful supports.

A manual, not THE manual

In diverse, dynamic field contexts, not all systems can be totally reliable. For example, a manual that is useful in one situation does not necessarily make sense in another situation. Judging whether a manual is applicable in a given context or not is left up to the staff because the manual itself does not specify the conditions in which it can make sense.[34] However, the danger is that a manual often acquires a strong authority to become THE manual and influences the staff to follow it blindly without judgement.[35] Facing this problem, a director of operations vividly presents his stance on the matter:

> One of the tasks I have is to keep reminding people, 'Yes it's good to write a manual, but don't forget why you wrote it.' Because what can happen is it becomes THE manual. We were in Somalia. The plane with food was coming into Mogadishu airport. But we were saying, 'We can't take it from the airport to the store.' Why? Because we haven't got a budget for the transport. I said, 'It's crazy.' If our field director doesn't have the money, borrow it. Pure nonsense. But that's what happens when you get [things on] paper and they become very formal. We were able to deploy in Bangladesh in a cyclone, right that instant. Our country director spent more than $400 000 without communication. He was actually carrying out the mission of organization. As long as that makes sense, as long as it's not doing something stupid, that's all about the quality of people. If you have field directors, you must trust[36] them to make decisions.

---

[33] Implementing even the simplest rules require judgement. See Howard (1994).

[34] '[T]he domain of practical deliberation is defined in terms of contingencies and particulars. The latter, especially, is seen as the characteristic mark of deliberative reason. Deliberation is assigned the role of applying universals in the midst of the particular. Practical wisdom must "be familiar with particulars, since it is concerned with action and action has to do with particulars" ' (Beiner, 1983, 92).

[35] See *Rules lead to more rules* in this chapter, 'Constructing their own worlds' for a discussion of similar tensions.

[36] Trust is not merely an interpersonal matter. It is seen as a key component for quality organizations. See, for example, Fox (1974) and Kramer and Tyler (1996) for discussions of risks and the contributions of trust to organizations.

The director emphasizes two important components that enable the staff to keep the manual in perspective. One is judgement and the other is trust. Judgement does not answer the question: how do the staff better follow the manual? Rather, it reframes the question to ask: what problems do the staff need to respond to in what manner? How does the manual help the staff respond to the problems? Should the staff follow the manual or not? This shift in questions reduces the authority of a manual from an 'unquestionable' document to a helpful guide that facilitates their judgement. The reframing releases the views of the staff from goal-oriented narrow ones and allows them to explore, reformulate and judge their issues.[37]

The director refers to trust as a vital resource for making judgements.[38] Trust motivates him to encourage the staff to make judgements rather than to follow manuals automatically. With trust, he argues, staff members can make courageous decisions. They can free themselves from the myth of the absoluteness of the manuals and even break rules and regulations to strive for their objectives based on their judgement.

Where, then, does trust come from? His trust appears to originate from a belief in the quality of people. He says at another part of his interview, 'people are not impotent like oxen'. He treats human beings as more than machines which can only follow manuals. Having said that, however, one cannot easily trust a person without knowing the person. A field officer emphasizes interpersonal relationships as the source of trust that goes beyond systems:

> Systems are not very flexible. Especially when it's there, unless you change that, it's there. But systems can become secondary when you have a very good relationship. Systems help, but not very much. I can give up, if I know you and I can trust you. The relationship is the key. When I was young, systems were everything. 'Follow the systems.' Now, I would say, 'Systems are good. They must be there. Otherwise, there would be chaos. But how flexible you are is something else. Flexibility comes when I know you more than systems. Systems must follow our needs rather than systems preaching.'

When the staff know and trust each other more than the systems, they can better manage systems. One way to manage systems is to treat them as support mechanisms, secondary to the relationships among the staff. As this field officer says, 'I can give up, if I know you and I can trust you.' While developing an ability to give up by establishing mutual

---

[37] Guide dog training shows that judgement is more important than sincerely following rules. Training dogs to be disobedient, to break trained rules, is the final step in teaching guide dogs to avoid having an accident. For human beings, deliberation, defined as 'an experiment in finding out what the various lines of possible action are really like' (Dewey, 1922, 190), offers a valuable means to broaden one's views.

[38] Beiner (1983, 79) argues, '[S]ympathetic understanding and capacity for forgiveness are essential moments of any judgement upon human affairs'.

relationships among the staff is one strategy, the next strategy, instead of giving up, explores the spirit of rules to address needs.

The spirit of a rule, not its literal meaning
Differentiating the spirit of a rule from its literal meaning depends on one's interpretation and thus requires wise judgement to embody the value of the rule. A field administrator identifies the difference between the spirit of a policy and its literal meaning:

> [When] the interests of the organization are not adversely affected, then something good is being done for the staff member in every way . . . Sometimes, it could be even a telephone call. The policy may be that no personal calls should be made. But somebody makes one personal call home or to somebody he or she wants. So you have to figure out what difference it makes to the person or to the organization. You may find that, by making that call, she will feel comfortable the rest of the afternoon and work properly. If you stick to the policy, she would not work properly because you've denied that call, and you find now you are affecting the organization. So it's a tricky situation.

Making a personal telephone call clearly violates the policy as far as its literal meaning is concerned. However, if the policy is aimed at helping the staff work for their missions more effectively and efficiently, making a personal call cannot simply be regarded as a violation of the policy. Several factors make the administrator carefully consider the differences between the spirit of the policy and its literal meaning.

First, a concrete case in front of him motivates the administrator to consider the spirit of the policy. Without the particular case in his mind, he could not have had an example to which the spirit of the policy is applied. The particular case, in which this particular individual wants to make a particular call in this particular organizational setting, prompts him to judge the policy in a more critical way instead of following its literal meaning. Generally, the more grounded one is in a specific context, the more interested one is in the real implications of the policy than in its literal meaning, because one's concerns arise from that involvement.

Second, the simple choice of allowing or denying a call does not guarantee a positive impact on the organization or the staff. Allowing all personal calls is clearly not what the organization seeks to do. Nevertheless, denying all personal calls does not necessarily contribute positively to the organization, as the administrator explains. In light of the spirit of the policy, a simple decision to allow or deny personal calls should not be the issue. Rather, when denying a personal call would negatively influence the person and the organization, then the staff members are required to judge whether to allow or deny the call based on its impact, both positive and negative, on the organization and the staff. This, of course, requires careful thinking and a better understanding of the situation.

Third, the spirit of the policy can take into account the people under the policy's influence because the policy is judged in light of its impact on those people. In contrast, the literal meaning of the policy does not take people into account, for the policy can be judged simply by the execution of what it literally says. Therefore, as the administrator knows the person, he tends to apply the spirit of the policy and to consider the expected impact of the personal call on the person and on the organization. Considering the personal call in terms of the spirit of the policy provides him with an insight into the possibly negative impact on the organization in the case that he denies the call.

The spirit of the policy embodies opportunities, within which the staff make full use of careful, thoughtful and contextually sound judgement. In light of the spirit of the policy, the staff can justify the violation of (the literal meaning of) the rule.

Relying on reciprocity, not systems

Practising reciprocity is another strategy to treat systems as a relative concept. Instead of putting systems at the heart of practices, reciprocity attempts to make the staff as persons the core motivation of practices.[39] A field officer describes his anticipation:

> My view might be selfish . . . but if I can make things easy for them, then I think they can make things easy for me as well. My feeling is that they wouldn't be asking this question or asking for this information unless they need it. So I will only serve from that perspective and it has been quite good.

While he characterizes his view as selfish, he hopes to develop a sense of reciprocity with other staff. He expects that the give-and-take relationships can be established voluntarily as he supports other staff. He believes that reciprocal practices can take place based on the common understanding among the staff that something in return can be expected some time in the future.

This symmetrical give-and-take interaction is different from a rational market economy that assumes that individual participants try to maximize their benefits. The motive of give-and-take in his case is to establish mutual support among his colleagues rather than to maximize his personal benefits.[40] The reciprocal practices are motivated by a sense of

---

[39] For discussions of conditions under which reciprocity can be practised and maintained, see Polanyi (1944, 47–8) who claims that reciprocity is 'not primarily associated with economics.' In contrast to economic analysis that would regard people as rational and selfish beings, Dawes and Thaler (1988), on the basis of experimental research, suggest that people tend to co-operate until they observe that others are taking advantage of them.

[40] 'The individual's economic interest is rarely paramount, for the community keeps all its members from starving . . . The maintenance of social ties, on the other hand, is crucial' (Polanyi, 1944, 46). Friedmann (1987, 20) argues that, in contrast with market rationality, which assumes that the individual is logically prioritized over society (Macpherson, 1962), social rationality assumes that social formations are prioritized over the individual.

commonality and common goals rather than by clear directions to get the job done.

'We are artists'

If the staff members think that they are artists performing development projects, they do not worry much about following systems or making mistakes. A field officer says:

> Because we are artists, artists are granted difference. Mistakes in art are not as [problematic] as mistakes in decision-making.

Any artistic performance may be inherently creative and thus can be distinguished from systematic performance, which is usually evaluated based on mistakes and successes.[41] The appreciation of artistic performance is so broad that the conceptual dichotomy – mistakes vs. successes – is too narrow to reflect adequately the quality of development work.[42] Consequently, artists may feel at ease exploring novel practices. They are rarely punished, for the terms on which their performance takes place are so broad that one cannot easily dismiss it as a mistake.[43] Moreover, using a positive term – 'lessons learned', instead of 'mistakes' – helps the staff artistically perform development. In fact, making a mistake can sow a seed of learning,[44] as a desk officer points out:

> By making mistakes. That's how you learn. . . . I've learned a lot because I've made so many mistakes.

Having said that, it is important to keep in mind that not all mistakes can be treated in such a positive manner. An assistant country director explains that although operational mistakes can be treated as 'lessons learned', managerial mistakes are usually serious enough that the staff cannot enjoy 'lessons learned'. A field officer articulates his concern about making a managerial mistake:

---

[41] John Dewey differentiates mechanical or purely objective construction from artistic production (*Webster's Third New International Dictionary*, 1981).

[42] Because art is 'the quality, production, expression, or realm of what is beautiful or of more than ordinary significance,' (*Webster's Third New International Dictionary*) it can be judged by a broad range of criteria, but not narrowly defined criteria.

[43] Bryson (1988, 203) suggests that 'If people are encouraged to make errors as a way of learning, but are rewarded for correcting the errors, not for persisting in them, then it will be easier to change directions and augment organizational knowledge and change-management skills. . . . The public sector is a particularly hard place for people to take risks – and therefore to learn – without punishment. Accountability often has been interpreted to mean the minimization of mistakes, rather than learning how best to achieve desired outcomes effectively and efficiently.' Sitkin (1996) also argues that failure is a vital prerequisite for an organization to learn effectively.

[44] Sandelands and Buckner (1989) refer to Dewey's (1934, 633) 'record of growth' to explain that 'art projects a course of development' (113).

181

In your employment situation, you can get fired. You can only admit your mistake if you feel you won't be penalized. I think if it costs your job or whatever, you might be in danger.

How can the staff address problems in a flexible and creative manner as opposed to following a set of procedures blindly? This strategy claims that the answer may depend on two factors: the characteristics of the staff and the organization. The more the staff can identify themselves as artists who perform their work in a creative way and the more the organization is willing to learn from mistakes, then the more the staff enable themselves to address diverse and changing problems in a flexible and creative way.

Using tensions

When NGO staff members face a dilemma, conventional rational approaches often fail to offer viable solutions. Yet the staff must somehow deal with the situation and determine a course of action designed to overcome the problem.[45] In fact, some paradoxical tensions may ultimately lead to desirable change in an NGO. For example, a budget cut, which put terrible stress on the staff and inculcated a sense of fatalism, in the end had an unexpected impact. A field officer says:

I really feel that if there had been no budget cut, then they probably wouldn't have made a change. We would still be having [the same undesirable project].

The two cases that follow present alternative strategies that field staff have pursued under contradictory circumstances.

Living in between two contradictory but correct answers

NGO staff members often face situations in which they must address two practices that contradict each other but that, independently, are both correct. This situation leads the staff to a logical impasse where taking one side means to negate the other and vice versa. In this situation, a rational approach,[46] which attempts to resolve the issue by selecting one practice or the other,[47] would involve trying to obtain more information, knowledge and theories to facilitate the selection of the right practice. In contrast to this rational approach, staff members have developed another strategy. A senior officer in HQ describes a new direction:

---

[45] Benson (1977) lists four aspects of contradictions in the organization. First, contradictions are a source of tensions and conflicts which lead to changes in the present situation. Second, contradictions frame the limit and possibility of reconstructing the organization. Third, contradictions may place the organization in a critical situation and thus motivate changes within it. Fourth, contradictions define the limits of a system.

[46] Allison (1971, 30) refers to rationality as 'consistent, value-maximizing choices within specific constraints'.

[47] The rational stance would assume that perfect information would lead to the selection of one of them as the correct approach.

There is a conflict, and people may say in Ethiopia, 'Development is the answer to people's problems. Long-term projects. We need integrated projects. We need self-sustainability in projects.' You get somebody who comes and denies that, 'You know, our people are starving to death, they need food, they need money, now. They need rehabilitation. Development is a mess to these people.' Now we are saying more as an organization, 'Wait a minute. You must live. This is a paradox. This is a dilemma.' Western people find it difficult to live with dilemmas. We want to solve the dilemma. We are very rational people. We want an answer. We want somebody who says, 'Development is correct', or 'Relief is correct.' We want to come down on one side. But we must live with this dilemma.

Living with a dilemma is different from neglecting to make a decision regarding the issue. Yet, it is also different from making a decision to select one approach or the other. It is a decision that the staff will intentionally stay in the tension that emerges in the midst of two contradictory but correct positions. What does this intentional endeavour entail? The officer continues:

I went to Bangladesh a few years ago. A lot of development projects. But you got a huge slot. One hundred fifty thousand people killed. You say, 'Well that's not our business.' I say, 'It is your business. Are we able to deal with this cyclone without destroying your long-term projects? That's your job.' Live with that tension and try and explain that. There is nothing wrong in this. Don't be saying that that's wrong.

His concern is reflected in his question, 'Are we able to deal with this cyclone without destroying your long-term projects?' How would this challenge affect the staff and the organization? Several interesting effects on the organization and the staff can be expected.

First, the staff take a risk by living with a dilemma, for they run a considerable risk of failing, not only in their relief efforts but also in their development projects. From the point of view of organizational resources, the risk of having development projects fail increases due to the reallocation of limited resources from development projects to relief efforts.[48]

Second, the staff members are forced to explore a new framework for understanding their situation and deciding what they should do.[49] When they live with a dilemma, the manual's rationality, on which staff members normally rely to make decisions and to draw conclusions, no longer

---

[48] Both the issue of resource availability and the difference in the methods, means, and prerequisites necessary for relief and for development work make it tremendously difficult for an NGO to carry out the two types of projects simultaneously. See Ati (1993).
[49] March (1996, 102) discusses the tensions between the exploration of new possibilities and the exploration of old certainties, 'Adaptive systems that engage in exploration to the exclusion of exploitation are likely to find that they suffer the costs of experimentation without gaining many of its benefits. . . . Conversely, systems that engage in exploitation to the exclusion of exploration are likely to find themselves trapped in suboptimal stable equilibria.'

helps guide the staff. A dilemma is by definition a logical impasse, where rational thinking does not yield appropriate answers.[50]

Third, staff members are required to invent their courses of action as they live within the dilemma. They do not have any manuals or guidelines on which they can rely in making decisions.

Fourth, the dilemma – the common enemy[51] of the staff – prompts them to identify themselves in a novel way. When staff members do not have a common issue that concerns all of them, their sense of commonality does not need to be strong. A commonly shared identity tends to be weak, and internal conflicts may be pronounced because of the different interests they represent. However, living with a dilemma places staff members under a lot of pressure, which drives them to work cooperatively for the sake of their survival.[52]

These effects of living within a dilemma all suggest that, under these circumstances, staff members are forced to rely more on their judgement than on systems. Because of the tensions, risks and uncertainty that accompany the situation, the staff need to be much more attentive, careful and responsive to their situations than if they were simply following established systems. In a sense, a dilemma provides an opportunity for the staff to go beyond systems and rely on their judgement about the situation.[53] Because they need to make judgements, they become seriously concerned about the situation. Consequently, the organization can remain flexible, adaptive and responsive.

Action-centred planning

NGOs usually follow reasonably ordered procedures in the hope of making wise plans and decisions and implementing a high-quality project.[54] NGOs would not be wise if they simply went ahead and implemented projects without enough information, planning and financial support. However, in practice, NGOs' working situations do not always offer enough resources to make wise decisions. NGOs must often make decisions under circumstances characterized by financial constraints, lack of information and limited time.[55] In particular, an emergency situation

---

[50] From a rational standpoint, constraints on resources, time and information are so high that the staff often have very little in the way of these components to help them make decisions.

[51] Identifying a common enemy can help people to build a sense of commonality (Said and Oe, 1995).

[52] In this sense, living with a dilemma can also be a relevant strategy to develop coherence within an organization. See the second half of Chapter 5 for a discussion of the strategies for developing coherence.

[53] Simon (1991) argues that decision-making can never be perfect, for one can never obtain perfect resources and information or unlimited time.

[54] See Daley and Angulo (1990) or Daley and Kettner (1986).

[55] When uncertainty is high, previous precedents are few, reliable facts are limited, time is limited, and many options exist, top leaders of organizations find that intuition is helpful for guiding their decisions (Agor, 1989, 11).

demands that an NGO make a decision with far less resources than necessary. In this tough situation, a director of operations takes strategic action:

> We've gone into a city under seizure. It was said that it was impossible to set up feeding centres. But our feeding centres were set up within five days, because we had people who cared, we had people who were prepared to make it happen. 'OK, we plan this operation, let's fund here, let's get a five-year plan, let's get a three-year plan, let's get a two-year plan, let's get a one-year plan. No, we go into the field, and we plan from there. We go there. We plan from there.' I mean, it's our job here to back up the people who are in the field and if we lose sight of that, we are losing sight of the organization. Our philosophy is to meet people where they are and then try to improve, taking to the next step on the ladder. Don't be trying to take the person who is starving and say, 'What we need is integrated rural development projects.' Nonsense. What we need here is to solve the problem first. We don't get to integrate very complex theories about development. People are our strength. People are to be there as a witness as well to what's going on, rather than writing reports about how people are there.

This organization cannot have enough resources to make an informed decision to go into the field or not. It is a Catch-22: without going into the field, you can hardly judge the decision. But once you go in the field, asking whether you should go in the field or not is irrelevant because you have already made a decision, whether it is right or not. Instead of asking whether going into the field is right or not, the staff question themselves about how much they care about people there. Then, the staff respond to the question by saying, 'Because we had people who cared, we had people who were prepared to make it happen'.[56]

This action-centred planning does not rely heavily on theories and systems.[57] The staff are always ready to give up theories and systems for the sake of people in the field.[58] 'People are our strength.' However, readiness is different from ignoring theories and systems from the beginning. When the staff are ready, they always pay attention to their situations to judge if, for example, collecting information before making a decision is a wise choice in an emergency situation or not. On the one hand, the staff need to take care of collecting necessary resources such as financial support, information, expertise and so forth to prepare them to address problems in a better way. On the other hand, the staff must

---

[56] '[S]trong democratic decision-making is predicated on will rather than choice and on judgement rather than preference' (Barber, 1984, 200). Here the issue is not how to select the right choice but how to make a choice correctly.

[57] Though this does not mean that the staff do not have theories in mind. In fact, no person can be totally free from theories that they use as their frameworks for decision-making.

[58] Compare with the elements of people-centred community planning. Daley and Angulo (1990) explain the elements from ideology and values, knowledge base and skills.

185

actively put the organization's missions into practice even if they have far less than enough resources available due to the constraints that their contexts entail.

For an organization to make a good decision, a set of criteria must be used to judge the decision. The criteria play a regulatory role in the organization. However, in this strategic, action-centred planning, the reference is not conventional criteria but people. When time to analyse emergent situations in the field is sharply limited for the very reason of emergency, the staff cannot spend time deciding whether to go or not. In this case, the staff with action-centred planning take actions motivated by their caring for people in the field. This planning strategy asserts that only after they go into the field to work on the issue can they know what to do.[59]

Using ambiguity

No organizational systems are free from ambiguity. Different interpretations are possible for any rules and regulations. Ambiguity, however, is not necessarily a constraint on the organization. Though ambiguity can often create misunderstanding among the staff, it can provide valuable room for the staff to put their intentions into practice with fewer constraints.[60] The ambiguous space, hence, increases their capacity to handle their work.[61] The strategies discussed below, in fact, actively make use of ambiguity's positive aspects.

Demanding vs. inviting

This strategy makes use of the ambiguity between demanding and inviting. A newsletter editor of an NGO worried that he did not receive enough reports from the field for newsletters. Upon hearing of his concern, the president of the organization sent a memo to the FOs to help this editor. What follows is the stimulating response of the editor after he observed the reaction of the field staff to the president's memo:

> One time the president sent a note to the offices under him saying, 'I want you each to send news items every week to him', and I said, 'Oh, no', because there are ten countries and there are bad items that I can't use. So I'm glad that they didn't obey him.

Ideally, he wants to receive a manageable number of publishable items consistently each week. As an editor, he strongly desires to receive

---

[59] See Horton and Freire (1990).

[60] 'We cannot play chess without agreeing on rules, nor drive a car without knowing traffic signs, nor live in a community without following social conventions, yet we routinely disagree about the best chess move, the safest response to an emergency, or a just solution to a social problem, and the more complicated the situation, the more room there is for the honest difference of opinion.' (Shalin, 1992, 263)

[61] For a discussion of the opportunities that ambiguity offers, see Krumholz and Forester (1990).

quality items from the field so that he can publish readable and attractive newsletters. On the other hand, as an HQ staff member, he feels accountable to the field staff who spend their valuable time writing reports. He wants to reward them by carrying their reports in the newsletters. However, when their reports are not good enough or are too numerous to use in the newsletter, he faces a dilemma between accountability to the writers in the field and accountability to the readers.

In this context, this president's memo happens to work well. Had this editor sent the same memo in his daily communication, it would have had little influence on the field staff compared with the president's memo. However, if the memo had been sent as a demand, the field staff members would have attempted to keep up the appearance of meeting the demand by sending reports, regardless of their quality. As a result, he would have received too many reports, including many under-qualified ones. When he contradictorily says, 'I'm glad that they didn't obey him', he is apparently glad that the memo is not taken as a demand.

Consequently, he welcomes the ambiguous meaning of the memo. The president's memo neither demands reports nor simply invites them. The ambiguity of the memo, in terms of the degree of enforcement over the field staff, provides them with room to review and judge their reporting practices without much obligation, yet with the editor's concern in mind. When a key person sends an informal memo, it can effectively draw the staff's attention to the sender's concerns, yet leave room for the staff to determine their response themselves. An ambiguous action by a formal authority is a strategy to draw careful attention and judgement from the staff concerning the issue at hand. While the ambiguity provides the staff with room to judge the degree of enforcement that the memo entails, the room for judgement can also be confusing and promote chaos. Thus, to avoid undesirable side effects, some measure, such as informing the field of the situation that this editor faces as the background of the memo, should carefully be considered and taken. Despite the chances of negative impact, however, ambiguity can present a strategy that provides the staff with room for judgement that enables the organization to remain flexible and responsive to changing needs.

'What' to do vs. 'how' to do

Making better use of the ambiguity that exists between 'what' and 'how' to do a job provides the staff with more strategic resources to handle the job properly. While the staff are usually told 'what' to do as their tasks, they are not clearly directed 'how' to accomplish the tasks in detail. Although an NGO may provide guidelines that suggest how to work on tasks, the staff still have a considerable degree of freedom to employ their own styles, so long as they can accomplish the tasks. While a result can easily be evaluated because people can easily look at it and compare it with the primary objective, processes to get the result cannot be evaluated easily due partially to the difficulty of observing them and partially to the presence of many alternatives that can achieve the same objectives. A field administrator identifies this 'how' as a rich resource for bringing about change.

> Accountants operate on principles which are very clear-cut. But for administrators, it's not like that. That is why you find one makes a bigger difference than the other. Whereas in accounts, personal style creates a very small impact, because the rules are usually very clear. But in administration, that is not really how it works. It's how you do things. Although we have rules in administration, I would advise somebody to really watch how they do things.

As the administrator explains, if little ambiguity exists, as in the case of accountants, the working processes are more mechanistic. However, when plenty of ambiguity exists, as in the case of administration, no single procedure can ensure the best result. Because each administrator can develop a different style of work, they have more chances to make a difference.

When the staff are assigned a certain task, the strategy suggests that the staff do not need to strictly follow conventional or popular procedures, but can flexibly explore alternatives that make more sense to them. Through the practices of exploring alternatives, the staff can remain flexible, adaptable and responsive to diverse issues.

An NGO strategically makes use of the ambiguity that a project entails in terms of actual, concrete activities in the field.[62] This NGO attempts to realize its objective of building relationships with the village through what it calls the Child Sponsorship Program, which provides financial support to children so that they can receive a better education. A deputy country director says:

> What we do is that under the guides of our Child Sponsorship Program, we are operating a development programme. Child Sponsorship gets us into the village, makes it known to all the people in the village, makes us known to all the government officials that we are doing Child Sponsorship Program. CSP is very straightforward: this is what we hope to see, this is what we expect from you. Once we are in the village, part of Child Sponsorship is visitation. We go visiting every family. And we live in the village. We are in the village building relationships. . . . That's the foundation of our development project. It's not a project where we develop infrastructure.

---

[62] Fowler (1993, 334–5) refers to this strategy as 'the onion skin strategy' and argues that it is characterized by 'an outer layer of welfare-oriented activity that protects inner layers of material service delivery that act as nuclei for a core strategy dedicated to transformation. Welfarism satisfies elites' demands in so far as they provide a supplementary source of placatory assistance to groups which may otherwise become radicalized. Development actions involving delivery of social services that complement the state are also unlikely to be perceived by the elite as being contrary to their interests. Simultaneously, NGOs must implement transformation-oriented activities and adopt methods, camouflaged by whatever packaging and labeling is required to cloud their actual intent.'

This strategy emerges in the tension between two different types of accountability. On the one hand, the country office is strongly encouraged to carry out the Child Sponsorship Program because of its popularity in the village, among government officials and among donors. On the other hand, the country office aims at building relationships in the village as its important development objective and thus is not interested in the service provision that the Child Sponsorship Program does. In the context of this tension, the staff pay attention to the ambiguity that the programme can hold in terms of actual activities in the field. The staff wisely carry out the programme not only to support children but also, and more importantly, to legitimize their stay in the village and build relationships. By wisely applying the ambiguity that the staff face, they can simultaneously accommodate the two different accountabilities, which otherwise might even conflict.

Fact vs. information

Nobody can write the same report as another even if everybody in the same organization writes a report on the same issue. A fact may appear to be similar to information but is actually significantly different from information. While a fact embodies some existence regardless of the people who observe it, information depends heavily on the people who interpret the fact. Thus, despite looking at the same issues and facts, everybody has different information, ideas, views, perspectives and interests in mind. A desk officer who works under a vice-president uses this ambiguity as a strategic tool:

> Anything we do as humans ends up being slanted one way or another, no matter how hard we try to be objective. So simply by my wording, even if I didn't believe something in the information I provided, simply the way I worded it could have a great effect on the vice-president's decision. There was a situation where a regional director was a particular friend of mine, I was sympathetic to the person, who had a problem. I would try and present that in as favourable a light as possible and, at the same time, I'd try to be honest to anyone. But I don't think there was anybody who could resist adding their own feelings to a job situation like that. When it involves someone who I know well, I will go the extra mile to help him out. That's human nature.

The strategic use of the ambiguity between fact and information has several practical implications. First, this officer can influence his boss's decisions. Through the ways he presents information to his boss, he may direct the boss's attention to certain aspects of issues instead of others. Thus, whether he intends it or not, his expression, wording and attention in his writing can play an important role in shaping his boss's decisions.

Second, he judges, intentionally or unintentionally, the way in which a situation is reported. In one's writing, one can never be totally objective, as he explains: 'Humans end up being slanted one way or another, no matter how hard we try to be objective.' No matter how accurately he tries to describe the situation, inevitably he has to select some information and disregard other information based on his judgement.

Lastly, his judgement is strongly influenced by personal relationships. An intention to 'go the extra mile to help him out' does not originate from his tasks. The intention comes from his care for the staff member as a person.

As he says, without telling a lie but shaping the attention of his boss by emphasizing certain types of information, he has a great effect on the boss's decisions. By proactively making better use of the ambiguity between fact and information, he can 'go the extra mile' to help the field staff.

Conclusion

Following the previous chapter's discussion of the problems that derive from regulatory systems, and of strategies to address those problems, this chapter has gone farther to discuss the problems derived from the self-perpetuating characteristics of systems such as rules and regulations, and has presented and examined practical strategies that the staff use to handle the problems. The first half of the chapter clarifies the impact of self-regulatory mechanisms that systems embody. Two major problems have been discussed. First, once rules construct their own world, they tend to begin serving themselves instead of serving the organization or the staff. Rules lead to more rules. Consequently, organizations and the staff members become resources for rules to perpetuate and serve themselves. Second, systems serve to reproduce hierarchy in various ways. For example, when some staff hold narrower views while others hold wider ones, interactions between the two systematically reproduce and augment the gaps between their views, and consequently serve to dichotomize the organization.

The second half of the chapter has presented and analysed practical strategies that the staff members actually use *vis-à-vis* the tensions caused by self-regulated systems. The first type of strategy attempts to delegitimize the autonomy of systems and put them under the control of the staff. The second type of strategy makes full use of tensions as a precious resource, instead of regarding them as obstacles, to help people give up systems and rely on their core values and missions. The third type of strategy actively employs ambiguity to increase the latitude the staff enjoy in exercising their own judgement to manage the issues they face by themselves, rather than being obliged to follow systems blindly.

PART IV

What Have We Learned?

PARTS I, II AND III have discussed three different sets of opposing pressures as tensions: tensions between programme-centred activities and organization-centred activities; tensions between diversity and similarity; and tensions between flexibility and consistency. Based on the problems and strategies that the three Parts have identified and discussed, this Part first draws lessons learned from the discussions in the preceding Parts, and then provides a summary of the study as a conclusion.

Parts I, II and III have not focused specifically on the relationships between HQ and FOs, for narrow framing may obscure other important issues that are not directly related to these relationships. Chapter 8, however, reintroduces the framework of the HQ–FOs relationship and presents the lessons in terms of their applicability to donors and governments, to NGO managers or leadership, and to NGO field staff for their future efforts. Finally, Chapter 9 is devoted to summarizing the problems and strategies that the study identified and discussed in the three preceding Parts.

CHAPTER 8

Lessons

By making mistakes. That's how you learn. . . . I've learned a lot because I've made so many mistakes.

Desk officer

THIS CHAPTER DRAWS lessons from the problems and strategies that previous chapters have identified and discussed. The lessons are divided into three categories, not mutually exclusive, based on their applicability to donors and governments, to NGO managers and leadership, and to NGO field staff.

Lessons for donors and governments

Donors and governments support NGOs financially and expect NGOs to carry out projects to which they and the NGOs have agreed. What lessons can this study offer donors and governments dealing with NGOs in this relationship? The following are several lessons that help donors and governments better work with NGOs.

When assessing NGOs

Do not treat an NGO as one unit.[1] An NGO's offices are situated in various social, cultural and political settings. It employs diverse staff members who have different cultural backgrounds, values, views and interests. This study examines the complex internal dynamics of NGOs as organizations. When donors deal with an NGO, they may benefit significantly from understanding the NGOs' internal dynamics.

Expect tensions between headquarters and field offices. When donors and governments interact with an NGO, they usually contact HQ and treat their views as representative of those of the entire organization. Donors, however, should remember that HQ does not always represent what the field actually implements, thinks and believes. The tensions between HQ

---

[1] Much NGO literature, as noted in Chapter 1, regards NGOs as a unit of analysis. In contrast to this conventional analytical view, this research has focused on individual staff members to show how an NGO is a complex, diverse and dynamic entity.

and FOs are enormous due to their differences in accountability, interests and tasks, as this study has argued. Moreover, donors and governments should understand that the connection between HQ and FOs is not as strong as they might expect. Normally, one or two people in leadership positions in the field can contact HQ. Consequently, the realities staff members face at the grassroots level are not readily apparent to donors.[2] Thus, donors and governments should understand and take into account differences and tensions between HQ and the field when they interact with a representative of the NGO.

Don't depend only on the proposal and reports. All papers from NGOs are expected to be sent to donors after careful examination by HQ.[3] During the process of managing the quality of papers (such as project proposals and reports) for donors, the reality in the field can easily be modified with input from HQ,[4] which has different interests. Thus, donors need to keep in mind that those papers are products not directly of the field but of internal co-ordination designed to reflect the interests of HQ. When they interact with NGOs, donors can gain a better sense of what the NGO is doing internally, and they can gauge the degree of credibility of proposals or reports, if they listen carefully to NGO staff while keeping the complex internal organizational dynamics in mind.[5] In particular, developing relationships with the staff and informally asking them about their project progress can still provide donors with a better understanding than if they simply demand proposals or reports.

When selecting an NGO to fund

Develop room for NGOs to show their own intentions. When donors attempt to select an appropriate NGO to fund, they are advised to understand what funding means for NGOs and how NGOs deal with donors. However, understanding NGOs' real intentions is difficult. Because the necessity of funding is '*the singular* most important reality',[6] NGOs expend significant effort in seeking funds and may even change their

---

[2] Both administration and the mindsets of the local staff make it difficult for them to articulate their concerns. See *Apathy and fears of raising voices,* in Chapter 7, 'Systems as a catalyst to reproduce hierarchy.'

[3] See *Organizational issues over operational issues,* in Chapter 7, 'Systems as a catalyst to reproduce hierarchy.'

[4] See 'Cultural differences,' and 'Differences in scope', in Chapter 4, 'Constructing identity', in Chapter 5 and 'Constructing their own worlds' in Chapter 7.

[5] 'Listening, we understand the meaning of what is said in the context of the speaker's life. . . . In listening, we pay attention not to the sound of the person, but to the person of the sound; we pay attention to practical meaning and possible implications, not to "dictionary meaning"' (Forester, 1989, 108–9).

[6] Quote from *Money: a powerful regulatory system,* in Chapter 6, 'Systems' undesirable impacts'. Italics reflect the speaker's emphasis.

missions for the sake of getting funds.[7] Thus, donors should understand that NGOs' proposals or reports do not necessarily represent the missions of NGOs.[8] In evaluating the compatibility of NGOs' goals with their own, donors should let NGOs reflect the NGOs' real intentions by not imposing or revealing what donors expect from them.

Try to determine whether or not NGOs simply strive to make donors happy. One way to judge the quality of NGOs is to examine carefully how they relate to donors. Because funding is a must for NGOs while being accountable to the field is also important, NGOs are pulled in two opposite directions.[9] However, for fundraisers of NGOs, the temptation to satisfy donors' requests even at the cost of sacrificing the field is strong.[10] In the face of these two opposing forces, capable NGOs attempt to balance the tensions by avoiding being trapped by either of them. A desk officer looks at both sides simultaneously to balance them:

> [I]f you feel that the project is not going in the right direction, or it needs to be redirected, there is a procedure. Because we are involved in a contract with funding agencies, we have to do that. But you can certainly approach us to say that we are doing A, B, C, we should be doing X, Y, Z. Then, we approach the funders and suggest that it should be redirected this way. In that situation, I don't know any case where funders say, 'No, you can't do it.'[11]

Donors should judge the quality of NGOs in terms of whether they deal flexibly with the tensions to judge each request from donors, or whether they simply make donors happy.[12] This study suggests that those NGOs that can sometimes disagree with donors are likely to have good working relationships between HQ and the FOs.[13]

Question conventional criteria. Conventional criteria for evaluating an NGO, such as the number of staff members, their education level, the organization's annual budget, the types of projects it conducts,

---

[7] See *Donor relations* in Chapter 5, 'Recruiting to homogenize the organization', *Money: a powerful regulatory system*, in Chapter 6, 'Systems' undesirable impacts,' and *Organizational issues over operational issues*, 'Systems as a catalyst to reproduce hierarchy' in Chapter 7.

[8] Most donors, whether they appreciate NGOs' own missions or attempt to achieve their own interests by employing NGOs as implementors, depend significantly on NGOs' written documents, such as reports and proposals, to make decisions.

[9] See Part I, 'Programme-Centred vs. Organization-Centred Activities'.

[10] See, for example, *Where you stand depends on where you sit* in Chapter 4, 'Differences in scope'.

[11] Quote from Chapter 3, 'Predeparture training'.

[12] Even if an NGO loses the balance, it does not necessarily mean that its organizational existence is at stake. Within a certain range of imbalance, NGOs can persist (Meyer and Zucker, 1989). For a collection of excellent articles related to NGO performance and accountability, see Edwards and Hulme (1996).

[13] See 'Predeparture training' in Chapter 3.

its organizational structure and so forth,[14] can hardly show how the NGO as an organization functions to attain its mission objectives. The nature of interactions among the staff members, ways in which the staff make decisions, and the staff's motivations to work for the organization cannot be expressed as formal criteria. However, these characteristics play crucial roles in their work for their mission goals as an organization. These can be evaluated by donors only by actively interacting with NGOs both formally and informally.

Be careful when an NGO can clarify projects too clearly. Field situations are diverse and changing. Thus, if an NGO really tries to carry out development projects that make sense in the field, it needs to carefully plan project processes to be flexible enough to accommodate unforeseen issues and unrecognized problems that it might encounter, rather than planning rigidly fixed objectives with clear but inflexible processes.[15] Donors must be aware, however, that proposals that persuasively spell out clear objectives with clear processes appear to be more attractive than proposals that can only explain a broad framework of processes. Because NGOs understand donors' preferences, writing attractive proposals and reports becomes their major work, whether they can carry out what they propose or not.

> People in the headquarters are more concerned about the accomplishments of the papers. Papers should be good. But that is not what development is all about.[16]

This exercise may exacerbate the gap between HQ and the FOs, the gap between the real projects and what reports or proposals say, and the gap between what the donors understand about the projects and what the NGO staff understand about them. When donors receive proposals or reports that do not address the issues and problems that arise in diverse, uncertain and dynamic contexts, donors should worry about these gaps.

When working with NGOs

Treat NGO staff as colleagues. When donors assume a position of superiority on the grounds that they are the source of funds for projects, NGOs

---

[14] Because much of the information available to donors is this kind of information (unless they have special informal connections), donors are tempted to form unreasonable judgements about the quality of NGOs based on these attributions. This tendency can be compared with a situation in which an NGO recruits a person with a good CV but an undesirable personality. For this case, see *Good CV but undesirable person* in Chapter 2, 'Inappropriate recruiting criteria'.
[15] The lack of flexibility in project plans is a death blow for implementing projects in NGOs' dynamic environments. For discussions of the impact of headquarters' communication mode on field activities, see the second half of *Devaluing differences* in Chapter 5, 'Constructing identity'.
[16] Quote from *Systematic gap between administration and operation* in Chapter 7, 'Constructing their own worlds'.

do not inform donors of their weak points, because doing so might place the funding at risk. If donors are really interested in projects, they should show their respect for the work of NGOs rather than using their financial power to pressure NGOs. They should also acknowledge the difficulties that NGOs face in dealing with projects. To the degree that they encourage NGOs in this manner, NGOs may also respect donors and openly discuss their issues, problems and worries. Remember the power of respect:

> When you oppose someone's idea, that person tends to regard you as an enemy. But if you smile . . . you convey a sense of respect to the person despite the difference in opinions. Only in that manner, they get to listen to you and understand the difference. Unless they feel respected, they do not listen to you.[17]

Embrace mistakes as lessons. A desk officer's comment that she 'learned a lot by making mistakes' conveys the pedagogical implications of error. However, people do not deliberately make mistakes. Even if you make a mistake, 'you can only admit your mistake if you feel you wouldn't be penalized'.[18] To use mistakes as lessons for the future, donors should make clear their positive attitudes toward NGOs before NGOs make mistakes. When NGOs understand that donors embrace mistakes as lessons, NGOs do not need to pretend that their projects function excellently without problems. Consequently, NGOs can be more candid with donors about their errors.

Lessons for NGO leadership

The main focus of this study is NGO leadership, although other people who are involved NGO activities in one way or another are not totally excluded. NGO leaders direct NGOs in many ways. They play major roles in contacting donors, recruiting staff members, communicating with the field, co-ordinating the staff, and making rules, regulations and policies, to name but a few of their functions. This study presents lessons in the hope of helping them improve their performance. The lessons apply to various occasions: when recruiting the staff, when working with the staff, when working with donors and when dealing with rules, regulations and policies.

When recruiting the staff

Understand the field situations. Recruiting the staff is not the same as matching required tasks with candidates' résumés.[19] Without

---

17 Quote from *Valuing emotions* in Chapter 6, 'Prioritizing the staff over systems'.
18 Quote from *We are artists* in Chapter 7, 'Judging systems.'
19 See Chapter 2, 'Inappropriate recruiting criteria'.

understanding the context in which a recruit works and with what kind of staff members, a recruiter cannot select suitable people for a position.[20]

Examine the intentions of candidates. Not only the abilities of candidates, but also and more importantly their intentions need to be carefully examined by asking how they want to work for the NGO and how they understand development. Candidates' expertise, skills and experiences do not reflect whether they can work co-operatively to fulfil organizational missions.[21]

Examine willingness to learn.[22] Candidates usually try to demonstrate that they have great expertise, skills and experience that fit the available positions. They show what they possess at the moment as their resources. However, this does not guarantee that they can handle the dynamic, diverse and uncertain situations they will face in the field. If a candidate has developed rigid values, views and *modus operandi*, he or she may be too stubborn to handle issues flexibly with other staff members.

Judge sincerity and honesty. If the field staff discuss only positive aspects of a project and do not say anything about its negative aspects, you cannot trust them:

> If I go into a programme, and somebody is continually pointing out to me only good and successful points, and I don't hear any of the negative aspects [of a programme], then I have a problem with this. Then I would begin to ask questions, and if the story that keeps on coming back is a very, very positive one, then I will begin to mistrust the person, because I think they are not telling the full story. But if they can tell me good things and bad things and explain to me why we should continue, then I have much more trust in that person because I feel they have been open.[23]

Recruiters should judge carefully whether a candidate tries to get a job by making the recruiters happy, or honestly tells the entire story of what the candidate really feels, is concerned about, is interested in and so forth.

Examine the ability of patience. Working in an NGO that is internally complex, and facing external uncertainties of dynamic environments, NGO staff usually cannot expect that they can carry out their work as they plan to. Their turbulent working environments tend to create a gap between what they plan to achieve and what they can actually accomplish. To address this problem without giving up too easily, they should be

---

[20] See Chapter 2, 'Ambiguous recruiting processes'.
[21] See *Expertise but discrepant values* in Chapter 2, 'Inappropriate recruiting criteria'.
[22] See *Sensitivity* and *Ability to listen and learn* in Chapter 2, 'Introducing alternative criteria'.
[23] See *Honesty* in Chapter 2, 'Introducing alternative criteria.'

patient enough to involve themselves actively and persistently in the issue at hand. In the words of a local manager, 'NGO staff should not stop dealing with issues but [should] keep on interacting . . . despite the differences.'[24]

When working with the staff

Embrace mistakes as lessons. In the same way that donors work with NGOs, NGO leadership should embrace mistakes as lessons so that the field can become more open to learning from their errors.

Exemplify what they want the staff to do. Requesting the staff to do what the managers themselves fail to do does not make sense for the staff, and ends up damaging the credibility of the leadership. If NGO leaders want the staff to adopt certain practices, they must exemplify those practices. As a country director says, 'We have to model the way we want them to interact with people in community.'[25] The leadership should consider their own practices as an important factor in attaining their goals. Without careful processes, managers cannot expect to attain a desired outcome. For example, managers need carefully to consider decision-making processes if they want to make wise decisions.

Develop enabling environments rather than closely supervising. When managers supervise the staff closely, the supervision can kill staff members' motivation, incentives and voluntary spirit. The staff may be content with their supervision or be fed up with it. In either case, the managers fail to draw on their latent abilities. In contrast to such supervision, when managers create environments that help the staff work effectively, the staff are willing to work to meet managers' expectations.[26]

Treat the emotions and feelings of the staff carefully.[27] When the managers do not listen attentively to staff members to understand their problems, concerns, frustrations, worries and so forth, staff members do not dare express their emotions and feelings. This situation destroys a precious opportunity for the staff to learn, because 'all learning has an emotional base'.[28] The managers should be aware that emotions in an organization are not something they should devalue, but rather something they can make use of actively.

---

[24] See *Active patience* in Chapter 2, 'Introducing alternative criteria'.
[25] See *Modelling exemplary life* in Chapter 3, 'Drawing on latent abilities'.
[26] See Chapter 3, 'Locals vs. expatriates' and 'Drawing on latent abilities.'
[27] See Chapter 6, 'Prioritizing the staff over systems'.
[28] Proverb of Plato from Fitzhenry (1993, 139).

Take a risk to develop trust.[29] Many staff members say that trust is important. How, then, can the staff develop trust? Trust cannot be developed through rational interactions; it requires risk. '[M]utual trust', Schön and Rein (1994, 179) assert, 'is a virtuous circle of anticipating and action whose initiation always requires a leap of faith beyond the available evidence'. Trust emerges when the staff act without evidence. Hence, the managers need to be aware that the chance of making a mistake always exists when they attempt to act based on trust.

When working with the donors

Treat donors not only as funders but also as a target of education.[30] When an NGO treats donors merely as a source of funds, it loses a vital chance to educate the public in the donors' industrialized home countries. Donors can play vital roles in educating the public. Thus, NGO managers are wise if they attempt to interact with donors not only as a financial source but as a target of the NGOs' advocacy projects. Their projects do not need to be in the Third World. Advocacy and development education in NGOs' as well as donors' home countries have become one major concern.[31]

Put NGOs' intentions up front. When NGO managers contact donors, they should put their intentions up front in order to clarify what the NGO is seeking.[32] If an NGO approaches donors without clarifying its intentions and tries to obtain support by any means, the NGO may face a serious problem when donors discover the gap between their own intentions and those of the NGO. Particularly if an NGO hopes to develop long-term relationships with donors, presenting its intentions clearly from the outset is vital to maintaining donors' trust.[33]

Tell donors the entire story. Donors cannot trust an NGO if the NGO staff informs the donors only of positive things. Just as the NGO leadership expects the full story from the staff, rather than only positive aspects of

---

[29] For vivid accounts that describe the relationships between developing trust and risk taking, see *Honesty* in Chapter 2; 'Introducing alternative criteria', 'Don't ask me but do it' and *Modelling exemplary life* in Chapter 3, 'Drawing on latent abilities'; and *A manual, not THE manual* in Chapter 7, 'Judging systems'.

[30] See *Donor relations* in Chapter 5, 'Recruiting to homogenize the organization'.

[31] For discussions of NGOs' advocacy roles, see Edwards (1994), Edwards and Hulme (1992a, 1992b) and Fowler (1991).

[32] Cf. *Consistently focusing on merit but not on the people involved* in Chapter 5, 'Dealing with differences.'

[33] In contrast to a strategy of articulating intentions up front, Frost (1987) presents several examples of literature that explain the disguise of real intent in the hope of minimizing the costs of others' disapproval or the unwilling mobilization of resources by others.

projects,[34] the leadership should, in turn, honestly tell donors the entire story of projects.

Develop multi-dimensional relationships.[35] When an NGO develops multi-dimensional links with donors, the NGO need not depend solely upon reports to be accountable to donors. Face-to-face contact, telephone conversations, informal discussions, joint workshops and so forth all aid mutual understanding.

Do not beat with a stick but invite. If NGO staff criticize government officers without constructive proposals for the future, the practice only helps build a barrier between NGO staff and government officers. But if NGO staff can help the government officers comprehend the field situation, the NGO staff can motivate the government officers to work on the issue:

> In an informal setting, we asked the foreign minister. But it's not aggressive, because they are human beings. They are caught within their own bureaucracy. . . . I think we have got a lot of respect from government circles, because we don't try and beat them with a stick. We . . . say, 'Why don't you visit our projects, why don't you see what's happening?' And he did. . . . He came back and fought for the budget.[36]

This lesson is also relevant for those field staff who work with their bosses.[37]

Encourage donors to participate in projects. As an NGO encourages donors to participate in projects in one way or another, the NGO can successfully share its accountability with donors. When a donor is involved in a project with an NGO, they become colleagues rather than forming implementer–funder relationships.[38]

When dealing with rules, regulations, and policies

Judge in a given context rather than simply following systems.[39] Systems such as rules, regulations and policies are not universally relevant. The staff are the ones to judge how systems can be used effectively to serve their purposes. Dewey and Tufts (1910, 334) argue that 'a tool is for

---

[34] See *Judge sincerity and honesty* in Chapter 8, 'When recruiting the staff'.
[35] See *Developing multi-dimensional relationships* in Chapter 6, 'Prioritizing the staff over systems'.
[36] Quote from *Developing multi-dimensional relationships* in Chapter 6, 'Prioritizing the staff over systems'.
[37] See *Do not demand but motivate* in Chapter 8, 'When working with bosses'.
[38] See *On-the-job training* in Chapter 3, 'Training in projects'.
[39] See Chapter 7, 'Judging systems'.

analyzing a specific situation, the right or wrong being determined by the situation in its entirety, and not by the rule as such'. Systems make sense when the staff use their judgement to make better use of systems relevant to the context. NGO managers' judgement is especially crucial because NGOs face diverse, dynamic problems.

Be aware of the side effects of systems. When an organization applies a rule, the staff usually do not worry much about its negative side effects on the organization. This study has found, however, that virtually all systems have undesirable and substantial side effects on organizations.[40] For example, an ill-suited *modus operandi* is subtly imposed on FOs by headquarters to subvert local value systems.[41] Introducing systems without careful consideration in advance can easily bring about this kind of destructive side effect.

Broadly accepted models obscure alternatives. When popular terms, such as participation and people-centred development, dominate staff discussions of development, the staff tend blindly to accept practices that bear the label of popular terms, whatever they actually are, without judging their relevance to a given situation. For example, in the name of 'participation', the NGO staff members can gather to fight and compete to maximize their personal interests instead of working in the interests of the whole organization.[42] The staff should consider carefully the relevance of models to a specific situation, and whether the models are popularly used and applied.

'System' is almost synonymous with 'hierarchy'. A desk officer explains the relationship between system and hierarchy:

> In the system, you need some standards. To have one system, you've got to agree on definitions, terms like data items. You almost need some hierarchy in order to get to an agreement.[43]

When the NGO staff employ systems such as rules, regulations, policies, language, money and so forth, hierarchy is likely to be introduced as a resource to sustain these systems. As hierarchy is introduced for systematic convenience such as hierarchy between organizational issues and operational issues, and hierarchy among the staff's titles in the organization, the staff, in turn, tend to shape systems in a hierarchical manner.[44]

---

[40] 'Problems: Gaps between the systems and reality' in Chapter 6 and 'Problems: Perpetuated control mechanisms' in Chapter 7 discuss various kinds of unexpected side effects.
[41] See *Modus operandi: a device to control field offices* in Chapter 6, 'Systems' undesirable impacts'.
[42] See *Battlefield called 'participation'* in Chapter 7, 'Constructing their own worlds'.
[43] Quote from Chapter 7, 'Systems as a catalyst to reproduce hierarchy'.
[44] See Chapter 7, 'Systems as a catalyst to reproduce hierarchy'.

Consequently, hierarchy and systems interact (through the medium of the staff) to reproduce and enhance hierarchy with the catalytic support of systems. The leadership must remember where the hierarchy comes from and must delegitimize the unnecessary impact of hierarchy by keeping in mind the reasons for the existence of systems and hierarchy.[45]

Lessons for NGO field staff

In contrast with much NGO literature that focuses on how the field staff work on projects and deal with field problems, this study focuses on how an NGO develops its internal capacity to act as it wants to act in the face of various tensions, pressures and problems. Thus, the lessons for NGO field staff presented here focus specifically on internal NGO dynamics, and attempt to address the issues that they face when they work under regulatory systems and when they work with their bosses, rather than when they work in the field.[46]

When working under regulatory systems

Make full use of informal work styles. Rather than breaking or ignoring regulatory systems, the staff can make use of informal interactions for their work to remain flexible, adaptable and responsive to diverse and changing problems. Rituals, narratives and emotions are some of the relevant strategies that the staff can use to serve their work without strict regulatory systems.[47]

Use formal structures to protect vulnerable informal interactions. When the field staff use informal ways of solving problems, the vulnerable informal style can be protected by wisely applying formal structures. For example, when misunderstandings between HQ and a field office hinder their interactions, formal structures secure room for them to interact:

> The beauty was that even though there was misunderstanding, the structure [allowed] the time to work it out and the process increased the level of trust.[48]

The staff should neither be content with formal structures nor rely solely on informal interactions, but should strategically make use of both to supplement each with the other.

---

[45] See *A manual not THE manual* in Chapter 7, 'Judging systems'.
[46] But this does not mean that field practices are not important.
[47] See Chapter 4, 'Rituals as a mediator', and 'Narratives', and Chapter 6, 'Prioritizing the staff over systems'.
[48] See *Protecting informal time* in Chapter 6, 'Broadening views.'

Actively look for ambiguity and make good use of it. Ambiguity around systems exists in several forms. For example, ambiguity between demanding and asking, ambiguity of what to do and how to do it, and ambiguity between fact and information can all be valuable resources with which the field staff address their problems and concerns:[49]

> Anything we do as humans ends up being slanted one way or another, no matter how hard we try to be objective. So simply by my wording . . . it could have a great effect on the vice-president's decision. . . . When it involves someone who I know well, I will go the extra mile to help him out.[50]

When facing a dilemma, don't give up, but hope for a better[51] change to emerge from the dilemma. Dilemmas invalidate systems and require the staff to judge, make decisions and act based on their understanding of the situation. Although dilemmas place heavy emotional burdens on the staff, the staff should not forget that dilemmas also offer unexpected yet precious opportunities for the staff to address their concerns, interests, agendas and so forth, effectively.[52] Dealing with a dilemma makes the staff remain flexible, responsive and adaptable to diverse problems. When the field staff faced a serious budget cut:

> [T]he local staff was very upset, very angry. There was a lot of yelling, shouting. . . . There was a sense of fatalism about their work.[53]

But, after going through the problem, the staff was grateful that the dilemma brought about a change for the better:

> I really feel if there had been no budget cut, then they probably wouldn't have made a change. We would still be having [the same undesirable project].[54]

The field staff should remember the difference between when they are having a problem and after the problem has been resolved, and should not lose hope when they face a tough time.

When working with bosses

Neither loyalty nor exit but voice. Hirschman (1970) nicely characterizes three courses of action that organization members can take: exit, voice, and loyalty. These three distinctive features clearly represent the practices available to NGO field staff. If staff members cannot stand their situations, they 'exit' from the organization and look for other job opportunities. If

---

[49] See Chapter 7, 'Using ambiguity'. Krumholz and Forester (1990) discuss how deeply ambiguous mandates become the resource of planners to address issues effectively.
[50] Quote from *'What' to do vs. 'how' to do* in Chapter 7, 'Using ambiguity'.
[51] Boone (1989) argues that faith in a better future is a characteristic of effective extension work.
[52] See Chapter 7, 'Using tensions'.
[53] Quote from *Expatriate vs. local staff* in Chapter 2, 'Discrepant employment terms'.
[54] Quote from Chapter 7, 'Using tensions'.

the staff expect that they can significantly benefit from the organization, they may show their 'loyalty' and become co-opted to support the *status quo* of the organization. The third path, which I recommend here, is to 'voice' when the staff feel that they need to address an issue at hand. This practice requires a continuous balancing effort not to 'exit' or remain silent out of 'loyalty'.[55] Because of the continuous effort required to avoid these pitfalls, the staff can remain responsive to issues in dynamic environments.

Do not demand but motivate. Demanding the boss's attention is not a wise stance for staff to take,[56] as it may discourage the boss from listening to them. In the words of a senior manager, quoted above,[57] 'unless they feel respected, they do not listen to you'. The staff should carefully examine, 'What incentives might motivate those in power to commit themselves to learning to share power?'[58] The language they use significantly influences the bosses.[59] The staff should keep in mind the voice from the field:

> I guess the tone is so important, how you deal with people. Deal with people in a respectful way. And in a way that underscores your respect for that individual, not constantly questioning, not being patronizing, but creating adult relationships, I think that's really important. You can be direct and respectful.[60]

Ask specific questions.[61] This lesson is, in fact, valid for anybody who asks questions. But because field staff are situated at the lower levels of the organizational ladder, it is especially important that they keep this lesson in mind if they need to get appropriate responses from their bosses. The field staff can benefit greatly from the strategy of asking questions, though this strategy comes from the HQ's context:

> If you are just saying a general thing, they don't have time for that. If you just tell me to rewrite it, it's not good. That doesn't help me. If you are very specific, and if you also offer them a consultant to help them do it, or some other resources and guidelines, then they will do it.[62]

---

[55] Korten (1995, 328) concludes his book by suggesting new 'ways of thinking that cannot be defined by the old categories', such as Left and Right, liberal and conservative.
[56] For discussions of the dialogue between unequal power groups, such as between headquarters and the field, see Burbules and Rice (1991) and Shor and Freire (1987).
[57] Quote from *Valuing Emotions* in Chapter 6, 'Prioritizing the Staff Over Systems.'
[58] Soedjamoko (1986, 25).
[59] See Liska (1991).
[60] See *Questioning what, how, when and who* in Chapter 4, 'Associating differences'.
[61] Ibid.
[62] Quote from *Questioning what, how, when and who* in Chapter 4, 'Associating differences'.

Understand bosses' contexts, interests, pressures and concerns. As a country director says, 'at where you stand depends on where you sit'.[63] Likewise, staff members' organizational positions strongly shape their behaviour. If they are managers, they have a set of issues, concerns, constraints and so forth that other staff do not have. Although their bosses can understand the issues in the field, they might not be able to act on those issues due to their positional constraints. If the field staff simply raise their voices to their bosses in HQ without understanding the bosses' contexts, constraints and issues, the field staff cannot expect a desirable response from the bosses.

---

[63] Quote from *'Where you stand depends on where you sit'* in Chapter 4, 'Differences in scope'.

CHAPTER 9

Problems and Strategies in Tensions

You have to model what you are telling people to do. If they are getting one message from their own experience within the organization, it's going to be very hard for them to do the opposite with the beneficiaries.

Country director

THIS CHAPTER SUMMARIZES and analyses the problems and strategies derived from the three tensions that the previous chapters have identified and discussed.

General lessons from the three tensions

Virtually all NGOs face three broad sets of tensions between two opposing pressures: programme-centred vs. organization-centred activities, diversity vs. similarity, and flexibility vs. consistency. Each of these tensions influences NGOs' capacities in different ways. Managing the tensions between programme-centred activities and organization-centred activities is the key to serving the field while maintaining the organization at the same time. Managing the tensions between diversity and similarity is the key to appreciating differences among the staff members in values, views and interests, and treating those differences as resources for the organization, while at the same time maintaining their similarity in having common missions. And managing the tensions between flexibility and consistency is the key to remaining adaptable and responsive to diverse, dynamic local problems while maintaining organizational consistency at the same time.

Programme-centred vs. organization-centred activities
Part I discussed the tensions between programme-centred activities and organization-centred activities through the processes of recruitment and staff training. As Table 4 indicates, NGOs need to balance two opposing pressures: the need to be accountable to project activities in the field as the output of the organization and the need to maintain and develop the organization's capacities to ensure its quality output in the long term.

When NGO leaders pay more attention to programme activities, they tend to value accountability to the field's immediate needs while sacrificing long-term benefits derived from developing organizational capacities,

Table 4. Tension in Organizational Activities: Recruitment and Training

Pathology	Area of Tension		Pathology
Self-destruction	Programme-centred ◄─────►	Organization-centred	Self-perpetuation

for example through investing in the staff. In the absence of organizational investments such as staff development, the decreased capability of the staff will lead the quality of projects to suffer. But when the leadership concerns itself with maintaining the organization, it then emphasizes the development of organizational capacities over the immediate needs in the field. In this case, the lack of accountability to the field's needs is the likely result. Hence, this tension can also be regarded as the tension between meeting short-term needs and meeting long-term needs.

Part I identified and discussed a set of problems derived from the tension between the two opposing pressures. Chapter 2 discussed the issues in light of staff recruitment. Chapter 3 identified and discussed problems associated with staff training. The research has shown that the pressure to meet immediate needs in the field creates the following problems:

Problem 1.1   NGOs tend to seek people with relevant CVs and expertise, and end up recruiting undesirable people whose values conflict with those of the organization. These recruits not only contribute little to the organization, they also disrupt its endeavours. (See Chapter 2, 'Inappropriate recruiting criteria'.)

Problem 1.2   NGOs tend to employ staff solely for the sake of organizational convenience and do not care about the staff members as persons. (See Chapter 2, 'Discrepant employment terms'.) Therefore, staff members feel fatalistic, work only for the sake of their survival and start to look for other jobs. Consequently, the staff can perform only at a minimal level.

Problem 1.3   Putting the right person in the right place is difficult due to the scarcity of effective local staff, the personal interests of the leadership, and requirements derived from organizational consistency. (See Chapter 2, 'Problems in matching a person to a position'.)

Problem 1.4   The ambiguity of recruiting processes, which take place between headquarters and the field, makes it difficult for the field to take the initiative of recruitment, despite its vital importance for the field. Consequently, the field ends up being content with recruiting an unsuitable person. (See Chapter 2, 'Ambiguous recruiting processes'.)

Problem 1.5 NGOs are discouraged from developing the staff due to high turnover and staff members' personal interests in making use of their training to pursue their careers in different organizations. Even if they train the staff, the training is limited to a technique-oriented focus that can yield only short-term returns. (See Chapter 3, 'Hard to expect long-range returns'.) The lack of training to develop the staff lowers the quality of their performance in the field and even negatively influences the field in the name of development projects.

Problem 1.6 NGOs tend to train the staff to meet the immediate needs of projects as quickly as possible by importing exogenous skills, knowledge and expertise. (See Chapter 3, 'Locals vs. expatriates'.) The consequences of this practice include the negation and subversion of indigenous knowledge and the creation of a gap between the field and HQ.

These problems all reflect pressures to meet immediate needs. To address these problems, the staff members practise the following strategies:

Strategy 1.1 The recruiters take into account not only task-oriented criteria such as skills, expertise and knowledge, but also criteria that measure various capacities such as flexibility, sensitivity, ability to listen and learn, honesty and the capacity to tolerate others. (See Chapter 2, 'Introducing alternative criteria'.)

Strategy 1.2 The recruiters and the field staff develop trust based on mutual understanding so that the field staff can delegate the whole recruitment process to the recruiters. (See Chapter 2, 'Recruiting based on trust'.)

Strategy 1.3 NGOs strategically make use of the recruitment process as a chance to make a difference in the organization, though doing so should not subvert organizational consistency. (See Chapter 2, 'Dealing with consistency and changes'.)

Strategy 1.4 The leadership broadens the staff members' views so that they gain the capacity to identify and address crucial issues properly instead of being trapped by a singular focus on their immediate needs. (See Chapter 3, 'Broadening views to identify the right questions'.)

Strategy 1.5 The leadership draw on latent abilities of the staff rather than importing expertise, knowledge and skills. (See Chapter 3, 'Drawing on latent abilities'.)

Strategy 1.6   The leadership train the staff in projects so that the organ-
                ization does not spend extra financial resources and time
                on training. In addition, by situating training in real work-
                ing contexts, the staff learn from the training more effec-
                tively than they would from training separated from the
                working context. (See Chapter 3, 'Training in projects'.)

In response to the problems staff members encounter, virtually all of
these strategies emphasize investing in the staff with a view to the long-
term return. However, the leadership must apply the strategies in such a
way that an NGO takes into account both programme-centred activities
and organization-centred activities simultaneously. Although these
strategies focus on developing organizational capacities, e.g., through
investing in the staff, the aim of the strategies is not to drive the organization to serve and perpetuate itself but to restore balance between the
opposing pressures of programme-centred activities and organization-
centred activities. Therefore, if the organization over-emphasizes
organization-centred activities, these strategies would be not merely
irrelevant but rather destructive. These strategies address the problems
identified here but do not attempt to achieve a pre-determined
outcome.

Diversity vs. similarity
Part II discussed the tensions between managing diversity and similarity
among staff members. As Table 5 indicates, NGOs need to balance two
pressures: the pressure to take advantage of differences among staff in
values, views and interests as a precious human resource for the organization, and the pressure to seek similarities among staff members in
terms of common understanding of organizational missions.

When NGO staff members emphasize diversity, they tend to value
differences over similarities, with fragmented performance the likely result of the organization's activities. But when staff members make fragmentation their biggest concern, they then emphasize the importance of
similarities over differences and introduce control mechanisms to enforce
similarity among staff members. In this case, homogeneity among staff
members, which diminishes the organization's capacity to handle diverse
problems, is the likely result.

Table 5. Tension among the Staff

Pathology	Area of Tension			Pathology
Fragmented performance	Diversity	⟵ ⟶	Similarity	Restricted performance

In Part II, Chapters 4 and 5 have identified and discussed a set of problems derived from two opposing pressures: diversity and similarity. Problems derived from the tensions between the two forces include the following:

Problem 2.1 Decentralization, which is an appreciation of diversity, tends to decrease order in the organization and divide it into fragmented pieces. Consequently, the organization suffers from fragmented performance. (See Chapter 4, 'Decentralization and loss of order'.)

Problem 2.2 Cultural differences often contribute to distrust between people with different cultural backgrounds and develop a schism among them. (See Chapter 4, 'Cultural differences'.)

Problem 2.3 Differences in experience, scope of knowledge, views and position make co-ordination among the staff difficult, if not impossible. Co-operative organizational endeavours suffer due to lack of co-ordination. (See Chapter 4, 'Differences in scope'.)

Problem 2.4 When the NGO leadership emphasize the importance of a coherent relationship among the staff members, they tend to recruit people with similar values, views, cultural backgrounds and interests. Consequently, they homogenize themselves and lose their capacity to address diverse local problems. In this case, restricted performance is the likely result. (See Chapter 5, 'Recruiting to homogenize the organization'.)

Problem 2.5 When an NGO attempts to build a sense of commonality among the staff, a sense of commonality among the leadership tends to dominate and is regarded as the identity of the entire organization. The identity of the field is subtly subsumed under the identity of the leadership. As a result, the organization fails to obtain valuable input from the field. (See Chapter 5, 'Constructing identity'.)

Problems 2.1 to 2.3 are the problems of fragmented performance caused by an emphasis on diversity, and Problems 2.4 and 2.5 are the problems of restricted performance caused by an emphasis on similarity. To address these problems, staff members use the following strategies:

Strategy 2.1 The staff employs rituals to develop a sense of community within the organization. (See Chapter 4, 'Rituals as a mediator'.) If the organization is based on religion, prayers can play a vital role in developing a common ground on which staff members discuss the issues at hand. Even if the organization is not based on religion, ritualized chatting enables the staff to protect room for constructing a common ground on which to build a sense of commonality.

Strategy 2.2   The staff use several variations of narratives to share their ideas, views and interests. The variations include coining terms, envisioning and articulating their missions together, and sharing their personal experiences with other staff members. (See Chapter 4, 'Narratives'.)

Strategy 2.3   By establishing a sense of commonality among the leadership first, the organization can prevent the staff from taking uncoordinated actions and can initiate coherent practices to promote common understandings among the staff. (See Chapter 4, 'Developing common understanding among leadership'.)

Strategy 2.4   Identifying and making use of any common ground instead of emphasizing their differences, the staff can more easily build a sense of commonality. (See Chapter 4, 'Associating differences'.)

Strategy 2.5   When the leadership intentionally protects time for the process of building a sense of commonality, the staff can avoid the pitfall of dealing with day-to-day tasks without having the big picture in mind. (See Chapter 4, 'Time is worth spending'.)

Strategy 2.6   When the staff are equipped and ready to deal with differences that they might face, they can tolerate unexpected, difficult situations that arise from differences among them. Moreover, they can even better use their differences as resources for contributing to their performance. (See Chapter 5, 'Dealing with differences'.)

Strategy 2.7   When the staff retain ownership of various activities in the organization, they have a better chance of employing their differences as relevant resources for organizational activities. (See Chapter 5, 'Taking charge of processes'.)

Strategies 2.1 to 2.5 address the issue of fragmented performance and attempt to build a sense of commonality among the staff. In the face of differences, the strategies aid staff members in developing relationships among themselves rather than minimizing their differences.

Strategies 2.6 and 2.7 tackle the issue of restricted performance. When an NGO consists of staff members who are similar in their views of organizational missions, the strategies help them to appreciate differences in values, views, ideas and so forth rather than concentrating on their sameness.[1]

---

[1] As I argue in Chapter 5, staff members can be distinctive while being similar in seeking to attain the same mission goals.

Flexibility vs. consistency

Part III discussed the tensions between flexibility and consistency. As Table 6 indicates, NGOs need to balance two more pressures: the pressure to remain flexible, adaptable and responsive to diverse local problems, and the pressure to remain consistent so that the organization can steadily and continuously seek to attain its objectives.

Table 6. Tension in Organizational Response

Pathology		Area of Tension		Pathology
Opportunism	Flexibility	◄─────►	Consistency	Unresponsive-ness

When NGO staff members pay more attention to flexibility, they tend to value responsiveness over systems, with opportunism the likely result. But when staff members worry about opportunism, they emphasize the importance of systems over responsiveness and introduce more formal systems. In this case, unresponsiveness is the likely result.

Chapter 6 has identified and discussed how NGOs struggle in the midst of the tensions between opportunism and unresponsiveness. Chapter 7 has identified and discussed how systems gain autonomy, perpetuate themselves, and bring about undesirable impacts on the organization. Once a system, such as a recruitment policy, is established, it begins functioning to perpetuate itself for its own sake. Thus, according to Table 6, the organization tends to be trapped by rigidity as systems self-perpetuate. The problems identified include:

Problem 3.1   Each system has its own reasonable rationale for its employment by the organization. Thus, employing systems aids in achieving the specific goals for which they were created. This rationale tempts the staff to establish new systems without careful consideration of their side effects. (See Chapter 6, 'Rationale for seeking systems'.)

Problem 3.2   Each system that is important for the targeted functionality is almost always accompanied by some side effect that disturbs the organization and turns it in different directions. Employment policy, money, language and *modus operandi* are all important and necessary for the organization. But they are, at the same time, accompanied by effects that prevent the organization from seeking to achieve its objectives. (See Chapter 6, 'Systems' undesirable impacts'.)

212

Problem 3.3   Systems such as rules, regulations, policies, procedures and so forth often possess self-perpetuating mechanisms and reproduce themselves to unjustly dominate the organization. The more the organization blindly and rigidly follows systems, the more the systems perpetuate themselves for their own sake. Under the perpetuation processes, the organization is exploited as the resource of the processes. (See Chapter 7.1, 'Constructing their own worlds'.)

Problem 3.4   Systematic interactions among the staff can play a catalytic role in enhancing and reproducing hierarchy in the organization. Perspectives, authority to make a decision, ability to express oneself, credibility, experiences and job titles are all hierarchically structured in the organization and the degree of hierarchy is systematically enforced as the staff interact to handle these issues. (See Chapter 7, 'Systems as a catalyst to reproduce hierarchy'.)

Problems 3.1 and 3.2 are side effects of systems, and Problems 3.3 and 3.4 are problems caused by the self-perpetuating mechanisms of systems. In the face of these problems, the staff members employ several alternative strategies:

Strategy 3.1   To avoid narrow-minded practices stemming from systems, the staff attempt to broaden views in many ways, such as sharing information, questioning, reminding themselves of their core values and protecting time for informal interactions. As the staff develop broader views, they are equipped with a variety of strategies from which they can select an appropriate one to deal with the issue at hand. Consequently, the staff can acquire the capability to judge situations rather than blindly following systems. (See Chapter 6, 'Broadening views'.)

Strategy 3.2   Prioritizing the staff over systems is another strategy to subvert the rigidity and narrowness of systems. By valuing various modes of communication such as face-to-face interactions, telephone conversations and personal letters, and by acknowledging each other's feelings and emotions, staff members treat each other as persons and can moderate the effects of their differences. As the staff develop mutual understanding by treating each other as persons, they can broaden their views and be in a better position to make wise judgements on the issues at hand. (See Chapter 6, 'Prioritizing the staff over systems'.)

Strategy 3.3	Critically examining the relevance of systems in specific contexts is a major strategy for addressing the problem of their self-perpetuation. Leaving room to make a decision to follow (or not follow) systems leads the staff to perform differently when they deal with systems and with other staff. The staff try to regard a rule as a mere support system but not as THE rule that they have to obey. The staff interact based on reciprocal relationships without much support from formalized systems. The staff identify themselves as artists who deal with issues in creative ways. (See Chapter 7, 'Judging systems'.)
Strategy 3.4	Actively making use of tensions that arise from intractable dilemmas is a wise strategy for making changes in the face of systems' rigidity. By deliberately living with two opposing but correct positions, the staff strategically embrace dilemmas for which systems do not offer an answer. As they face and live with a dilemma, they regain their capacity to remain flexible, responsive and adaptable to diverse and dynamic problems in the field. (See Chapter 7, 'Using tensions'.)
Strategy 3.5	Identifying and making better use of ambiguity is another novel but powerful strategy for revitalizing flexibility, responsiveness and adaptability among the staff. Focusing on the area of ambiguity where systems do not reach their regulatory power, the staff can act flexibly to address diverse problems. Ambiguity has been found in the degree of enforcement, the degree of freedom to employ one's own style to accomplish assigned tasks, and the degree of bringing one's own intentions and interpretation to the task of conveying information about a given situation. (See Chapter 7, 'Using ambiguity'.)

Conclusion

Five important general lessons suggest themselves. First, these tensions between opposing pressures themselves are neither problems nor the target of the strategies. Losing the balance between the opposing pressures causes problems in an NGO, and diverse strategies seek to rebalance the tensions.

Second, the strategies always address problems. Without problems, strategies do not make sense. In fact, problems motivate the staff to create new strategies. Hence, identifying problems is important. The more the problems are clarified, the more effective strategies can be applied to address the problems.

214

Third, continuous reflection helps to maintain the balance of an organization. So long as the staff continuously strive to identify issues, reconsider their understanding, views and values, and explore new strategies, they can remain flexible to balance the tensions.

Fourth, the strategies are not a panacea. Each strategy is applicable to a particular situation. Misusing the strategies can cause a situation to deteriorate rather than improve. Thus, the relevance of strategies must always be judged in context.

Lastly, strategies can facilitate staff learning as long as staff treat processes carefully; take a long-term stance; are willing and empowered to take risks; make better use of mistakes; and are ready to deconstruct their own frameworks to seek new, alternative understandings.

This research has overviewed problems that NGO staff face and strategies they employ to address these problems. The analysis remains general because the research interviews aimed mainly at identifying and probing problems and strategies rather than analysing certain problems or strategies that were identified a priori. These overviews lay the groundwork for more focused, critical and deep analyses of the three sets of tensions between two opposing pressures – analyses from which those working in and with NGOs should benefit considerably. In particular, various informal practices identified here – such as making use of rituals, narratives, emotions, ambiguities, trust and dilemmas – are rich and invaluable yet unexplored resources, which, with deeper understanding and proper application, can be employed to improve profoundly the performance of NGOs and NGO staff members. The exploration of these rich resources awaits future research.

APPENDIX A

The Origin of NGOs

SINCE THE 16TH CENTURY, many charitable organizations in Europe and North America have played roles as important trans-national actors. The earliest international agencies in Western societies were church-related organizations. According to Eggins (1967), the oldest is a Canadian society in Montreal founded in 1653.[1] Along with missionary organizations, educational institutions were founded in an attempt to 'educate' people in colonized countries in Africa and Asia.[2] Eggins (1967) also shows that the first secular voluntary organizations were medical aid organizations such as The American Medical Association, founded in 1847, and Save the Children in London (currently SF/UK), founded in 1919. These organizations have engaged in socio-economic development activities such as religious evangelization, education and disaster relief.

While these early trans-national activities were all voluntary, governments in the organizations' home countries valued the role that these organizations played as complements to, and even surrogates for, their own foreign policies. Some of these organizations received significant financial support from their home governments because their missionary objectives, such as the promotion of Western cultural values in colonial societies, were welcomed and encouraged by the governments.

In the United States, the government did not want to get involved in aid overseas until the end of the 1890s. However, from the period of the Spanish-American War in 1898 to the end of the 1930s, the government demonstrated a magnificent amount of giving to foreign countries. This was to be expected in view of the country's economic growth and its new role as a world power. This period was marked by an expansion of the government's role in overseas philanthropy.[3]

The majority of NGOs that have emerged in the last 100 years clearly served their governments' interests abroad through the various cultural

---

[1] The Canadian society 'Les Soeurs de la Congregation de Notre-Dame'.
[2] The first two educational institutions were founded in England: The Royal Society, founded in 1660, and the National Adult School Union, founded in 1798. French institutions followed: Ligue Française de l'Enseignment, founded in 1866, and Alliance Française, founded in 1883.
[3] Curti (1963).

and relief activities they performed. Nevertheless, this fact does not necessarily compromise the quality of NGO activities, at least on the surface. By the 1980s, over 2200 NGOs received donations and grants from industrialized countries and transmitted them to counterpart private non-profit institutions in the Third World. Twenty thousand organizations in developing countries now receive this assistance and attempt to work for the poor.[4] NGOs in the United States, Canada and Europe have gained reputations for their efficient and cost-effective activities in disaster situations. During disasters such as famines, floods, earthquakes and refugee crises, they are seen as having the capacity to react more quickly and efficiently than government agencies in bringing aid to the victims of such miseries.[5]

Throughout the history of NGOs, most of these organizations and the governments of their home countries have related to each other interdependently and have complemented each other in the fields of religious evangelization, disaster relief and 'education' (in the sense of promoting Western cultural values). While these activities have 'helped' people in the Third World, they have also been used as a device to maintain the *status quo* of the relationshps between industrialized countries and Third World countries.

Although the problems facing Third World countries apparently require social change to be solved, many NGOs, especially church-related ones, have declined to take political stances on social issues due to their missionary philosophies. More important, they are strictly observed by their home governments as a means to ensure that they behave apolitically. On the other hand, some progressive NGOs have begun to address both local government and their home governments about political issues, with an emphasis on the importance of development. These NGOs have tried to redirect NGO activities by redefining development as not merely the fulfilment of physical needs, but as a dynamic process to seek better socio-political conditions, such as broad participation in decision-making at all levels, a high degree of social justice, respect for cultural diversity and so forth. NGOs have undergone a transition from traditional charity-oriented organizations to social change-oriented organizations.

---

[4] OECD (1987).
[5] Van Der Heijden (1985).

APPENDIX B

Types of Development NGOs

DEVELOPMENT SCHOLARS CATEGORIZE NGOs in different ways and name them differently. The following are lists of NGO types categorized by four scholars.

Three types of NGOs are categorized by Fisher (1993, 8):

(1) Grassroots Organizations (GROs): locally-based groups that work to improve and develop their own communities, either with community-wide membership or more specific membership groups, such as women or farmers.

(2) Grassroots Support Organizations (GRSOs): groups that are concerned with development, the environment, the role of women and primary health care. They are nationally- or regionally-based development assistance organizations, usually staffed by professionals, that channel international funds to grassroots organizations (GROs) and help communities other than their own to develop.

(3) International Non-governmental Organizations (INGOs): groups that include all private overseas organizations working in development.

Private Agencies Collaborating Together (PACT) identifies three types of NGOs as follow (1989, 4):

(1) Voluntary Resource Organizations (VROs): organizations that support service or serve national non-governmental organizations (NGOs) rather than conducting village-based field programmes. This support takes the form of co-ordination, delivery of specific services and facilitation of far-reaching programme strategies.

(2) National Non-governmental Organizations (NGOs): organizations that are indigenous agencies that conduct village-based field programmes.

(3) International Private Voluntary Organizations (IPVOs): organizations that are external, non-governmental agencies working in the Third World.

Korten (1990a, 95) divides NGOs into four types:

(1) Voluntary Organizations (VOs): groups that pursue a social mission driven by a commitment to shared values.

(2) Public Service Contractors (PSCs): entities that function as market-oriented non-profit businesses serving public purposes.

219

(3) People's Organizations (POs): groups that represent their members' interests, have member-accountable leadership and are substantially self-reliant.

(4) Governmental Non-governmental Organizations (GONGOs): organizations that are creations of governments and serve as instruments of government policy.

Six types are classified by Clark (1991):

(1) Relief and Welfare Agencies (RWAs): agencies that concentrate on alleviating disasters.

(2) Technical Innovation Organizations (TIOs): organizations that operate their own projects to pioneer new or improved approaches to problems, and which tend to remain specialized in their chosen fields.

(3) Public Service Contractors (PSCs): groups that are mostly funded by Northern governments and that work closely with Southern governments and official aid agencies. They are contracted to implement components of official programmes.

(4) Popular Development Agencies (PDAs): agencies that are Northern NGOs and their Southern intermediary counterparts that concentrate on self-help, social development and grassroots democracy.

(5) Grassroots Development Organizations (GDOs): organizations that are locally-based Southern NGOs whose members are the poor and oppressed themselves, and which attempt to shape a popular development process.

(6) Advocacy Groups and Networks (AGNs): which have no field projects but exist primarily for education and lobbying.

Based on these classifications, relationships among the different types of NGOs can be depicted as in Table 7.

Regarding the types of Northern NGOs, RWAs and Northern TIOs (Clark) cannot be considered Northern development-oriented NGOs, for they do not serve development objectives. Hence, Clark's Northern PDAs and Northern AGNs, which are a part of INGOs in Fisher's taxonomy, a part of IPVOs in PACT's schema, and a part of Northern VOs in Korten's classification, are considered Northern NGOs working in development.

All four scholars seem to agree that Southern NGOs can at least be divided between those that work on grassroots development by themselves, as the first party, and those that support grassroots organizations, as the third party. While GROs in Fisher, NGOs in PACT, POs and Southern VOs in Korten, and GDOs in Clark can all be considered development organizations, some types within the range of Southern NGOs may not be considered development organizations. Korten's GONGOs and PSCs, and Clark's Southern TIOs, are basically interested in their own agendas, which differ from development agendas. Therefore, in Clark's categories, GDOs, Southern PDAs and Southern AGNs can be considered

Table 7. Types of NGOs in South and North

	Fisher	PACT	Korten	Clark
	GROs	NGOs	POs	GDOs
Southern NGOs			Southern VOs	Southern PDAs
	GRSOs	VROs		Southern AGNs
				Southern TIOs
			GONGOs	PSCs
			PSCs	RWAs
Northern NGOs	INGOs	IPVOs	Northern VOs	Northern TIOs
				Northern PDAs
				Northern AGNs

Sources: Fisher, 1993; PACT, 1989; Korten, 1990a; Clark, 1991.

Southern development-oriented NGOs, which are GSOs and a part of GRSOs in Fisher, NGOs and a part of VROs in PACT, and POs and a part of Southern VOs in Korten.

Research

Concept

Point of view

This research applied a critical stance in its methodology to focus not only on providing insight into an individual's sense-making practices (organizational practice), but also on uncovering the deeper structure of power relations which partly determines these practices (organizational praxis).[1] This approach was taken in the hope of developing an organizational analysis capable of changing organizational processes rather than developing 'scientism', which is an institutionalized form of reasoning that accepts the idea that the meaning of knowledge is defined by what the sciences do.[2]

The study regarded the interpretation of practitioners' storytelling as an important component of the research, for such storytelling is a pervasive aspect of organizational life, socializing members by providing the appropriate experiential base to make sense of organizational practices.[3] Throughout the research, tensions that the staff express in their storytelling were considered a crucial factor for understanding their practices and praxis because tensions not only cause problems but also provide opportunities to develop strategies to address problems.

Position of the researcher

Clarifying the position of the researcher should be important as it makes

---

[1] Organizational practices refer to institutionalized or habitual activities that are goal-directed problem-solving actions. By contrast, organizational praxis refers not only to the technical efforts to solve practical problems, but also to the attentive self-transformation of collective actors. This requires a thorough understanding and insight into the relationship among actors, social structures and history (Heydebrand, 1983). Feminist perspectives may also help us understand organizational praxis. See, for example, Frost (1987) and Gould (1979).

[2] See Steffy and Grimes (1986). The purpose of this study was not to test whether the logic was correct or not but to provide new insights into the ways issues might be identified and analysed.

[3] 'Thinking about an experience requires that we remember it and recount it to ourselves. This invariably takes the form of telling a story. Telling a story, then, is the "thinking completion" of the event, it is the form of dialogue in which I think with myself about what has happened . . . everybody feels that need to think about their experience in this way, because it is the only way we can become reconciled to reality' (Hill, 1979, 288).

the research itself and the outcome of the research considerably different.[4] In this research, the researcher viewed himself as a historically-produced entity made sensitive to NGO issues by his work experience in Ethiopia in a Japanese NGO; he recognized his biases in engaging in research by focusing on internal issues; and he considered the specific contexts in which data were collected by seeking multiple interviews to check single conversations. The researcher also understood that he needed to expand his critique to include the aim of research to maintain a self-reflective stance.[5]

Throughout the research process, the researcher tried to be honest with those who were involved in the research, and explained truthfully his aim, his background and his status if they asked. In each interview, he identified himself, briefly explained the outline of the study, and answered interviewees' questions until they were ready to accept the interviewer's role without coercion.

Data

Data source

This study is based on field research that was conducted in both HQs and FOs of NGOs between December 1993 and July 1994. Data were collected from staff members working in the HQs and four FOs of each of four international NGOs (four HQs and 16 FOs in total).

The four NGOs were selected based on the following criteria: (1) they were operational (implementing projects rather than funding other NGOs); (2) they were large enough to have several FOs in the Third World and several staff members in each office; (3) they agreed to co-operate with this research; and (4) they had FOs in the same countries so

Table 8. Profiles of the Four NGOs

NGO	No. of staff	No. of field offices	Total	Annual budget (US$ million) (Private, Public, Self-financing %)		
A	<500	<20	<100	(<30%	>60%	<10%)
B	<500	<20	<100	(>60%	<40%	<2%)
C	>5000	>50	>200	(<20%	>80%	<2%)
D	>5000	>50	>200	(>90%	<10%	<2%)

Sources: InterAction *Member Profiles* (1991), *Directory of Non-Governmental Environment and Development Organizations in OECD Member Countries* (OECD, 1992), and *Human Rights, Refugees, Migrants & Development: Directory of NGOs in OECD Countries* (OECD, 1993).

---

[4] Astley (1985) argues that the knowledge of administrative science does not stem from objective data but from subjective views, which are the product of social definition.
[5] See McCarthy (1978).

that the researcher could cover all of their FOs in a country. The four NGOs happened to include two Christian NGOs and two non-religiously-based NGOs. All four NGOs are involved in a variety of development projects as their main activities and relief operations as emergency situations arise.

Kenya, Ethiopia, Thailand and Cambodia were chosen as research countries. The countries were selected from those countries in which the selected NGOs have their FOs. Two countries from Asia and another two from Africa were selected to cover the diversity of the FOs of the NGOs.

Data collection

This research mainly used interviews as its method to collect data. Although the researcher did not ignore other methods such as observation, documents and artefacts, the time constraints involved in visiting many offices in different countries within a limited time frame led the researcher to rely mainly on interviews.

i) Interviews

Semi-structured, open-ended interviews were conducted with a total of 76 respondents who were staff members of the four NGOs. In each of 20 offices (four HQs and sixteen FOs in total), the researcher interviewed an average of about four staff members (from a minimum of one to a maximum of seven) who had worked with FOs or HQs respectively. The respondents included: eight senior manager-level staff in HQs who play major roles in directing the organizations; 16 desk officer-level staff in HQs who deal with day-to-day work with FOs and donors; 11 country directors in FOs; 20 deputy country director-level staff; 14 project managers; and seven administrators/accountants.

During each interview, the researcher tried to explore the problems and strategies of respondents through their day-to-day work. Instead of directly asking, 'What are your problems and strategies?' the researcher began the interview by asking, 'What do you do in your day-to-day work?' By letting the respondents tell the story of their daily work, the researcher, but not the respondents themselves, tried to explore their problems, concerns, interests, strategies for addressing issues, and so forth.

Most interviews were conducted by appointment, in staff members' offices during office hours for about 45 minutes to an hour each. Interviews were conducted in English with a few exceptions.[6] Assuring the confidentiality of the interviews, the researcher took notes and, by agreement with interviewees, tape-recorded 74 out of 76 interviews.[7]

---

[6] A few respondents whose mother tongue is Japanese were interviewed in that language.
[7] For the two respondents who showed uneasiness about the recording, the researcher did not tape-record but only took notes in the interviews.

All recorded interviews were transcribed after the field research for deeper analysis. However, ongoing inductive analysis took place, as data were collected in the field. After each interview, the researcher tried to: (1) understand the meaning and implications that emerged from the interview based on interview notes; (2) analyse what he queried and what response he received; (3) refine research questions and develop working themes; and then (4) prepare the next interview based on the emergent questions and themes. Interactions between data collection and data analysis contributed to the improvement of interviews.

ii) Observations
Minimal time was available to observe staff activities. However, the researcher observed what happened during his visits to the offices and took notes on whatever he noticed.

iii) Documents
The researcher collected documents that seemed to help with understanding the HQs–FOs relationship. Collected documents include: (1) internal organizational structure descriptions; (2) job descriptions for staff members; (3) intraorganizational and interorganizational networks; (4) lists of funding sources; (5) descriptions of programme activities; (6) documents on organizational history; (7) programme evaluation reports; and (8) statements of organizational missions.

Analysis

After the field research, deeper analysis began based mainly on the transcribed texts. Recurring themes emerged from inductive analysis during the field research, and the researcher's initial, broad framework concerning the HQs–FOs relationships was scrutinized, deconstructed and reframed in light of the transcribed texts. The researcher tried to focus on the transcribed texts and field notes with the help of, but not relying heavily on,[8] his initial framework and literature[9] to pose several main issues as he coded data and developed a category system for framing data.

---

[8] To avoid failing to identify issues that are important in their own terms but not important for the researcher, the researcher attempted to interpret the texts in various ways. As an example of multiple ways to interpret a text, see Martin (1990). For its philosophical root, see Derrida (1973).

[9] Mumby and Putnam (1992) caution that researchers tend to take their languages for granted so that they are often unable to recognize that their languages are the products of their own unique backgrounds and are different from others'. Foucault (1979, 1980) argues that truth-claims depend upon the particular power-knowledge arrangements within which they are found. From a feminist perspective, Devault (1990) says, '[T]o fully describe women's experiences, we often need to go beyond standard vocabulary – not just in our analyses, but also in the ways that we actually talk with those we interview.'

Three broad problem areas emerged as relevant analytical tools after several attempts to process the data coding and to develop the system of categories. The problem areas are separated according to types of tensions that NGOs and NGO staff members experience: (1) tensions between programme-centred and organization-centred activities, (2) tensions between diversity and similarity of the staff members, and (3) tensions between the flexibility and consistency of an NGO. Each problem area embodies two opposing pressures under which the staff members face problems and employ strategies to address them.

While areas of problems and strategies are too diverse to apply a single theory to analyse or explain all of them, most of the problems and strategies are considered as issues related to NGOs' internal organizational hierarchies. In particular, the hierarchical relationships between HQs and FOs become the major focal point of analysis. Because the HQs–FOs relationships are multi-dimensional, the study employs various analytical tools to examine the relationships. Specifically, skills, knowledge, languages, cultures, values, perspectives and their socio-economic contexts are important components that influence the relationships to a great extent. HQs and FOs are not merely different in these components but are hierarchically ordered by the components.[10]

Having identified the internal issues, however, this study does not ignore the interactions of an NGO with its environments. Rather, the research attempts to understand the impact of the environments (e.g., donors/governments and projects/beneficiaries) on the internal dynamics of an NGO.[11]

To analyse this type of issue properly, the research views an NGO as a political entity[12] in which staff members with different interests, values, authorities, power, cultures and languages interact not only with each other but also with their environments outside the organization. Based on this theoretical framework, the research examines how the staff members are influenced in problematic ways through internal interactions within the organization and external interactions with their environments on the one hand; and how they strategically influence the organization and the environments through their attempts to address the problems, on the other.[13]

---

[10] These categories value and favour HQs' experiences more than FOs' experiences. Feminist analyses of knowledge also hold that different sets of knowledge held by men and women are hierarchically ordered.

[11] The research perceives an NGO as an open system that interacts with its environments rather than a closed system. For discussions and clarification of open systems, see Scott (1992).

[12] For discussions of the relationship between power and discourse in organizations, see Deetz and Mumby (1990).

[13] See the theory of structuration (Giddens, 1979, 69–73).

References

Agor, Weston H. 1989. *Intuition in Organizations: Leading and Managing Productively.* Newbury Park, California: Sage Publications.

Aldrich, Howard E. 1979. *Organizations and Environments.* Englewood Cliffs, New Jersey: Prentice-Hall.

Aldrich, Howard E. 1992. Incommensurable Paradigms? Vital Signs from Three Perspectives. In Reed, Michael and Michael Hughes (Ed.), *Rethinking Organization: New Directions in Organization Theory and Analysis* (pp. 17–45). London: Sage Publications.

Allison, Graham T. 1971. *Essence of Decision: Explaining the Cuban Missile Crisis.* Boston: Little, Brown.

Antrobus, Peggy. 1987. Funding for NGOs: Issues and Options. *World Development*, 15(Supplement): 95–102.

Arendt, Hannah. 1958. *The Human Condition.* Chicago: University of Chicago Press.

Argyris, Chris and Donald A. Schön. 1974. *Theory in Practice: Increasing Professional Effectiveness.* San Francisco: Jossey-Bass Publishers.

Argyris, Chris and Donald A. Schön. 1978. *Organizational Learning: A Theory of Action Perspective.* Reading, Massachusetts: Addison-Wesley Pub. Co.

Asian NGO Coalition for Agrarian Reform and Rural Development. 1987. *NGO Management Development and Training: Recent Experiences and Future Possibilities.* ANGOC/ICVA. 18–23 January, 1987.

Astley, W. Graham. 1985. Administrative Science as Socially Constructed Truth. *Administrative Science Quarterly*, 30(4): 497–513.

Ati, Hassan Ahmed Abdel. 1993. The Development Impact of NGO Activities in the Red Sea Province of Sudan: A Critique. *Development and Change*, 24(1): 103–30.

Axelrod, Robert. 1984. *The Evolution of Cooperation.* New York: BasicBooks.

Baker, Randall. 1989. Institutional Innovation, Development and Environmental Management: An 'Administrative Trap' Revisited. Part II. *Public Administration and Development*, 9(2): 159–67.

Barber, Benjamin. 1984. *Strong Democracy: Participatory Politics for a New Age.* Berkeley: University of California Press.

Barley, Stephen R. 1986. Technology as an Occasion for Structuring: Evidence from Observations of CT Scanners and the Social Order of Radiology Departments. *Administrative Science Quarterly*, 31: 78–108.

Barley, Stephen R. 1990. The Alignment of Technology and Structure through Roles and Networks. *Administrative Science Quarterly*, 35: 61–103.

Baum, Howell S. 1987. *The Invisible Bureaucracy: The Unconscious in Organizational Problem Solving*. New York: Oxford University Press.

Bebbington, Anthony and John Farrington. 1993. Governments, NGOs and Agricultural Development: Perspectives on Changing Inter-Organizational Relationships. *The Journal of Development Studies*, 29(2): 199–219.

Becker, Howard S. 1970. Whose Side Are We on? In Filstead, William J. (Ed.), *Qualitative Methodology: Firsthand Involvement With the Social World* (pp. 15–25). Chicago: Markham Publishing Co.

Beiner, Ronald. 1983. *Political Judgment*. Chicago: Chicago University Press.

Béjar, Héctor and Peter Oakley. 1996. From Accountability to Shared Responsibility: NGO Evaluation in Latin America. In Edwards, Michael and David Hulme (Ed.), *Beyond the Magic Bullet: NGO Performance and Accountability in the Post-Cold War World* (pp. 91–100). West Hartford, Connecticut: Kumarian Press.

Belenky, Mary Field, Blythe McVicker Clinchy, Nancy Rule Goldberger and Jill Mattuck Tarule. 1986. *Women's Ways of Knowing: The Development of Self, Voice, and Mind*. New York: BasicBooks.

Benson, J. Kenneth. 1977. Organizations: A Dialectical View. *Administrative Science Quarterly*, 22: 1–21.

Berman, Edward H. 1980. Educational Colonialism in Africa: The Role of American Foundations, 1910–1945. In Arnove, Robert F. (Ed.), *Philanthropy and Cultural Imperialism: The Foundations at Home and Abroad*. Boston, Massachusetts: G.K. Hall and Co.

Billis, David. 1992. Planned Change in Voluntary and Government Social Service Agencies. *Administration in Social Work*, 16(3/4): 29–44.

Billis, David. 1993. *Organising Public and Voluntary Agencies*. London, New York: Routledge.

Billis, David and Joy MacKeith. 1992. Growth and Change in NGOs: Concepts and Comparative Experience. In Edwards, Michael and David Hulme (Ed.), *Making a Difference: NGOs and Development in a Changing World* (pp. 118–126). London: Earthscan Publications.

Billis, David and Joy MacKeith. 1993. *Organising NGOs: Challenges and Trends in the Management of Overseas Aid*. London: Centre for Voluntary Organization, London School of Economics.

Blunt, Peter. 1990. Strategies for Enhancing Organizational Effectiveness in the Third World. *Public Administration and Development*, 10(3): 299–313.

Boone, Edgar J. 1989. Philosophical Foundations of Extension. In Blackburn, Donald J. (Ed.), *Foundations and Changing Practices in Extension* (pp. 1–9). Guelph: University of Guelph.

Booth, Alan, Douglas Higgins and Robert Cornelius. 1989. Community Influences on Funds Raised by Human Service Volunteers. *Nonprofit and Voluntary Sector Quarterly*, 18(1): 81–92.

Boulding, Kenneth E. 1989. *Three Faces of Power*. Newbury Park, California: Sage Publications.

Bowden, Peter. 1990. NGOs in Asia: Issues in Development. *Public Administration and Development*, 10(2): 141–52.

Bratton, Michael. 1989. The Politics of Government-NGO Relations in Africa. *World Development*, 17(4): 569–87.

Brinkerhoff, Derick W. 1979. Inside Public Bureaucracy: Empowering Managers to Empower Clients. *Rural Development Committee, Cornell University*, 1(1): 7–9.

Brown, John Seely and Paul Duguid. 1996. Organizational Learning and Communities-of-Practice: Toward a Unified View of Working, Learning, and Innovation. In Cohen, Michael D. and Lee S. Sproull (Ed.), *Organizational Learning* (pp. 58–82). Thousand Oaks, London, New Delhi: Sage Publications.

Brown, L. David. 1985. People-Centered Development and Participatory Research. *Harvard Educational Review*, 55(1): 69–75.

Brown, L. David. 1988. Organizational Barriers to NGO Strategic Action. In *NGO Strategic Management in Asia: Focus on Bangladesh, Indonesia, and the Philippines* (pp. 21–31). Asian NGO Coalition for Agrarian Reform and Rural Development, Philippines.

Brown, L. David. 1991a. Bridging Organizations and Sustainable Development. *Human Relations*, 44(8): 807–31.

Brown, L. David. 1991b. Methodological Considerations in the Evaluation of Social Development Programmes – An Alternative Approach. *Community Development Journal*, 26(4): 259–65.

Brown, L. David. 1993. Social Change Through Collective Reflection with Asian Nongovernmental Development Organizations. *Human Relations*, 46(2): 249–73.

Brown, L. David and Jane G. Covey. 1989. Organization Development in Social Change Organizations: Some Implications for Practice. In Drexler, S.W. and J. Grant (Ed.), *The Emerging Practice of Organizational Development*. NLT, Institute for Applied Behavioral Science.

Brown, L. David and David C. Korten. 1989. *Understanding Voluntary Organizations: Guidelines for Donors*. Washington, D.C.: The World Bank.

Brown, Roger. 1965. *Social Psychology*. New York: Free Press.

Bruner, Jerome. 1990. *Acts of Meaning*. Cambridge, Massachusetts: Harvard University Press.

Bryant, Coralie and Louise G. White. 1982. *Managing Development in the Third World*. Boulder, Colorado: Westview Press.

Bryson, John M. 1988. *Strategic Planning for Public and Nonprofit Organizations: A guide to Strengthening and Sustaining Organizational Achievement*. San Francisco: Jossey-Bass Publishers.

Burbules, Nicholas C. and Suzanne Rice. 1991. Dialogue Across Differences: Continuing the Conversation. *Harvard Educational Review*, 61(4): 393–416.

Cameron, Kim S. and David A. Whetten. 1983. *Organizational Effectiveness: A Comparison of Multiple Models*. New York: Academic Press.

Carr, Irene Campos. 1990. The Politics of Literacy in Latin America. *Convergence*, 23(2): 50–67.

Carroll, Thomas F. 1992a. *Capacity-Building for Participatory Organizations*. Washington, D.C.: The World Bank. 26–27 February, 1992.

Carroll, Thomas F. 1992b. *Intermediary NGOs: The Supporting Link in Grassroots Development*. West Hartford, Connecticut: Kumarian Press.

Casse, Pierre and Surinder Deol. 1985. *Managing Intercultural Negotiations: Guidelines For Trainers and Negotiators*. Washington, D.C.: SIETAR International.

Chamberlain, Neil W. and James W. Kuhn. 1965. *Collective Bargaining* (2nd edn). New York: McGraw-Hill.

Chambers, Robert. 1985. *Managing Rural Development: Ideas and Experience from East Africa*. West Hartford, Connecticut: Kumarian Press.

Chambers, Robert, 1996. The Primacy of the Personal. In Edwards, Michael and David Hulme (Ed.), *Beyond the Magic Bullet: NGO Performance and Accountability in the Post-Cold War World* (pp. 241–53). West Hartford, Connecticut: Kumarian Press.

Clark, John. 1991. *Democratizing Development: The Role of Voluntary Organizations*. West Hartford, Connecticut: Kumarian Press.

Clark, John. 1995. The State, Popular Participation, and the Voluntary Sector. *World Development*, 23(4): 593–601.

Clegg, Stewart R. 1989. Radical Revisions: Power, Discipline and Organizations. *Organization Studies*, 10(1): 97–115.

Cohen, John M. and Norman T. Uphoff. 1980. Participation's Place in Rural Development: Seeking Clarity through Specificity. *World Development*, 8(3): 213–35.

Cohen, Michael D. and Lee S. Sproull. 1996. *Organizational Learning*. Thousand Oaks, London, New Delhi: Sage Publications.

Collion, Marie-Hélène and Ali Kissi. 1993. Learning by Doing: Developing a Programme Planning Method in Morocco. *Public Administration and Development*, 13(3): 261–70.

Constantino-David, Karina. 1992. The Philippine Experience in Scaling-Up. In Edwards, Michael and David Hulme (Ed.), *Making a Difference: NGOs and Development in a Changing World* (pp. 137–47). London: Earthscan Publications.

Conyers, Diana and Mohan Kaul. 1990. Strategic Issues in Development Management: Learning from Successful Experience. Part I. *Public Administration and Development*, 10(2): 127–40.

Craig, Gary, Marjorie Mayo and Marilyn Taylor. 1990. Editorial Introduction: Empowerment: A Continuing Role for Community Development. *Community Development Journal*, 25(4): 286–90.

Curti, Merle. 1963. *American Philanthropy Abroad: A History*. New Brunswick, New Jersey. Rutgers University Press.

Daley, John Michael and Julio Angulo. 1990. People-Centered Community Planning. *Journal of the Community Development Society*, 21(2): 88–103.

Daley, John Michael and Peter M. Kettner. 1986. The Episode of Purposive Change. *Journal of the Community Development Society*, 17(2): 54–72.

Daniels, Doug and Tim Dottridge. 1993. Managing Agricultural Research: Views from a Funding Agency. *Public Administration and Development*, 13(3): 205–15.

Davis, Murray S. 1971. That's Interesting: Towards a Phenomenology of Sociology and a Sociology of Phenomenology. *Philosophy of the Social Sciences*, 1: 309–44.

Dawes, Robyn M. and Richard H. Thaler. 1988. Anomalies: Cooperation. *Journal of Economic Perspectives*, 2(3): 187–97.

De Graaf, Martin. 1987. Context, Constraint or Control? Zimbabwean NGOs and Their Environment. *Development Policy Review*, 5: 277–301.

De Senillosa, Ignacio. 1992. Beyond NGDOs: Is Utopia Still Viable? *Development in Practice*, 2(2): 114–20.

Deetz, Stanley A. and Dennis K. Mumby. 1990. Power, Discourse, and the Workplace: Reclaiming the Critical Tradition. In Anderson, James A. (Ed.), *Communication Yearbook 13* (pp. 18–47).

Derrida, Jacques. 1973. *Speech and Phenomena*. Evanston: Northwestern University Press.

Deshler, David. 1993. *Learning Approaches From the Critical Reflection Tradition* (Mini-lecture No. 2). Cornell University. 24 March, 1993.

Devault, Marjorie L. 1990. Talking and Listening from Women's Standpoint: Feminist Strategies for Interviewing and Analysis. *Social Problems*, 37(1): 96–116.

Dewey, John. 1922. The Nature of Deliberation, & Deliberation and Calculation. In *Human Nature and Conduct* (pp. 189–209). New York: Carlton House.

Dewey, John. 1934. Art as Experience. Reprinted in Albert Hofstadter and Richard Kuhns (Ed.). 1964. *Philosophies of Art and Beauty: Selected Readings in Aesthetics from Plato to Heidegger*. Chicago: University of Chicago Press.

Dewey, John and James H. Tufts. 1910. *Ethics*. New York: Henry Holt and Company.

DiBella, Anthony J. 1992. Planned Change in an Organized Anarchy: Support for a Postmodernist Perspective. *Journal of Organizational Change Management*, 5(3): 55–65.

DiBella, Anthony J. 1993. The Role of Assumptions in Implementing Management Practices Across Cultural Boundaries. *The Journal of Applied Behavioral Science*, 29(3): 311–27.

Dichter, Thomas W. 1989. Development Management: Plain or Fancy? Sorting Out Some Muddles. *Public Administration and Development*, 9(4): 381–93.

DiMaggio, Paul J. and Walter W. Powell. 1983. The Iron Cage Revisited: Institutional Isomorphism and Collective Rationality in Organizational Fields. *American Sociological Review*, 48(April): 147–60.

Dolnick, Sandy F. 1987. *Fundraising for Nonprofit Institutiions*. Greenwich, Connecticut: JAI Press.

Drabek, Anne Gordon. 1987. *Development Alternatives: The Challenge for NGOs*. Oxford, New York: Pergamon Press.

Driver, Tom F. 1991. *The Magic of Ritual: Our Need for Liberating Rites that Transform Our Lives and Our Communities*. San Francisco: HarperSan Francisco.

Drucker, Peter F. 1990. *Managing the Nonprofit Organization: Principles and Practices*. New York: HarperCollins.

Duffield, Mark. 1991. Where Famine is Functional: Actual Adjustment and the Politics of Relief in Sudan. *Middle East Report*, (September–October): 27–30.

Eaton, Joseph W. 1972. *Institution Building and Development: From Concepts to Application*. Beverly Hills, California: Sage Publications.

Edwards, Michael. 1994. NGOs in the Age of Information. *IDS Bulletin*, 25(2): 117–24.

Edwards, Michael and David Hulme. 1992a. Scaling Up NGO Impact on Development: Learning from Experience. *Development in Practice*, 2(2): 77–91.

Edwards, Michael and David Hulme. 1992b. Scaling-Up the Developmental Impact of NGOs: Concepts and Experiences. In Edwards, Michael and David Hulme (Ed.), *Making a Difference: NGOs and Development in a Changing World* (pp. 13–27). London: Earthscan Publications.

Edwards, Michael and David Hulme. 1996. *Beyond the Magic Bullet: NGO Performance and Accountability in the Post-Cold War World*. West Hartford, Connecticut: Kumarian Press.

Eggins, Edwin. 1967. *Development Aid of Non-Governmental Non-Profit Organizations*. Paris: OECD-ICVA.

Ellsworth, Elizabeth. 1989. Why Doesn't This Feel Empowering? Working Through the Repressive Myths of Critical Pedagogy. *Harvard Educational Review*, 59(3): 297–324.

Erikson, Erik H. 1959. *Identity and the Life Cycle*. New York: W.W. Norton & Company.

Esman, Milton J. 1988. The Maturing of Development Administration. *Public Administration and Development*, 8(2): 125–34.

Esman, Milton J. 1991. *Management Dimensions of Development: Perspectives and Strategies*. West Hartford, Connecticut: Kumarian Press.

Faludi, Andreas. 1987. *A Decision-Centred View of Environmental Planning*. Oxford: Pergamon Press.

Fanon, Frantz. 1967. *Black Skin White Masks*. New York: Grove Press.

Fieldhouse, David Kenneth. 1982. *The Colonial Empires: A Comparative Survey from the Eighteenth Century*. London: Macmillan.

Fineman, Stephen. 1993. Organizations as Emotional Arenas. In Fineman, Stephen (Ed.), *Emotion in Organizations* (pp. 9–35). London: Sage Publications.

Fischer, Frank and Carmen Sirianni. 1984. *Critical Studies in Organization and Bureaucracy*. Philadelphia: Temple University Press.

Fisher, Julie. 1993. *The Road from Rio: Sustainable Development and the Nongovernmental Movement in the Third World*. Westport, Connecticut: Praeger.

Fisher, Roger and William Ury. 1991. *Getting to Yes: Negotiating Agreement Without Giving In* (2nd edn). New York: Penguin Books.

Fishkin, James S. 1991. *Democracy and Deliberation: New Directions for Democratic Reform*. New Haven, Connecticut: Yale University Press.

Fitzhenry, Robert I. 1993. *The Harper Book of Quotations*. New York: Harper Perennial.

Forester, John. 1989. *Planning in the Face of Power*. Berkeley, California: University of California Press.

Forester, John. 1993. *Critical Theory, Public Policy, and Planning Practice: Toward a Critical Pragmatism*. Albany: State University of New York Press.

Foucault, Michel. 1979. *Discipline and Punish: The Birth of the Prison*. New York: Vintage Books.

Foucault, Michel. 1980. Two Lectures. In Gordon, Colin (Ed.), *Power/Knowledge: Selected Interviews and Other Writings 1972–1977* (pp. 78–108). New York: Pantheon.

Fowler, Alan. 1990. What is Different About Managing Non-Government Organisations (NGOs) Involved in Third World Development. *NGO Management*, 12(January–March).

Fowler, Alan. 1991. The Role of NGOs in Changing State Society Relations: Perspectives from Eastern and Southern Africa. *Development Policy Review*, 9(1): 53–84.

Fowler, Alan. 1992a. Decentralisation for International NGOs. *Development in Practice*, 2(2): 121–4.

Fowler, Alan. 1992b. Distant Obligations: Speculations on NGO Funding and the Global Market. *Review of African Political Economy*, 55: 9–29.

Fowler, Alan. 1993. Non-Governmental Organizations as Agents of Democratization: An African Perspective. *Journal of International Development*, 3(3): 325–39.

Fowler, Alan. 1996. Assessing NGO Performance: Difficulties, Dilemmas, and a Way Ahead. In Edwards, Michael and David Hulme (Ed.), *Beyond the Magic Bullet: NGO Performance and Accountability in the Post-Cold War World* (pp. 169–86). West Hartford, Connecticut: Kumarian Press.

Fox, Alan. 1974. Discretion, Status, and Rewards in Work. In *Beyond Contract: Work, Power and Trust Relations* (pp. 13–65). London: Faber.

Franks, Tom. 1989. Bureaucracy, Organization Culture and Development. *Public Administration and Development*, 9(4): 357–368.

Friedmann, John. 1987. *Planning in the Public Domain: From Knowledge to Action*. Princeton, New Jersey: Princeton University.

Friedmann, John. 1992. *Empowerment: The Politics of Alternative Development*. Cambridge, Massachusetts: Blackwell Publishers.

Frost, Peter J. 1987. Power, Politics, and Influence. In Jablin, Fredric M., Linda L. Putnam, Karlene H. Roberts and Lyman W. Porter (Ed.), *Handbook of Organizational Communication: An Interdisciplinary Perspective* (pp. 503–48). Beverly Hills, California: Sage Publications.

Frye, Marilyn. 1983. *The Politics of Reality: Essays in Feminist Theory*. Trumansburg, New York: The Crossing Press.

Garain, Swapan. 1994. Government–NGO Interface in India: An Overview. *The Indian Journal of Social Work*, 55(3): 337–46.

Giddens, Anthony. 1979. *Central Problems in Social Theory: Action, Structure and Contradiction in Social Analysis*. Berkeley, California: University of California Press.

Giddens, Anthony. 1990. *The Consequences of Modernity*. Stanford, California: Stanford University Press.

Goldsmith, Arthur. 1996. Strategic Thinking in International Development: Using Management Tools to See the Big Picture. *World Development*, 24(9): 1431–9.

Gould, Meredith. 1979. When Women Create An Organization: The Ideological Imperatives of Feminism. In Dunkerley, David and Graeme Salaman (Ed.), *The International Yearbook of Organization Studies 1979* (pp. 237–52). London: Routledge and Kegan Paul.

Gouldner, Alvin W. 1963. The Secrets of Organizations. In *The Social Welfare Forum 1963* (pp. 161–77). New York: Columbia University Press.

Gutmann, Amy. 1993. The Challenge of Multiculturalism in Political Ethics. *Philosophy and Public Affairs*, 22(3): 171–206.

Hage, Per and Frank Harary. 1983. *Structural Models in Anthropology*. Cambridge: Cambridge University Press.

Handy, Charles. 1988. *Understanding Voluntary Organizations*. New York: Penguin Books.

Handy, Charles. 1990. *The Age of Unreason*. Boston, Massachusetts: Harvard Business School Press.

Handy, Charles. 1993. *Understanding Organizations*. New York, Oxford: Oxford University Press.

Hashemi, Syed M. 1996. NGO Accountability in Bangladesh: Beneficiaries, Donors, and the State. In Edwards, Michael and David Hulme (Ed.), *Beyond the Magic Bullet: NGO Performance and Accountability in the Post-Cold War World* (pp. 123–31). West Hartford, Connecticut: Kumarian Press.

Hayek, Friedrich A. 1945. The Use of Knowledge in Society. *American Economic Review*, 35(4): 519–30.

Herman, Robert D. and Richard D. Heimovics. 1989. Critical Events in the Management of Nonprofit Organizations: Initial Evidence. *Nonprofit and Voluntary Sector Quarterly*, 18(2): 119–32.

Heydebrand, Wolf V. 1983. Organization and Praxis. In Morgan, Gareth (Ed.), *Beyond Method: Strategies for Social Research* (pp. 306–20). Beverly Hills: Sage Publications.

Hill, Melvyn, A. 1979. The Fictions of Mankind and the Stories of Men. In Hill, Melvyn (Ed.), *Hannah Arendt: The Recovery of the Public World* (pp. 275–300). New York: St. Martin's Press.

Hirschman, Albert O. 1967. The Principle of the Hiding Hand. *The Public Interest*, 6(Winter): 10–23.

Hirschman, Albert O. 1970. *Exit, Voice, and Loyalty: Responses to Decline in Firms, Organizations, and States*. Cambridge, Massachusetts: Harvard University Press.

Hodgkinson, Virginia A. and Russy D. Sumariwalla. 1992. The Nonprofit Sector and the New Global Community: Issues and Challenges. In *The Nonprofit Sector in The Global Community: Voices from Many Nations* (pp. 485–508). San Francisco: Jossey-Bass Publishers.

Horkheimer, Max. 1974. *Critique of Instrumental Reason*. New York: Seabury.

Horton, Myles and Paulo Freire. 1990. *We Make the Road by Walking: Conversations on Education and Social Change*. Philadelphia: Temple University Press.

Howard, Philip K. 1994. *The Death of Common Sense: How Law is Suffocating America*. New York: Random House.

Howes, Mick. 1992. Linking Paradigms and Practice: Key Issues in the Appraisal, Monitoring and Evaluation of British NGO Projects. *Journal of International Development*, 4(4): 375–96.

Hughes, Terence Stirling. 1991. *Organizational Learning in Rural Development Agencies*. Ph.D. Dissertation, Cornell University.

Hulme, David and Michael Edwards. 1997. NGOs, States and Donors: An Overview. In Hulme, David and Michael Edwards (Ed.), *NGOs, States and Donors: Too Close For Comfort?* (pp. 3–22). New York: St. Martin's Press.

234

Hunter, Albert and Suzanne Staggenborg. 1988. Local Communities and Organized Action. In Milofsky, Carl (Ed.), *Community Organizations: Studies in Resource Mobilization and Exchange* (pp. 243–76).

Ingram, Larry C. and Ann Carol King. 1995. Organizational Mission As Source of Vulnerability: Comparing Attitudes of Trustees and Professors in Southern Baptist Colleges. *Review of Religious Research*, 36(4): 355–68.

InterAction. 1991. *Member Profiles*. Washington, D.C.: The American Council for Voluntary International Action.

Israel, Arturo. 1987. *Institutional Development: Incentives to Performance.* Baltimore, Maryland: Johns Hopkins University Press.

Jackall, Robert. 1983. Moral Mazes: Bureaucracy and Managerial Work. *Harvard Business Review*, (September/October): 118–30.

James, Estelle. 1989. *The Nonprofit Sector in International Perspective: Studies in Comparative Culture and Policy.* New York: Oxford University Press.

Jurmo, Paul. 1985. *'Dialogue is not a Chaste Event.' Comments by Paulo Freire on Issues in Participatory Research*. Amherst, Massachusetts: Center for International Education.

Kabeer, Naila. 1991. Gender, Development, and Training: Raising Awareness in the Planning Process. *Development in Practice*, 1(3): 185–95.

Kelleher, David and Kate McLaren. 1996. *Grabbing the Tiger by the Tail: NGOs Learning for Organizational Change.* Canadian Council for International Co-operation.

Khleif, Bud B. and N.H. Durham. 1993. Minoritization of Languages in Their Traditional Historical Territories: Issues of Autonomy and Identity in the Nation-State. *Sociologia Internationalis*, 31(2): 159–78.

Kiggundu, Moses N. 1989. *Managing Organizations in Developing Countries: An Operational and Strategic Approach.* West Hartford, Connecticut: Kumarian Press.

Korten, David C. 1980. Community Organization and Rural Development: A Learning Process Approach. *Public Administration Review*, 40(5): 480–511.

Korten, David C. 1988. New Roles and Challenges for Asian NGOs. In *NGO Strategic Management in Asia: Focus on Bangladesh, Indonesia, and the Philippines* (pp. 9–19). Asian NGO Coalition for Agrarian Reform and Rural Development, Philippines.

Korten, David C. 1990a. *Getting to the 21st Century: Voluntary Action and the Global Agenda.* West Hartford, Connecticut: Kumarian Press.

Korten, David C. 1990b. *NGO Strategic Networks: From Community Projects to Global Transformation.* The People-Centered Development Forum. 24 November, 1990.

Korten, David C. 1995. *When Corporations Rule the World.* West Hartford, Connecticut: Kumarian Press; San Francisco, California: Berrett-Koehler Publishers.

Korten, David C. and Rudi Klauss. 1984. *People Centered Development: Contributions toward Theory and Planning Frameworks.* West Hartford, Connecticut: Kumarian Press.

Kramer, Roderick M. and Tom R. Tyler, 1996. *Trust in Organizations: Frontiers of Theory and Research.* Thousand Oaks, California: Sage Publications.

Krumholz, Norman and John Forester. 1990. Possibilities. In *Making Equity Planning Work: Leadership in the Public Sector* (pp. 209–23). Philadelphia: Temple University Press.

Laponce, Jean A. 1987. *Languages and Their Territories*. Toronto: University of Toronto Press.

Lawrence, Paul R. and Jay W. Lorsch. 1967. *Organization and Environment: Managing Differentiation and Integration*. Boston: Harvard University.

Levitt, Barbara and James G. March. 1988. Organizational Learning. *Annual Review of Sociology*, 14: 319–40.

Levy, Charles S. 1982. *Guide to Ethical Decisions and Actions for Social Service Administrators: A Handbook for Managerial Personnel*. New York: The Haworth Press.

Liska, Jo. 1991. Dominance-Seeking Language Strategies: Please Eat the Floor, Dogbreath, or I'll Rip Your Lungs Out, Okay? In *Communication Yearbook 15* (pp. 427–56). New Brunswick, New Jersey: International Communication Association.

Lissner, Jørgen. 1977. *The Politics of Altruism: A Study of the Political Behaviour of Voluntary Development Agencies*. Geneva, Switzerland: Lutheran World Federation.

Lovell, Catherine H. 1992. *Breaking the Cycle of Poverty: The BRAC Strategy*. West Hartford, Connecticut: Kumarian Press.

Macpherson, Crawford Brough. 1962. *The Political Theory of Possessive Individualism: Hobbes to Locke*. Oxford: Clarendon Press.

Magendzo, Salomón. 1990. Popular Education in Nongovernmental Organizations: Education for Social Mobilization? *Harvard Educational Review*, 60(1): 49–61.

March, James G. 1981. Decision Making Perspective: Decisions in Organizations and Theories of Choice. In Van de Ven, Andrew H. and William F. Joyce (Ed.), *Perspectives on Organization Design and Behavior* (pp. 205–44). New York: Wiley-Interscience Publication.

March, James G. 1996. Exploration and Exploitation in Organizational Learning. In Cohen, Michael D. and Lee S. Sproull (Ed.), *Organizational Learning* (pp. 101–23). Thousand Oaks, London, New Delhi: Sage Publications.

March, James G. and Johan P. Olsen. 1988. The Uncertainty of the Past: Organizational Learning Under Ambiguity. In *Decisions and Organizations* (pp. 335–58). Cambridge, Massachusetts: Basil Blackwell.

March, James G. and Johan P. Olsen. 1989. *Rediscovering Institutions: The Organizational Basis for Politics*. New York: The Free Press.

Martin, Joanne. 1990. Deconstructing Organizational Taboos: The Suppression of Gender Conflict In Organizations. *Organization Science*, 1(4): 339–59.

Mazrui, Ali A. 1975. *The Political Sociology of the English Language*. The Hague: Mouton.

McCarthy, Thomas A. 1978. *The Critical Theory of Jurgen Habermas*. Cambridge: MIT Press.

Meyer, Marshall W. and Lynne G. Zucker. 1989. *Permanently Failing Organizations*. Newbury Park, California: Sage Publications.

Meyerson, Debra and Joanne Martin. 1987. Cultural Change: An Integration of Three Different Views. *Journal of Management Studies*, 24(6): 623–47.

Miller, Jon. 1991. Institutionalized Contradictions: Trouble in a Colonial Mission. *Organization Studies*, 12(3): 337–64.

Milofsky, Carl. 1988a. Scarcity and Community: A Resource Allocation Theory of Community and Mass Society Organizations. In Milofsky, Carl (Ed.), *Community Organizations: Studies in Resource Mobilization and Exchange* (pp. 16–41). New York: Oxford University Press.

Milofsky, Carl. 1988b. Structure and Process in Community Self-Help Organizations. In Milofsky, Carl (Ed.), *Community Organizations: Studies in Resource Mobilization and Exchange* (pp. 183–216). New York: Oxford University Press.

Mintz, Beth and Michael Schwartz. 1981. Interlocking Directorates and Interest Group Formation. *American Sociological Review*, 46(6): 851–68.

Mintzberg, Henry. 1979. *The Structuring of Organizations: A Synthesis of the Research*. Englewood Cliffs, New Jersey: Prentice Hall.

Mizrahi, Terry and Beth B. Rosenthal. 1993. Managing Dynamic Tensions in Social Change Coalitions. In Mizrahi, Terry and John Morrison (Ed.), *Community Organization and Social Administration: Advances, Trends, and Emerging Principles* (pp. 11–40). New York: The Haworth Press.

Mumby, Dennis K. 1993. Introduction: Narrative and Social Control. In Mumby, Dennis K. (Ed.), *Narrative and Social Control: Critical Perspectives* (pp. 1–12). Newbury Park, California: Sage Publications.

Mumby, Dennis K. and Linda L. Putnam. 1992. The Politics of Emotion: A Feminist Reading of Bounded Rationality. *Academy of Management Review*, 17(3): 465–86.

Nadler, David A. and M. Tushman. 1988. *Strategic Organization Design: Concepts, Tools and Processes*. Glenview, Illinois: Scott, Foresman.

Narkwiboonwong, Werachai and Walter E.J. Tips. 1989. Project Identification, Formulation and Start-Up by Voluntary Organizations (NGOs) in Thailand's Rural Development. *Public Administration and Development*, 9(2): 201–14.

Ndegwa, Stephen N. 1996. *The Two Faces of Civil Society: NGOs and Politics in Africa*. West Hartford, Connecticut: Kumarian Press.

O'Brien, Jim. 1991. How Can Donors Best Support NGO Consortia? *Grassroots Development*, 15(2): 38–45.

O'Neill, Michael and Dennis R. Young. 1988. *Educating Managers of Nonprofit Organizations*. New York: Praeger.

OECD. (1987). *Voluntary Aid for Development: The Role of Nongovernmental Organisations*. Paris: OECD.

OECD. (1992). *Directory of Non-Governmental Environment and Development Organisations in OECD Member Countries*. Paris: OECD.

OECD. 1993. *Human Rights, Refugees, Migrants & Development: Directory of NGOs in OECD Countries*. Paris: OECD.

PACT. 1989. *Asian Linkages: NGO Collaboration in The 1990s: A Five-Country Study*. New York: Private Agencies Collaborating Together.

Perlmutter, Howard V. 1991. On the Rocky Road to the First Global Civilization. *Human Relations*, 44(9): 897–920.

Perrow, Charles. 1972. *Complex Organizations: A Critical Essay*. New York: McGraw-Hill.

Pettigrew, Andrew M. 1979. On Studying Organizational Cultures. *Administrative Science Quarterly*, 24(4): 570–81.

Pfeffer, Jeffrey. 1982. Organizations as Paradigms and Processes. In *Organizations and Organization Theory* (pp. 226–53). Boston: Pitman.

Pfeffer, Jeffrey. 1992. *Managing with Power: Politics and Influence in Organizations*. Boston, Massachusetts: Harvard Business School Press.

Pfeffer, Jeffrey and Gerald R. Salancik. 1978. *The External Control of Organizations: A Resource Dependence Perspective*. New York: Harper & Row Publishers.

Polanyi, Karl. 1944. *The Great Transformation: The Political and Economic Origin of Our Time*. Boston: Beacon Press.

Postma, William. 1994. NGO Partnership and Institutional Development: Making it Real, Making it Intentional. *Canadian Journal of African Studies*, 28(3): 447–71.

Quizon, Antonio B. 1989. A Summary of NGO Issues on GO/NGO Relationships and Collaboration. In *A Strategic Assessment of Non-Governmental Organizations in the Philippines* (pp. 31–9). ANGOC Asian Nongovernmental Organizations Coalition for Agrarian Reform and Rural Development.

Rafaeli, Anat and Robert I. Sutton. 1989. The Expression of Emotion in Organizational Life. In Cummings, L.L. and Barry M. Staw (Ed.), *Research in Organizational Behavior* (pp. 1–42). Greenwich, Connecticut: JAI Press Inc.

Rahnema, Majid. 1990. Participatory Action Research: The 'Last Temptation of Saint' Development. *Alternatives*, 15(2): 199–226.

Rappaport, Roy A. 1979. *Ecology, Meaning, and Religion*. Richmond, California: North Atlantic Books.

Rondinelli, Dennis A. 1989. Decentralizing Public Services in Developing Countries: Issues and Opportunities. *Journal of Social, Political, and Economic Studies*, 14(1): 77–98.

Rose, Randall A. 1988. Organizations as Multiple Cultures: A Rules Theory Analysis. *Human Relations*, 41(2): 139–70.

Sager, Tore. 1994. Striking a Balance Between Opportunism and Rigidity. In *Communicative Planning Theory* (pp. 174–94). Aldershot: Avebury.

Said, Edward W. 1993. *Culture and Imperialism*. New York: Vintage Books.

Said, Edward W. and Kenzaburo Oe. 1995. Sei no Owari wo Mitsumeru Sutairu (A Style: Staring the End of Live). *Sekai*, (611): 22–41.

Salamon, Lester M. and Helmut K. Anheier. 1996. *The Emerging Nonprofit Sector: An Overview*. Manchester: Manchester University Press.

Sandelands, Lloyd E. and Geogette C. Buckner. 1989. Of Art and Work: Aesthetic Experience and The Psychology of Work Feelings. In *Research in Organizational Behavior* (pp. 105–31). Greenwich, Connecticut: JAI Press.

Schein, Edgar H. 1985. *Organizational Culture and Leadership*. San Francisco: Jossey-Bass Publishers.

Schön, Donald A. 1982. *The Reflective Practitioner: How Professionals Think in Action*. New York: BasicBooks.

Schön, Donald A. 1983. Organizational Learning. In Morgan, Gareth (Ed.), *Beyond Method: Strategies for Social Research* (pp. 114–28). Beverly Hills, California: Sage Publications.

Schön, Donald A. 1987. *Educating the Reflective Practitioner*. San Francisco: Jossey-Bass Publishers.

Schön, Donald A. and Martin Rein. 1994. *Frame Reflection: Toward the Resolution of Intractable Policy Controversies*. New York: BasicBooks.

Scott, Richard W. 1992. *Organizations: Rational, Natural, and Open Systems*. Englewood Cliffs, New Jersey: Prentice-Hall.

Shalin, Dmitri·N. 1992. Critical Theory and the Pragmatist Challenge. *American Journal of Sociology*, 98(2): 237–79.

Shor, Ira and Paulo Freire. 1987. What is the 'Dialogical Method' of Teaching? *Journal of Education*, 169(3): 11–31.

Silverman, David. 1971. Action Analysis of Organisations. In *The Theory of Organisations: A Sociological Framework* (pp. 147–74). New York: Basic Books.

Simon, Herbert A. 1991. Bounded Rationality and Organizational Learning. *Organization Science*, 2(1): 125–34.

Sitkin, Sim B. 1996. Learning Through Failure: The Strategy of Small Losses. In Cohen, Michael D. and Lee S. Sproull (Ed.), *Organizational Learning* (p. 541–77). Thousand Oaks, London, New Delhi: Sage Publications.

Smillie, Ian. 1994. Changing Partners: Northern NGOs, Northern Governments. *Voluntas*, 5(2): 155–92.

Smillie, Ian. 1995. *The Alms Bazaar: Altruism Under Fire – Non-Profit Organizations and International Development*. London: Intermediate Technology Publications.

Smith, Brian H. 1987. An Agenda of Future Tasks for International and Indigenous NGOs: Views From the North. *World Development*, 15(Supplement): 87–93.

Smith, Brian H. 1990. *More than Altruism: The Politics of Private Foreign Aid*. Princeton, New Jersey: Princeton University Press.

Soedjamoko. 1986. Social Energy as a Development Resource. In Korten, David (Ed.), *Community Management: Asian Experience and Perspectives* (pp. 19–31). West Hartford, Connecticut: Kumarian Press.

Starbuck, William H. 1965. Organizational Growth and Development. In March, James (Ed.), *Handbook of Organizations* (pp. 451–533). Chicago: Rand McNally Company.

Staudt, Kathleen. 1991. *Managing Development: State, Society, and International Contexts*. Newbury Park, California: Sage Publications.

Steen, Odd Inge. 1996. Autonomy or Dependency? Relations between Non-Governmental International Aid Organizations and Government. *Voluntas*, 7(2): 147–59.

Steffy, Brian D. and Andrew J. Grimes. 1986. A Critical Theory of Organization Science. *Academy of Management Review*, 11(2): 322–36.

Suharyanto, Her and Winfred Hutabarat. 1993. The Politics of NGO Funding. *Indonesia Business Weekly*, 1(45): 7–8.

Susskind, Lawrence and Jeffrey Cruikshank. 1987. *Breaking the Impasse: Consensual Approaches to Resolving Public Disputes*. New York: BasicBooks.

Tayko, Perla Rizalina M. 1988. *Organization Development for NGOs: An Introduction*. Manila: Phildhrra.

Thomas-Slayter, Barbara P. 1992. Implementing Effective Local Management of Natural Resources: New Roles for NGOs in Africa. *Human Relations*, 51(2): 136–43.

Tongsawate, Maniemai and Walter E.J. Tips. 1988. Coordination between Government and Voluntary Organizations (NGOs) in Thailand's rural development. *Public Administration and Development*, 8(4): 401–20.

Toynbee, Arnold. 1947. *A Study of History*. New York: Oxford University Press.

Tsoukas, Haridimos. 1992. Panoptic Reason and the Search for Totality: A Critical Assessment of the Critical Systems Perspective. *Human Relations*, 45(7): 637–57.

Tuckman, Howard P. and Cyril F. Chang. 1992. Nonprofit Equity: A Behavioral Model and Its Policy Implications. *Journal of Policy Analysis and Management*, 11(1): 76–87.

Uphoff, Norman. 1988. Assisted Self-Reliance: Working With, Rather than For, the Poor. In Lewis, John P., Valeriana Kallab and Richard E. Feinberg (Ed.), *Strengthening The Poor: What Have We Learned?* (pp. 47–59). New Brunswick: Transaction Books.

Uphoff, Norman. 1993. Grassroots Organizations and NGOs in Rural Development: Opportunities with Diminishing States and Expanding Markets. *World Development*, 21(4): 607–22.

Uphoff, Norman. 1996. Why NGOs are Not a Third Sector: A Sectoral Analysis with Some Thoughts on Accountability, Sustainability, and Evaluation. In Edwards, Michael and David Hulme (Ed.), *Beyond the Magic Bullet: NGO Performance and Accountability in the Post-Cold War World* (pp. 23–39). West Hartford, Connecticut: Kumarian Press.

Urban, Greg. 1993. Culture's Public Face. *Public Culture*, 5: 213–38.

Uyangoda, Jayadeva. 1989. *Voluntary Organizations and Political Participation*. Sri Lanka: Marga Institute.

Van Der Heijden, Hendrik. 1985. *Development Impact on Effectiveness of Non-Governmental Organizations: The Record of Rural Development*. Paris: OECD.

Van Der Heijden, Hendrik. 1987. The Reconciliation of NGO Autonomy, Program Integrity and Operational Effectiveness with Accountability to Donors. *World Development*, 15(Supplement): 103–12.

Van Maanen, John and Gideon Kunda. 1989. 'Real Feelings': Emotional Expression and Organizational Culture. In Cummings, L.L. and Barry M. Staw (Ed.), *Research in Organizational Behavior* (pp. 43–103). Greenwich, Connecticut: JAI Press.

Vansant, Jerry. 1989. Opportunities and Risks for Private Voluntary Organizations as Agents of LDC Policy Change. *World Development*, 17(11): 1723–31.

Vergara, Ricardo. 1994. NGOs: Help or Hindrance for Community Development in Latin America? *Community Development Journal*, 29(4): 322–8.

Verhagen, Koenraad. 1987. *Self-Help Promotion: a Challenge to the NGO Community*. Amsterdam/Oegstgeest: CEBEMO/Royal Tropical Institute, The Netherlands.

Ward, Haskell George. 1989. *African Development Reconsidered: New Perspectives from the Continent*. New York: A Phelps-Stokes Institute Publication.

Weiler, Kathleen. 1991. Freire and a Feminist Pedagogy of Difference. *Harvard Educational Review*, 61(4): 449–73.

Weiner, Myron E. 1988. Managing People for Enhanced Performance. In Patti, Rino J., John Poetner and Chales A. Rapp (Ed.), *Managing for Service Effectiveness in Social Welfare* (pp. 147–60). New York: Haworth Press.

Weisbrod, Burton, Allen. 1988. *The Nonprofit Economy*. Cambridge, Massachusetts: Harvard University Press.

Weiss, Janet A. 1988. Substance Versus Symbol in Administrative Reform: The Case of Human Services Coordination. In Milofsky, Carl (Ed.), *Community Organizations: Studies in Resource Mobilization and Exchange* (pp. 100–18). New York: Oxford University Press.

Young, Dennis R. 1989. Local Autonomy in a Franchise Age: Structural Change in National Voluntary Associations. *Nonprofit and Voluntary Sector Quarterly*, 18(2): 101–17.

Zeleny, Milan. 1987. Management Support Systems: Towards Integrated Knowledge Management. *Human Systems Management*, 7(1): 59–70.

RELATED TITLES FROM IT PUBLICATIONS

Managing for a Change: How to run community development projects
Anthony Davies

This book provides an insight into development project planning and management by guiding the reader, chapter by chapter, through the stages from concept to completion.

There is advice on all aspects of the process including problem analysis, meetings, letter-writing, decision-making, leadership, employment of contractors, and quality control. The last chapter includes sections on profitable and non-profit-making enterprises, and each chapter ends with exercises to help test the reader's new knowledge and reinforce the lessons in good practice.

Managing for a Change will be invaluable to community-group leaders and trainers, as well as to individuals who are involved in community organizations, and the not-for-profit sector.

ISBN 1 85339 399 1. 160pp. 1997

Manual of Practical Management for Third World Rural Development Associations
Fernand Vincent

Volume I: Organization, administration, communication
This comprehensive and simple guide will clarify management problems for those involved with non-governmental associations in developing countries. With numerous examples in annexes, together with a glossary of unfamiliar technical terms.

ISBN 1 85339 404 1. 240pp. 1997

Volume II: Financial management
Written in a simple and direct style, useful for training administrators of small groups or associations and those who manage development projects. Covers all aspects of financing an association, with annexes and a glossary.

ISBN 1 85339 405 X. 208pp. 1997

For more information on these titles or our full Books by Post catalogue, please contact:
Intermediate Technology Publications, 103–105 Southampton Row, London WC1B 4HH, UK

JOURNALS AVAILABLE FROM IT PUBLICATIONS

Waterlines
Appropriate technologies for water supply and sanitation

Waterlines is the world's only journal devoted entirely to low-cost water supply and sanitation. It contains practical help and advice on the problems that face policymakers, water practitioners, engineers and fieldworkers in their work. *Waterlines* also includes news and views from the field, the latest resource materials, and jobs, courses and training opportunities in the water and sanitation sector.

Waterlines is designed for the professional – both specialist and non-specialist – whether administrator or engineer, project manager or policymaker, trainer or fieldworker.

Appropriate Technology
Practical approaches to development

Wherever you are in the world, you are bound to find plenty to interest you in *Appropriate Technology*. By concentrating on real-life experiences and problems, *Appropriate Technology* deals with the issues in practical development in a clear, straightforward way – and the lessons can be applied in every part of the globe.

Every issue is based around a popular theme, with up to eight different articles giving a range of viewpoints from across the development sector, as well as an up-to-date resource guide, diary of key events, a pull-out-and-keep Appropriate Technology Brief, practical question-and-answer sections, and news on the latest technologies being used and developments throughout the North and South.

Small Enterprise Development
An international journal

Small Enterprise Development provides a forum for those involved in the design and administration of small enterprise development programmes in developing countries.

Detailed articles report on original research, programme evaluations and significant new approaches, and there are case studies of small enterprise development projects implemented by donor agencies, short practice notes from the various regions of the world describing programmes in operation and work of wider interest, as well as a regular review of resource materials, forthcoming conferences and events, and letters from readers.

Small Enterprise Development tackles the major themes and pressing concerns of small enterprise development, and is an invaluable resource to those involved in the small enterprise development sector.

For information on how to obtain a sample copy, or how to subscribe to any of these journals, please contact Intermediate Technology Publications, 103–105 Southampton Row, London WC1B 4HH, UK.

Printed in the United Kingdom
by Lightning Source UK Ltd.
113372UKS00001B/376-378